How to Write Better Essays

2013

Palgrave Study Guides

A Handbook of Writing for Engineers *Joan van Emden*
Authoring a PhD Thesis *Patrick Dunleavy*
Effective Communication for Arts and Humanities Students
    Joan van Emden and Lucinda Becker
Effective Communication for Science and Technology *Joan van Emden*
How to Manage your Arts, Humanities and Social Science Degree
    Lucinda Becker
How to Write Better Essays *Bryan Greetham*
Key Concepts in Politics *Andrew Heywood*
The Mature Student's Guide to Writing *Jean Rose*
The Postgraduate Research Handbook *Gina Wisker*
Professional Writing *Sky Marsen*
Research Using IT *Hilary Coombes*
The Student's Guide to Writing *John Peck and Martin Coyle*
The Study Skills Handbook *Stella Cottrell*
Studying Economics *Brian Atkinson and Susan Johns*
Studying History (second edition) *Jeremy Black and Donald M. MacRaild*
Studying Mathematics and its Applications *Peter Kahn*
Studying Psychology *Andrew Stevenson*
Teaching Study Skills and Supporting Learning *Stella Cottrell*

Palgrave Study Guides: Literature

General Editors: John Peck and Martin Coyle

How to Begin Studying English Literature (second edition)
    Nicholas Marsh
How to Study a Jane Austen Novel (second edition) *Vivien Jones*
How to Study Chaucer (second edition) *Rob Pope*
How to Study a Charles Dickens Novel *Keith Selby*
How to Study Foreign Languages *Marilyn Lewis*
How to Study an E. M. Forster Novel *Nigel Messenger*
How to Study James Joyce *John Blades*
How to Study Linguistics *Geoffrey Finch*
How to Study Modern Drama *Kenneth Pickering*
How to Study Modern Poetry *Tony Curtis*
How to Study a Novel (second edition) *John Peck*
How to Study a Poet (second edition) *John Peck*
How to Study a Renaissance Play *Chris Coles*
How to Study Romantic Poetry (second edition) *Paul O'Flinn*
How to Study a Shakespeare Play (second edition) *John Peck and
    Martin Coyle*
How to Study Television *Keith Selby and Ron Cowdery*
Linguistic Terms and Concepts *Geoffrey Finch*
Literary Terms and Criticism (third edition) *John Peck and
    Martin Coyle*
Practical Criticism *John Peck and Martin Coyle*

How to Write Better Essays

Bryan Greetham

palgrave

First published 2001 by
PALGRAVE
Houndmills, Basingstoke, Hampshire RG21 6XS and
175 Fifth Avenue, New York, N.Y. 10010
Companies and representatives throughout the world

PALGRAVE is the new global academic imprint of
St. Martin's Press LLC Scholarly and Reference Division and
Palgrave Publishers Ltd (formerly Macmillan Press Ltd).

ISBN 0–333–94715–0
ISBN 13–9780–0333–94715–9

This book is printed on paper suitable for recycling and
made from fully managed and sustained forest sources.

A catalogue record for this book is available
from the British Library.

Library of Congress Cataloging-in-Publication Data

Greetham, Bryan, 1946–
    How to write better essays/Bryan Greetham.
        p.   cm. – (Palgrave study guides)
    Includes bibliographical references (p.   ) and index.
    ISBN 0–333–94715–0
    1. English language – Rhetoric.   2. Exposition (Rhetoric)   3. Essay –
    Authorship.   4. Academic writing.   I. Title.   II. Series.

    PE1429 .G74 2001
    808'.042 – dc21

                                                            2001032790

10   9   8
10   09   08   07   06   05

Printed and bound in Great Britain by
Creative Print and Design (Wales), Ebbw Vale

For Pat, without whom nothing is possible, and two great men – my father, Robert Greetham, and Harry Rowe, whose rich and interesting life is still an inspiration.

Contents

Introduction

▶ About this book

By the time we reach university a surprising number of us are convinced that we should know all we need to know about researching and writing essays. We're inclined to argue that if we've got this far we should know how to analyse the implications of questions, read efficiently, take notes, plan and structure arguments, use evidence, and write light and interesting prose. Indeed these skills are the very thing that has got us this far in the first place, so to admit that we could be better at essay writing seems to be an admission that we're lucky to have got this far.

Instead of seeking help, then, to improve our skills, we settle for the strategy of just learning by our mistakes, or by example in those rare moments when we might see our tutor think through and analyse a difficult concept, or pull ideas together from different sources and synthesise them into a new way of looking at a problem. If we recognise the significance of the moment, and most of us don't, then we might be lucky enough to retain a small inkling of what went on in the hope that we, too, might be able to do the same.

But it need not be like this. The two types of skills that we all need to be successful in our courses – study skills (reading, note-taking, writing, organisation, and revision) and thinking skills (analysis, synthesis, discussion, argument, and use of evidence) – can be taught. There is nothing mysterious about them. They need not be the exclusive preserve of a few. And there is nothing particularly difficult about them either. Indeed, most of us have the abilities to succeed, if only we can unlock and use them by learning these simple skills.

▶ Learning the skills

In this book you will learn not just the study skills, but the thinking skills too. What's more, you won't do this alone. At every step of the way a tutor will be by your side, showing you clear and simple ways of overcoming the most difficult problems. And *you* choose the essay you want to work on, drawn from the courses you're taking at your school, college or university.

You will be taken carefully through each stage of writing the essay from interpreting the question to the research, planning, writing and revision. In each of these you will be given practice exercises to work on, along with their answers, with an assignment at the end of each section. As you work through each stage you will get practical help right up until the essay has been completed. In this way not only will your work improve, but you'll develop those skills necessary to tackle successfully all your future writing assignments.

All of this means this book is significantly different from any other writing or study-skills book you may have read before:

- **It's an integrated approach**

  It doesn't deal with writing skills in isolation from the thinking skills and the other study skills involved, like note-taking, reading and organisation. If you've taken study-skills courses before, you'll know that dealing with any skill in isolation results in us just tacking on this new skill to our existing pattern of study. It's not integrated within it. As a result, after a short time we come to realise it's not relevant to the way we use our other skills and we quietly abandon it.

- **It's a purposeful approach**

  Because it's directed at a specific goal of producing a certain essay that you have chosen yourself, it has a clear purpose that's relevant to what you're studying. Unlike more general books and courses, you're not working in a vacuum. In effect you have your own personal writing tutor, who will be by your side to help you with the problems you confront at each stage in the production of an essay that you have to complete for one of your courses.

- **The book takes account of the syllabus objectives of your courses**

  Unlike most books on this subject, this one will help you develop the skills you need to meet the syllabus objectives of the courses you're taking at school, college or university. You will develop the skills and techniques that allow you to explore more effectively in your writing those abilities your syllabuses set out to develop. As many of us know from our experience with other books and courses, any book that doesn't do this we are likely to abandon, realising it doesn't address our needs, because it's divorced from the abilities we are expected to use and develop in the courses we are studying.

- **The book is a comprehensive essay writing guide**
  After you've read the book and completed the course you're left with an invaluable guide that you can use to diagnose and deal with any problem you might have in your writing in the future. As it's broken up into stages it's easy to identify where the problem is and what you need to do to tackle it. To help you in this, the index can be used to diagnose a problem you might be experiencing, so that you can easily locate the relevant section of the guide.

With these unique characteristics this is a book that will ensure you develop the skills and techniques to unlock your abilities and your potential.

The Stages

This book is not just about the actual writing of essays; it's also about the various stages you need to go through to produce a good essay, and about the ways in which this can improve your learning. Once you've worked your way through it, you'll find you have an invaluable guide that you can keep by your side as you write your essays, to give you answers to problems as they arise.

▶ Why write essays?

If you understand the value of doing something, you normally find you're more confident and positive about tackling it. So, what are the reasons for writing essays?

- **It forces you to organise your thinking and develop your ideas on the issues**
  In one sense writing is *the* crucial step in the process of learning a subject, in that it helps you to get to grips with the new ideas. Without this it's difficult, if not impossible, to know clearly just how well you've understood the subject.

- **Feedback**
  In the same way, it also provides you with the opportunity to get feedback from your tutor, not just on how well you've understood the subject, but on how well you've communicated this, and where your strengths and weaknesses are, so you can concentrate your energies more effectively.

- **Revision material**
  If you've planned the essay well, so that it's got a clear structure, you'll find, when it comes to preparing for the final exam, that the plan itself is just about the most important revision material you have. It shows you how you've come to understand the topic, and how you've organised the ideas. As such, it is the one thing that

you will be able to recall and use most effectively under timed conditions. In fact many students who plan well use just these clearly organised thought patterns as their only revision material.

Writing an essay, then, is a valuable opportunity for learning, which ought to be approached positively. If you hide behind the text, just paraphrasing or copying what you've read, without processing those ideas and making them your own, your tutor will rarely see you, your abilities, or your problems, and you will never glimpse the extent of your abilities, or just how much you understand.

▶ The five stages

For any essay to achieve high marks it's essential to go through five distinct stages:

1 Interpretation of the question
2 Research
3 Planning
4 Writing
5 Revision

If you omit any of these or just rush them, certain familiar problems will emerge in your writing: irrelevance, weak structure, insufficient evidence and examples to support your arguments, lack of fluency between paragraphs, inconsistent arguments, and many others.

It's also as important to separate each stage, so that you leave, say, at least a day between each of them. Of course, it may not always be possible for you to do this. You may have a number of competing obligations that leave you only a few days to complete the essay. On these occasions the skills you'll learn in this book to manage your time will help you cope more effectively. They will also help you organise your time so that with most pieces of work you can in fact find sufficient time between each stage. Not only does this allow you to return to your ideas fresh, so that you're able to see which of them needs to be edited out, but you will also find that your ideas and arguments have developed in the meantime.

Ideas are organic. Hardly ever are they the complete and finished article the moment you grasp them, like products on a supermarket shelf. They grow and develop over time. So, for example, returning to your plan after a day or two, you will almost inevitably discover new ideas, new evidence and new ways of developing your arguments. You're also likely to see a more sensible and logical way of ordering your ideas.

And the same goes for all the other stages. Each time you return to your work after leaving it to lie unattended for a while, you will find your subconscious has worked on the ideas, restructuring them, answering questions that you weren't sure of, and critically evaluating the arguments you've read in your texts.

But, be reassured, this is not an endless, confusing process, in which your ideas are thrown up in the air each time you return to your work. Within a short time, after revising your plan a couple of times, you will realise that it's ready and you can begin writing. The same is true of your interpretation of the question, your research and the revision of your work. You will know when enough is enough. It may take three or four essays before you feel confident about your judgement, and during these you will have to rely on your tutor's judgement, but it will come.

Stage 1
Interpretation of the Question

INTRODUCTION

Often, and for the best of motives, our problems in essay writing begin the very moment we are given the question. Anxious to get on with the work and not fall behind, we skip the interpretation stage and launch straight into our research. As a result, we read sources and take notes without a clear idea of what's relevant, beyond some very general idea of the subject of the essay. Then finally, after hours of toil, tired and frustrated, and no clearer about what we're doing, we're left with a pile of irrelevant, unusable notes.

Yet, just an hour or two interpreting the question would not only have saved us this wasted time, but would have given us a clear idea of what the question is getting at and a better understanding of what the examiner is looking for in our work. And even more, it would have given us the opportunity to get our own ideas and insights involved at an early stage. Without this our work can seem routine and predictable: at best just the re-cycling of the ideas that dominate the subject.

So, what should you be looking for when you interpret a question? All essay questions tell you two things: the structure your essay should adopt for you to deal relevantly with all the issues it raises; and the range of abilities the examiner is expecting to see you use in answering the question.

▶ Structure

Take the first of these: the structure. In the following chapters you will learn how to unwrap the meaning and implications of the question, so that, before you go off to do your research, you will have prepared for yourself a clear structure of the issues that the question raises, so you know what you're looking for. In many questions this will develop out of your analysis of the key concepts in the question. Most of us struggle to do this well, but the skills involved can be easily learnt. You will be shown a simple three-step technique for analysing the most difficult concepts.

Once this has been done you will be shown how to brainstorm the question. Again, this is not a time-consuming task, but it will help you to use more of your own ideas and avoid wasting time in your research. Once you've learnt to do this, you will be able to make two important things clear to yourself before you start your research: what *you* know about the issues the essay question raises, and the questions you want your sources to answer. Without this the authors of the texts you read are likely to dictate to you and you'll find it difficult to distinguish between what's relevant and what's not.

▶ Range of abilities

Then, once you've brainstormed your ideas and know what questions you want your sources to answer, there's just one more thing you need to be sure about before you begin your research. You must be clear about the range of abilities the examiner wants to see you use. Otherwise you may find yourself tackling the essay in a way that doesn't answer the question, and noting information that is irrelevant.

1 Revealing the Structure

In this chapter you will learn:

- how to avoid irrelevance in your essay by carefully interpreting the meaning and implications of the question;
- how to reveal from the question the structure your essay should adopt;
- how to make sure your essay qualifies for the highest marks on offer.

Obviously it's important to realise that you're not embarking on a piece of open-ended research. You're answering a particular question that raises particular sharply focused issues. You must, therefore, be rigorously selective in collecting your material in the research stage, and in planning and writing the essay. You should use only material that is relevant to answering *this* question.

There are times in the research of every essay when you find yourself collecting material that is interesting and so closely argued that you find it difficult not to take notes from all of it, particularly when it's relevant to the wider implications of the topic. But if it's not relevant to the problems raised in *this* essay, ditch it! File it away for other essays, by all means, but don't let it tempt you in this essay. Otherwise it will lose focus and the reader will fail to understand what you're doing and why.

▶ Analyse the key concepts

With these warnings in mind it's essential to pin down two things: how many parts there are to the question and what weight you will need to give to each part. With many questions these structural problems can be solved by analysing the key concepts used in the question. Indeed, in most, if you fail to do this, the examiners will deduct marks: they will expect to see you show that you can analyse difficult abstract concepts and allow this to influence, if not determine, the structure of the essay.

For example, markers for the University of London are told to award the highest marks (70–100%) to those students who 'note subtlety, complexity and possible disagreements, [which they] . . . will discuss', while only average marks (40–60%) are to be awarded to the student who adopts a 'More relaxed application' of the question, and who 'follows [an] obvious line . . . [and] uncritically accepts the terms of the question'.[1]

Similarly, in the Department of Sociology at the University of Harvard students are told:

> Papers will be graded on the basis of the completeness and clarity of your analysis and the persuasiveness of your recommendations. As always, we will be appreciative of well-organised and well-written papers.[2]

The same emphasis can be found at the University of Oxford, where examiners look for a good analytical ability, to distinguish first class and upper second class scripts from the rest. In the marking criteria it's only in these two grades that any mention is made of analytical ability, with those failing to display it more likely to end up with lower seconds and below. A first class script should show:

> analytical and argumentative power, a good command of facts, evidence or arguments relevant to the questions, and an ability to organise the answer with clarity, insight and sensitivity.[3]

An upper second class script also displays these qualities, but 'less consistently' or 'to a lesser degree' than a first class script.

▶ Questions

To give you an idea of what this means in terms of actual questions, listed below is a selection of essay questions from different departments at different universities around the world. You will see that the answer to each of them hinges upon the same 'clarity, insight and sensitivity' that we can bring to the analysis of the key concepts in the question.

- Do the narrators of *Pride and Prejudice* and *Great Expectations* speak with the same kind of irony?
  (The English Novel, University of Harvard)

- Are there any good reasons for supposing that historical explanation is, in principle, different from scientific explanation?
  (History, University of Kent at Canterbury)

- Did the years 1603–4 witness a crisis in the history of English Protestantism?   **(History, University of Kent at Canterbury)**

- Consider Duncan Kennedy's claim that people who favour casting the law in the form of rules are individualists while people who favour the use of standards are altruists. Do you agree that the debate between rules and standards reflects that sort of deep difference in general moral outlook?
  (Law, University of Cornell)

- Hobbes insists that covenants extorted by force oblige. (Sovereignty by acquisition is a good example.) Is his argument consistent with his theory? What problems does his insistence pose for his theory? In your answer, be sure to address Hobbes's account of obligation, in particular the obligation to obey the sovereign.
  (Philosophy, University of Harvard)

- 'Mill has made as naïve and artless a use of the naturalistic fallacy as anybody could desire. "Good," he tells us, means "desirable", and you can only find out what is desirable by seeking to find out what is actually desired . . . The fact is that "desirable" does not mean "able to be desired" as "visible" means "able to be seen".' G. E. Moore. Discuss.
  (Philosophy, University of Kent at Canterbury)

- 'Authority amounts to no more than the possession of power.' Discuss.   **(Philosophy, University of Maryland)**

- Is there any important sense in which all men are equal? If so, what is it?   **(Politics, University of Maryland)**

- Is democracy always compatible with individual freedom?
  (**Politics, University of York**)

- Are concepts of anomie and subculture still of value in the explanation of criminality?   (**Sociology, University of Oxford**)

- What considerations determine the efficient levels of (a) smoking, (b) immunisation against infectious diseases? Is it practical to achieve these?   (**Economics, University of Oxford**)

- 'Free Trade leads to a Paretian Optimum.' 'Free Trade leads to unacceptable inequalities.' Discuss.
  (**Economics, University of Oxford**)

▶ Key concepts

As you can see, no matter what the subject, the analysis of the important concepts is the main focus when we come to interpret questions like these. They may be couched subtly in everyday language, like 'unacceptable inequalities', 'oblige', or 'efficient levels', or they may stand out like beacons warning the unwary not to ignore them, like 'Paretian Optimum', and 'anomie and subculture'. Historians, for example, are fond of using concepts like 'revolution' and 'crisis': seemingly inoffensive and untroubling words. But then, look at the British Industrial Revolution and you find yourself wondering, was this a revolution or just accelerated evolution? Indeed, what is a revolution? Is it all a question of the speed of change? In which case, the Industrial Revolution was more an evolution than a revolution, spread as it was over seventy to a hundred years. Or is it more to do with the scale of change? If this is the case, then there's little doubt that it was a revolution, what with the mechanisation of labour, factory production, the growth of cities and the development of mechanised transport.

Much the same could be argued for a concept like 'crisis'. Again it appears to be inoffensive and untroubling; that is until you ask yourself, what do we really mean by the word? It comes from the Greek, *Krisis*, meaning a decisive moment or turning point. So are we really justified in arguing that the years 1603–4 were not only a time of serious challenge to Protestantism, but also a decisive turning point in its history? Whatever your answer, you now have a structure emerging: on the one hand you can argue that it was a time of serious challenge to Protestantism, but on the other you might question whether it really was a genuine turning point in its history.

The same analysis of concepts and arguments can be found in just about every subject. In politics there are concepts like freedom, ideology, equality, authority, power, political obligation, influence, legitimacy, democracy and many more. Do we really harbour not a single fear of ambiguity when we use such a large and important concept like freedom, or was Donovan Leitch right when he admitted in the sixties that, 'Freedom is a word I rarely use without thinking'? What do we mean by legitimacy and how does it differ from legality? And when we use the word 'democracy' do we mean direct or indirect democracy, representative or responsible, totalitarian or liberal, third world or communist?

In literature what do we mean by concepts like tragedy, comedy, irony, and satire? Indeed, it's not unusual to find universities devoting complete courses to unravelling the implications of these and others like them: concepts like class, political obligation, punishment, revolution, authority and so on. In the following course outline, the concepts of punishment and obligation, and the distinction between law and morality, are central concerns that run throughout the course. Entitled 'Moral Reasoning – Reasoning In and About the Law', it is part of the programme at the University of Harvard:

> How is law related to morality? How is it distinct? Do we have an obligation to obey the law? What, if anything, justifies the imposition of legal punishment? These issues, and related issues dealing with the analysis and justification of legal practices, will be examined using the writings of philosophers, judges, and legal theorists.[4]

Take just about any course at any university and you will see the same: that many of the challenges we face are questions about concepts. For example, the Philosophy Department of the University of Southampton describes its Philosophy of Science course in the following terms:

> This course examines concepts of evidence, justification, probability and truth, in relation to scientific explanation, causality, laws of nature, theory and fact; the distinctions between science and pseudo-science, as well as between science and metaphor, are among the topics explored. Examples

illustrating the philosophical argument will be drawn from the histories of the physical, biological and social sciences.[5]

▶ Qualifying for the highest marks on offer

Syllabuses like these indicate the importance of key concepts both in the courses you're studying, and in the essays you're expected to write. By analysing them you not only give your essay a relevant structure, but, equally important, you qualify for the highest marks on offer.

If, at this stage, you don't acknowledge the significance of these concepts by analysing their implications, you will almost certainly fail to analyse them in your essay. This will indicate not only that you haven't seen the point of the question, but, more seriously, that you haven't yet developed that thoughtful, reflective ability to question some of the most important assumptions we make when we use language. It is as if you're saying to the examiner that you can see no reason why these concepts should raise any particular problem and, therefore, they deserve no special treatment.

▶ In the next chapter

In the next chapter we'll look at a particular concept and show how you can prise it open to reveal its implications. In so doing you'll see how you can capture more of your own ideas and insights.

Notes

1 *General Marking Instructions* (London: University of London, 1987).
2 Peter V. Marsden, *Sociology, 25: Introduction to the Sociology of Organizations* (Cambridge, Mass.: University of Harvard, 2000).
3 *Greats Handbook* (Oxford: University of Oxford, 2000), p. 46.
4 Michael Blake, *Moral Reasoning, 62: Reasoning in and about the Law* (Cambridge, Mass.: University of Harvard, 2000).
5 *What is Philosophy?* (Southampton: Department of Philosophy, University of Southampton, 1986), p. 16.

2 A Practical Example

In this chapter you will learn:

- the difference between closed and open concepts: those that can be left to a dictionary, and those that need to be analysed;
- how to prise open the structure of a concept by looking at the way we use it in everyday language and examples;
- how to capture your ideas and follow your train of thoughts in a clear structure of notes, while you analyse a concept.

Despite what we said in the previous chapter, there will still be those who ask, 'But why can't we just look up the meaning of these words in a dictionary, rather than go through the process of analysis?' And, of course, they're right: with some words this is all you need to do.

▶ Open and closed concepts

What you might describe as 'closed concepts' usually have an unchanging, unambiguous meaning. Words like 'bicycle', 'bachelor' and 'triangle' each have a structure to their meaning, which is bound by logical necessity. We all agree to abide by certain conventions that rule the meaning of these words. So, if you were to say 'this is a bicycle with one wheel', or 'this triangle has four sides', no-one would be in any doubt that you had made a logical mistake. When we use these words according to their conventions we are, in effect, allowing our understanding of the world to be structured in a particular way.

But with 'open concepts' it tends to be the reverse: our experience of the world shapes our concepts. As a result, such words cannot be pinned down just by looking them up in a dictionary. Their meaning responds to and reflects our changing experience: they change through time and from one culture to another. A dictionary definition, then, can only ever be a single snapshot taken in a constantly moving reel of images.[1]

If you take concepts like 'aunt' and 'democracy', you can see that in some societies and at some times they have a fairly unambiguous, unchanging meaning. The concept of 'aunt', for example, in some societies, has a narrow definition exclusively grounded in relations by blood and marriage. But in other societies it is more open, encompassing not just relatives in the strict sense, but also older, long-standing friends of the family. This is likely to be a reflection of the social practices prevalent in different societies and at different stages in their development. A predominantly rural society with limited social mobility might use 'aunt' in the narrow sense. In contrast, in a society undergoing rapid industrialisation, with greater social mobility and less permanent communities, the concept is likely to be applied more loosely to close friends of the parents of a child. A young couple, having recently moved to a city some distance from their parents' homes, may seek to reconstruct the security of an extended family by including close friends as aunts and uncles to their children.

Much the same can be said for a concept like 'democracy'. We might all agree that it implies government in accordance with the popular will, but beyond this principle everything is open. Western liberal democracies, believing that democracy implies one-man-one-vote, regular elections, secret ballots, multi-party politics and freedom of expression, are just one adaptation of the principle, serving the needs of a particular type of society: a liberal society with its emphasis on the importance of individualism, competition, free trade and consumer sovereignty.

In other societies, under different cultural influences, democracy has taken on different forms where accountability, participation, multi-party politics, even regular elections and voter sovereignty, are much less important. More significant is the progress that is being made towards achieving democratic goals, like the eradication of epidemic diseases, alleviation of poverty, improvement in literacy, even industrialisation. The achievement of these goals, rather than voter approval at elections, is seen as evidence of the democratic nature of government.

▶ Start with the way we use them

As you can see from this, if any of the concepts in essay questions are up for grabs in this way, if there is any doubt about the way we use them, then we need to analyse them. In most cases this means we start with words we use in everyday speech, in some cases sharpening and tightening them, in others just unpacking their ambiguities. In the process, this will more often than not give us the structure of our essay, in terms of the arguments we need to explore and develop.

So, start by asking yourself, 'How do I use the concept – do I use it in more than one way?' Take the concept of freedom. We tend to talk about being free *from* things, like repression, constraints, and restrictions of one form or another. I might say with some relief that I am finally free from pain having taken tablets for pain relief, or that a political prisoner has at last been freed from imprisonment. In both cases we're using the word in a negative way, in that something is being taken away, the pain or the imprisonment.

In contrast, we also tend to use the word in what we might describe as a positive way. In this sense the preposition changes from being free *from* something to being free *to* do something. We may say that, because a friend has unexpectedly won a large amount of money, she is now free to do what she has always wanted to do – to go back to college, or to buy her own home. Governments, too, use the concept in this way, arguing that the money they are investing in education will free more people to get better, more satisfying jobs and to fulfil more of their dreams.

Try it for yourself. Take the following question, which uses the concepts of authority and power. As you tackle the exercise below, think about how you use a concept like authority. If you find you use it in more than one way, then you have a structure emerging: each way in which you use it needs to be explored and its implications unwrapped.

Consider the question below and complete the exercise that follows

'Authority amounts to no more than the possession of power.' *Discuss.*

Practice exercise   *1*
Interpreting the question

Underline what you consider to be the key concepts and then analyse what you think are the main implications of the question.

This can be done in the form of sentences, but a more useful way is a short structure of notes that allows you to capture your ideas effectively and follow your train of thoughts quickly. Something like the structure shown on p.19 would be a useful way of outlining the central implications of the question, which you can then follow up in your research and, later, in the essay. If you find any of the abbreviations in these notes mystifying, you can find the meaning of them in Chapter 14.

Answer
Clearly in this question the key concepts that have to be examined are 'power' and 'authority', and the relationship between them. Start, then, by asking yourself how you use these words. For this you need to summon up a few examples of situations in which both of these concepts might come up. These might involve figures of authority, like police officers, teachers, parents and other people who have the power and influence to get you to do what you might not otherwise want to do.

From these examples you might conclude that the most obvious way in which we use the word 'power' is to describe somebody as having force, the capacity to compel us to do something against our wishes. A police officer has this sort of power, or a mugger, if he possesses a weapon with which to threaten us. But we also use it in the phrase 'the power of persuasion', in which the force involved is the force of an argument or the ability to persuade us to do something we would not otherwise do, by giving us good and persuasive reasons for doing it.

If the concept of power breaks down in this sort of way, then that of authority probably does too. We talk about somebody being *in* authority, somebody like a police officer or a judge. In this case we might not respect the person or the reasons they may give us for doing as they demand, but we might respect the institution they represent, or we might just comply with their orders because we fear the consequences of not doing so. Police officers have powers at their disposal that can seriously affect us, even denying us our liberty.

And, of course, there are others, like a mugger or a local gang leader, who can also compel us to do things, through force or threats of force, but who have no authority, although they still have this sort of power. This leads us to the conclusion that authority doesn't simply amount to the possession of power alone: the gang leader has no authority, in the usual sense, to command us to do anything, unlike the police

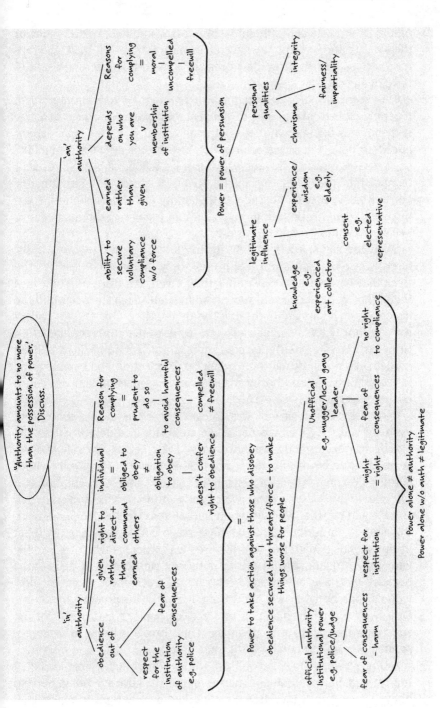

"Authority amounts to no more than the possession of power." Discuss.

'in' authority

obedience out of
- respect for the institution of authority e.g. police
- fear of consequences

given rather than earned

right to direct + command others

individual
= obliged to obey
≠ obligation to obey
|
doesn't confer right to obedience

Reason for complying
= prudent to do so
|
to avoid harmful consequences
|
compelled ≠ freewill

=

Power to take action against those who disobey
obedience secured thro threats/force – to make things worse for people

official authority
Institutional power
e.g. police/judge
- fear of consequences – harm
- respect for institution

Unofficial
e.g. mugger/local gang leader
- might = right
- fear of consequences
- no right to compliance

Power alone ≠ authority
Power alone w/o auth ≠ legitimate

'an' authority

ability to secure voluntary compliance w/o force

earned rather than given

depends on who you are
v
membership of institution

Reasons for complying
= moral
|
uncompelled
|
freewill

Power = power of persuasion

legitimate influence
- knowledge e.g. experienced art collector
- experience/ wisdom e.g. elderly
- consent e.g. elected representative

personal qualities
- charisma
- integrity
- fairness/ impartiality

officer, who has been appointed by representatives in parliament or the local council, whom we have elected. In this sense, then, the representatives and, in turn, their officially appointed officers are said to have democratic legitimacy.

This seems to suggest that the word 'authority' has an alternative meaning; something similar to the sense we mean when we describe somebody as being *an* authority. It may be that someone is an experienced art collector, so we are right to be persuaded by the arguments she presents because she knows what she's talking about. No force or compulsion is needed here, beyond, that is, the force of her arguments, her power of persuasion. She has the ability to secure voluntary compliance to her way of seeing things without the use of threats or force, because she has earned her authority.

We could say she has a 'right' to her authority, although it's a different sense of 'right' from that exercised by the police officer; it's the right that has been earned rather than given. It's also different from the authority of the elected representative, although they can both be described as being 'an' authority. The difference is that the art collector's authority has been earned as a result of her study and devotion to her work, whereas the elected representative's authority has been earned as a result of putting himself up for election and campaigning for votes. Both have authority and exercise legitimate influence because of the respect they have earned.

Of course, others fit into this category of legitimate influence, too, even though they have earned their authority in different ways. The elderly in our communities have earned respect as a result of their years of experience and the wisdom this has brought. Others have certain personal qualities that have given them a reputation for integrity and honesty; people we might go to for advice and support.

We could say that we have good 'moral' reasons for complying with this sort of authority: that is we have reasons that convince us to act in this way as a matter of our own free will; whereas when we comply with orders of those who are *in* authority we do so not necessarily because we have any moral reason, that we respect them as individuals, but because we know that it would be prudent to do so. Otherwise we might suffer in one way or another as a result of the sanctions they can bring upon us. This threat is likely to force us, against our will, to comply with their orders.

In this sense we may be 'obliged' to obey, if the local gang leader or the mugger is threatening to harm us, but we have no 'obligation' to obey, because such threats are not backed by any right to make such orders. Whereas the art collector has earned the right through many years of study, and police officers, while not having earned the same respect for themselves as a person, have been given the 'rightful', legitimate authority by our elected representatives.

▶ In the next chapter

Some people find this sort of exercise easy to do. If, however, you've found it particularly difficult, don't despair. It is a lot simpler than it appears. Over the next three chapters you will learn a simple three-step technique for analysing the most difficult concept.

Note
1 Those who want to read more about open and closed concepts should read Leon J. Goldstein's paper 'Reflections on Conceptual Openness and Conceptual Tension', in F. D'Agustino and I. C. Jarvie (eds), *Freedom and Rationality: Essays in Honour of John Watkins* (London: Kluwer Academic, 1989), pp. 87–110.

3 Learning to Analyse

In this chapter you will learn:

- that of all the thinking skills, analysis is probably the most useful in opening up rich sources of ideas for you to use in an essay;
- how to free yourself from your own preconceptions, so that you can think more freely and see more of the implications of questions;
- how techniques similar to the three-step technique have been the source of some of the most important intellectual achievements.

Of course, not all the questions you tackle will offer up their concepts so easily as the authority/power question. In many of them the concept will hide, lurking behind the most innocent word. And in some questions it will be difficult to decide whether it's worth analysing the concept at all – it may not be central to the issues the question raises, taking you in a direction that's irrelevant. In these cases you just have to take the concept and analyse it carefully to see what's there. In most questions you'll find that by doing this you will open up a treasure of all sorts of ideas you can use. The question just seems to unfold before your eyes and you know exactly the arguments to pursue and the research you need to do.

But, obviously, the key to this is to learn to analyse the concepts well. Of all the thinking skills we use this is the most neglected, even though it's probably the most useful. Without it we have no means of seeing a problem clearly, so that we can use our creative abilities to fashion a solution. Similarly, we have no means of seeing what it is about an argument that we dislike, so we can go on to criticise and improve it. In fact almost every intellectual activity begins with some form of analysis to make it clear what we're trying to tackle. It gives direction and purpose to our work. Without it we're likely to be at a complete loss as to how to set about the question.

Unfortunately, we all seem to assume that everyone knows how to do it, so there's no need to teach it. This, however, is far from the case. Most of us do it poorly because, rather than it being a natural thing to do, something we do almost by second nature, it seems to most of us to be the most *unnatural* thing. We have to force ourselves to ask the most deliberate questions about things that appear obvious. This seems to be unwarranted: it seems forced and unnecessary. I often ask students that most annoying and awkward of all questions, which begins, 'But what do you mean by . . . ?' Usually their response is to gasp in amazement that anyone, particularly one bearing the heavy responsibility for their education, could have any difficulty understanding a concept or the meaning of a word they use everyday of their lives. Their usual response is, 'But everyone knows what that means!'

But then, once they've begun thinking about the word and arguing what they all understand by it, they begin to realise that there is anything but consensus over its meaning. And, to their delight, as they analyse the implications of the concept they uncover for themselves rich sources of ideas they never knew they had, and the most perceptive observations that surprise even themselves.

▶ Blinded by preconceptions

In fact, the more awkward and deliberate this process feels the better the results are likely to be. In this lies the strength of the analytical method. We all carry around with us patterns of ideas through which we're able to structure unfamiliar experience and give it meaning. But, while this can be useful in giving us emotional safety, particularly in times of rapid change, it can be quite deceptive: we see what we want to see, even when it's perfectly obvious that we've got it wrong.

We've all heard police officers explain that, if they have, say, twelve eyewitnesses to a crime, they will more than likely have twelve different accounts of what happened. We all carry certain preconceptions that prepare our minds to see what they want to see. For example, read the phrases in each of the triangles below.

Most people read them as 'Paris in the spring', 'Once in a lifetime', 'Bird in the hand'. But when they're urged to look a little closer, sooner or later they see the extra words, which their minds have selectively ignored because they were already prepared to see the familiar expressions. There are other examples, too, illustrating the same point: our preconceptions prepare our minds to see what they want to see.

▶ Progress through analysis

It should come as no surprise, then, that analysing those concepts and explanations that we've become accustomed to accept almost without thinking, has been the source of the most remarkable breakthroughs in almost all areas of thought. Indeed, the ruling paradigms that structure our thinking in many areas do so even when it's clear they're no longer effective in explaining what we see.

In 1847, if Ignaz Semmelweis had allowed his thinking to be ruled by the prevailing paradigm of his time, he would have agreed with his colleagues that the high death-rate from puerperal, or childbed, fever among women in labour in the General Hospital in Vienna was due to the prevailing miasma that hung over the hospital. This was the conventional wisdom accepted by all the medical authorities, even though it failed to explain why there were five times more deaths in the doctors' division of the hospital than there were in the midwives' division. So, he wondered, how could a miasma settling over the whole hospital have such a strong differentiated effect?

Divesting himself of all the assumptions handed down by previous generations, he set about analysing the facts he had gathered by comparing the evidence in the two divisions. Unblinkered by any preconceptions, eventually he came to realise that the fever was a blood disorder made worse in the doctors' division by him and his students coming straight from the autopsy room to examine women in labour. Without disinfecting themselves they were transferring into the bloodstream of their female patients infections they had picked up from examining the 'cadaveric matter' in the autopsy room.

His refusal to accept the conventional wisdom of his day was to cost Semmelweis his job, his career and the respect of his peers, but it became the inspiration for the work of Louis Pasteur and the great advances in bacteriology that were to come. Without his courage the development of this field, considered by many to be the greatest single advance in the history of medicine, might never have occurred.

▶ A simple technique

In fact, looking at the way Semmelweis set about analysing the problem is very useful in learning how to do it ourselves. Most of us can do this just as well: we have the abilities, if only we can develop the skills to use them. What follows is a simple technique that you can learn quickly. But first:

Consider the question below and complete the exercise that follows

'Advertisers seek only to ensure consumers make informed choices.'
Discuss.

Practice exercise   2
Interpreting the question

Do what you did with the previous practice exercise and underline what you consider to be the key words. Then write a statement about the meaning and implications of the question.

Most students underline words like 'informed' and 'choices'. Some underline 'consumers', even 'advertisers'. But only those who feel confident about their analytical skills underline the word 'only'. Yet it not only alerts the reader to the suspicion that this may be a question largely about concepts, it also reveals the structure of the question.

Without it the statement is much weaker and the questions that are raised are much less contentious. The claim that advertisers try to inform the public is one that most of us would concede, albeit with certain reservations. But to claim that this is *all* they do is far more contentious and throws light on what we mean by the concept of 'advertisement'. Without it we might have been willing to accept the concept as if it raised no particular problem. Of course, it still might raise no particular problem, but you have to be sure.

▶ In the next chapter

Given this, then, we have to work our way deliberately through three simple steps to analyse the concept. Once you've done this a few times and begin to feel confident about what you're doing, you'll be surprised at just how quickly you develop your skills. You'll be able to identify subtle distinctions and shades of meaning, and you'll bring to your analysis the sort of perceptive insight that you might never have suspected you possessed.

4 The Three-Step Technique – Steps 1 and 2

In this chapter you will learn:

- how we create our own concepts, even when we start out knowing nothing about the subject;
- how to start with your own examples and identify the common pattern of characteristics that underlies each one;
- how to analyse concepts into their essential characteristics.

The three-step technique for analysing concepts begins at the same point where Semmelweis began. In Step 1 we gather the evidence: the examples of the concept we want to analyse. Then, in Step 2, we analyse these examples to extract a common pattern of characteristics.

▶ Step 1: Gather your typical examples

First, like Semmelweis, spend some time gathering the evidence. With the idea of 'advertisement' clearly in your mind, list what you think might be five or six of the most typical examples. Try to make them as different as possible. Avoid those for the same type of product or service, the same producer, and the same medium through which they are advertised. In this way you'll be able to strip away their differences to reveal more clearly their essential similarities.

▶ Step 2: Analyse your examples

Now, using these examples, create your concept. In other words, analyse the common characteristics in each of your examples, isolating them so that you can then put them together to form the concept. This is one of those things we all know how to do, but most of us would be hard pressed to explain just how we do it. In effect it's simple pattern recognition. By recognising the common pattern of characteristics that each example possesses, we visualise what the concept might look like that underlies all the examples.

It's always surprising how many people are willing to argue that they don't know how to do this, and they've never done it in their lives, even though it's something they do every day, almost without thinking. When it comes to the advertising question there are always a sizeable number of students who claim they know nothing about advertising – certainly not enough to analyse the concept into its essential characteristics.

But we all know much more than we let on. Even with the briefest of acquaintances with a concept, after confronting just four or five examples of it for the first time, most people are quite clear about its core characteristics. Indeed, they can be surprisingly dogmatic in a discussion with others as to what is and what is not an example of it just minutes after declaring they knew nothing about it and had no idea how to analyse it.

For example, in the following case the concept is represented by a number of unfamiliar abstract patterns. As a result we're freed from all those preconceptions that might otherwise have forced our thinking down pre-programmed routes. Nothing has been said about the concept to lead us to believe that those who are authorities in these sorts of matters think the concept has certain definite characteristics. The concept is ours to form without assistance from anyone else.

Practice exercise 3
Analysing the concept

Examine in turn each of the figures on pp. 29–30. As you do this you will see a concept emerge. For want of a better name, let's call it an 'Olic'.

Not all of the figures are olics, so you will have to form your idea of the concept and then use it to distinguish between the olics and the non-olics.

Once you've looked at all the figures, answer the following:

1. Which of the figures are olics?
2. Analyse the concept of an olic and list three of the essential characteristics common to all.

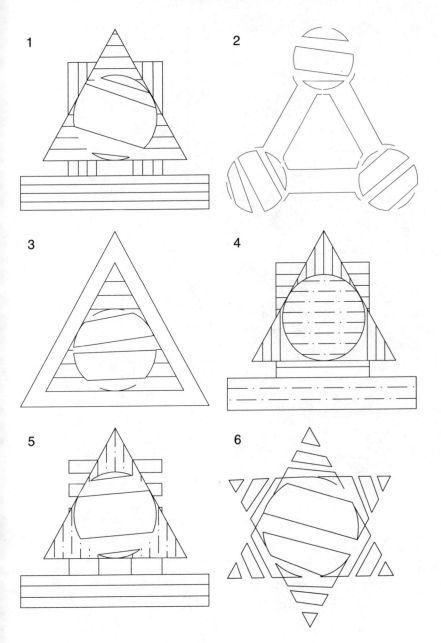

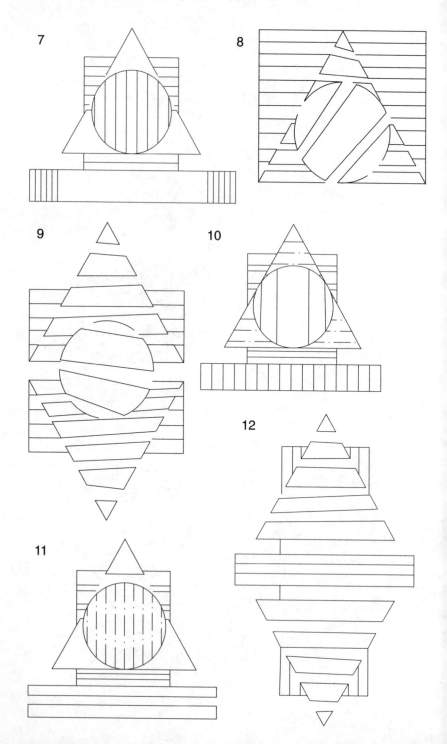

Answers

1. 1, 4, 5, 7, 10, 11.
2. You could have chosen your three characteristics from any of the following:
    2.1 long rectangular base
    2.2 a circle at the centre
    2.3 a triangle surrounding the circle
    2.4 a rectangle surrounding the circle and intersecting the triangle

As you can see from this, even though you haven't come across an olic before, the concept emerges, leaving you in no doubt about its essential characteristics. Now consider the advertising question again.

Question

'Advertisers seek only to ensure consumers make informed choices.'
Discuss.

Go through the first two steps, one at a time, deliberately and carefully. Don't rush them; they're important. If you need to, look back at the way we analysed the concepts of authority and power: you're doing exactly the same. It also helps if you can use a note-taking strategy, like the pattern notes we used with the authority/power question. This will allow you to capture your ideas effectively and follow your train of thoughts quickly.

Step 1:   Gather your typical examples
First choose, say, five or six examples of advertisements, that you may have seen on the television or in magazines.

Step 2:   Analyse your examples
Now do the same, with the concept of advertising, as you've just done with the concept of olic. Using the question as your guide, ask yourself if there are certain essential characteristics that are always present, without which it would be wrong to describe something as an advertisement.

From your examples it will no doubt be clear that they are all trying to persuade you in various ways. Yet, at the same time, it might be just as reasonable to conclude that they are also trying to inform you. In some cases this might not amount to much, but in most advertisements it's likely to be more than just the name of the product.

In the light of this and the implications of the question that you revealed earlier, you should be asking yourself if an advertisement is always persuasive, or can it be just informative without attempting to get you to choose or act in one way or another? You might conclude that almost all advertisements are informative, but that's not all they do. This analysis suggests there are two kinds of advertisement: those that seem largely preoccupied with passing on information, yet in fact are covertly manipulative; and those that are overtly manipulative, in that their intention is obvious – to persuade us as consumers to buy their product. Now you have a simple structure for the concept, which you can develop in the light of your examples in the same way we did for the olic and for the authority/power question.

As you have no doubt already discovered, there are a number of ways in which you can develop your analysis of ideas from this point. One of the most useful is to organise your ideas into their logical opposites, so that you create a continuum or a spectrum with opposites at either end. The analysis into overt and covert manipulation is an example of this. Although in terms of our examples they may not be exact logical opposites, they work just as well in mapping out the territory. Then, within this, you could use another method of organising your ideas by thinking about the types into which your ideas break down. Of course the number of types will depend on how many you can reasonably think of.

As we have a spectrum of opposites in this question, first take one side, then the other. You could begin with those advertisements which appear to be covertly persuasive. Some, like those concerned with public information, say about a new tax or changes in regulations, or government health warnings about smoking or the use of fire alarms, seem to be entirely concerned with informing us. However, that's not to say there isn't a message hidden in the information. The government no doubt would like to persuade you not to continue to smoke, or to organise yourself so that you pay your taxes promptly.

Others clearly are intent on promoting the sales of their products. But, nevertheless, they do this through a strategy of promoting awareness about new products, new designs and new technology. New computer games, mobile phones, and new types of household goods are all promoted, at least in the initial stages, by advertisements that are designed to inform and to promote awareness of the new type of product or design that's on the market.

In the same way, at the other end of the spectrum, the overtly manipulative advertisements can similarly be broken down into their types. At the very least they attempt to manipulate the consumer by using information selectively to emphasise what's good about their product and to omit what's bad. Others will use comments and information taken out of context to promote their product, even though these may be taken from reports and reviews that are highly critical of it. An unfavourable report from a consumer association might contain just a single sentence of praise, but it will be this that finds its way into the advertisement.

Equally effective are advertisers who appeal to a convincing, though distorted, picture of what is taken for common-sense or accepted values in our societies. Archetypal characters and scenarios are created to evoke predictable responses that advertisers believe we will all share. Those promoting slimming products try to convince us that everyone wants to be slim, that it's associated with success, and that if you're overweight this is a sign of social failure and self-indulgence.

But perhaps the most common strategy is for advertisers to sell their products by associating them with our strongest feelings, desires and prejudices. In this way they can by-pass our reason, thereby short-circuiting our ability to make conscious choices. As our understanding of the psychology of the individual has grown, so too has the advertiser's capacity to tap into our deepest motivations and develop more effective means of manipulation by exploiting the sex, status and prejudices of the consumer. Indeed, the most effective means of doing this, subliminal advertising, is now banned or regulated by many governments.

Answer
Once you've done this, look at the analysis in the structure on p. 34. It's unlikely that yours will be a lot different. You may use different examples and you may have seen things that I haven't, but the final structure is likely to be quite similar.

If you think you haven't gone far enough in your analysis, or you haven't seen enough, don't worry too much. You will get better at this with practice. And you've still got Step 3 to come.

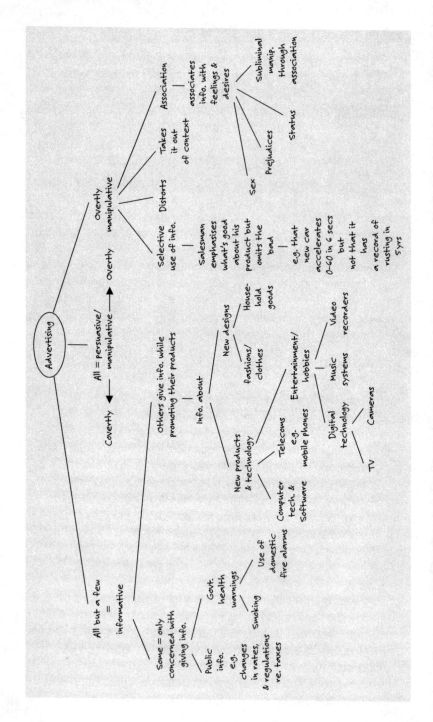

▶ In the next chapter

Now that you've mapped out the concept, the next step is to test it in much the same way you did when you compared an olic with a non-olic. In this way you will sharpen and tighten up the concept, and in the process you will begin to see the best way of tackling the essay in terms of the structure you should adopt.

5 Step 3 – Test your Concept

In this chapter you will learn:

- how to distinguish between those characteristics that are essential to the concept and those that are merely accidental;
- how to create a clear structure for the concept, which you can then use to catch the relevant ideas and evidence as you research the topic;
- how to test and refine your original analysis of the concept to uncover subtle distinctions and shades of meaning, for which you will earn high marks.

Now that you have your concept clearly analysed in a structure, it's time to test it. Like Semmelweis with his hypothesis, you may have the overall structure broadly right, but there may be details that are wrong, or subtle distinctions you haven't seen. When Semmelweis formulated his hypothesis he thought he and his students should disinfect their hands by washing them in a solution of chlorinated lime each time they came out of the autopsy room. In fact he was right about this, but it's quite possible he might have discovered, after testing it, that this was ineffective and another solution was needed.

In much the same way, by testing your concept you will shake out those characteristics that are essential and ditch those that are only accidental to it. In the process you will have sharpened up your understanding of the core characteristics. As a result you'll have a fairly well defined structure to catch the relevant ideas and evidence as you research the topic, and in most questions you'll probably find that you already have the broad structure on which you'll be able to build the plan of your essay.

To test it in this way you need only take some simple, but quite deliberate steps.[1]

▶ 1 Borderline cases

First, with your structure in front of you try to think of a borderline case, an example of advertising that doesn't fit comfortably within your structure. Then analyse its characteristics to see if, in fact, it does fit after all. You may find there's more to this form of advertising than you first thought and it does, in fact, fit within the structure. Alternatively, after thinking through all the possibilities it may become clear that it doesn't fit and you will have to adjust your structure to take account of it.

For example, take a form of advertising that appears to be wholly informative, say a bus or railway timetable. This is just a list of routes with times for arrivals and departures. There may be no enticing message at the top inducing you to 'Come to sunny Bognor, children travel free!' There may be no catchy jingles encouraging you to 'Let the train take the strain!' It might be just a simple notice containing travel information, erected in a prominent position in a bus or train station.

So, the question we have to ask is, does this suggest that advertisements can be just informative after all, or are we right in assuming that behind all of this information lies the covert message that we ought to travel by train or bus because it's more convenient and easier, and therefore less stressful than the alternatives? We could argue that in putting out this sort of information, the intentions of the managers of the bus and train companies are not just to give us information, but to so impress us with their efficiency and convenience, that we will travel this way more frequently.

▶ 2 Contrasting cases

If this is the conclusion you come to, move to the second stage and test your analysis again, this time by imagining an example that is the complete contrast to this – one that is composed of nothing but factual information, where the intention of the advertiser seems to amount to nothing more than to inform the public.

For example, you might be travelling through the countryside one summer afternoon, and you come into a small village. At the centre of the village is a small green, dominated by a huge tree. On this tree someone has attached a small hand-written notice with the words:

August 31st.
The Annual Village Fête.
On the Village Green.
Starting 3pm.

There is no enticing message with promises of gifts and untold wealth for the lucky person who wins the fête raffle, not even the simple appeal 'Come to the village fete!' There is nothing but information.

In this case, if we are still to assume that it is the *intentions* of those who put out the information, that define a notice as an advertisement, then they are more deeply hidden here than those of the people who framed the bus and railway timetables. Nevertheless, we might still be justified in arguing that the writer of the village fête notice had one unmistakable intention in putting up the notice: to encourage more people to attend and participate. This would no doubt mean more money for the local appeal to restore the church bells or to build an extension to the old people's day centre.

▶ 3   Doubtful cases

If this is the case, we've now reached a stage where we seem to have shaken out a core characteristic of advertising that was not sufficiently clear in our original analysis. We seem to be saying that even though an announcement is concerned with imparting information, with advertisements this is only surface appearance. What matters above all is the intentions of those who frame the notice. In an advertisement they are suggesting or attempting to persuade us to adopt a certain course of action. Whereas with a simple statement of information there are no ulterior motives: they are just presenting information and leaving it there.

Given this, we must move to the next stage and test the consequences of adopting this distinction. We need to imagine cases in which it would be difficult for us to accept these consequences. Clearly, if we're right in thinking this way, then any announcement or statement of fact that suggests a possible course of action is an advertisement. For example, a factual statement made in a television programme that smoking cigarettes is responsible for over 80 per cent of cases of lung cancer, or a report by a health authority that a diet containing large quantities of salt is likely to lead to high blood pressure, are both suggestive of a course of action. But it would be odd to describe either of these two statements as an advertisement.

If this is right, then we have reached a point where we can refine another of the distinctions that was in our original analysis. Each time we do this we inject more subtle shades of meaning for which we will earn high marks from an examiner who reads the arguments we've developed so far. You might consider arguing that these are not advertisements in the normal sense, by virtue of their subject matter. They are concerned with contentious political and social issues, not commercial products and services that businesses or local communities are trying to sell.

Indeed, those who suspect the intentions of the people making this type of statement might describe it as propaganda. This might include tobacco companies, who at one stage might have criticised governments for warning people about the dangers of smoking cigarettes. If this is right, we might conclude that advertising and propaganda, in so far as they share the same intention of trying to get people to choose and act in a particular way, are of the same family, only distinguishable by their different subject matter.

As you can see, as we have worked our way through each of these stages we have deliberately asked awkward questions to test and refine the distinctions we made in our original analysis. By doing so we've not only revealed some important subtle shades of meaning, for which the examiner will award us high marks, but in effect we have rehearsed some of the more complex arguments we'll develop when we come to write the essay.

Assignment 1
Analysing concepts

- Choose an essay question from one of the subjects you are studying. As you've already done in the practice exercises, underline the keywords and write a short statement outlining the meaning and implications of the question. This will help you clarify the key concept in the question, which you will need to analyse.

- Now analyse the concept deliberately, step by step. First, think up three or four **typical examples** that reflect the way the concept is

Continued

used in the question. Then **analyse** the core characteristics, those that are common to each of your examples. This will take a little thought, but remember the 'olic': your mind will have a fairly clear idea of the concept. You've just got to bring it in front of your mind's eye so that you can list the core characteristics. You may only come up with three or four, but that's fine.

- Then, **test it**. Think up a **borderline case**, one that doesn't easily fit. This will lead you to refine your original concept. Other characteristics may appear that are far more important, or you may adjust one or two of those you've listed. Once this is done, test your new refined concept by imagining a **contrasting case** that seems to conflict with it. This might lead you to adjust your concept again – either that or you will realise that there's more to your example and it does fit within your concept after all. Either way, after you've done this you will no doubt feel that you've mapped out the concept: you've got all the core characteristics sharply in focus.

- Armed with this you can now go back and reveal more of the implications of the question by imagining a **doubtful case**. This will throw a sharper light on the consequences of using the concept in the way it was used in the question. At the end of this, as a result of your careful analysis, you're quite likely to have in front of you in your notes the structure that will form the basis of the final essay.

Now that you've analysed the concepts and unwrapped the implications of the question, you're in a better position to research the essay. You should have a clear structure of the key issues raised. In a great many questions these will develop out of your analysis of the key concepts in the question. In others they will come from your initial attempt to describe what you believe to be its meaning and implications. Either way, you cannot begin your research without arming yourself with a clear idea of what the question is getting at and what you should be looking for when you begin to read and take notes.

▶ In the next chapter

In the next chapter we will look at the best way of getting your own ideas down, so that when you begin your research you know what questions you want answered and you're less likely to be dictated to by the texts you read.

Note

1 A similar approach was first used by John Wilson in *Thinking with Concepts* (Cambridge: Cambridge University Press, 1963), which provided the initial idea for this method.

6 Brainstorming

In this chapter you will learn:

- how to use more of your own ideas through effective brainstorming;
- why it is important to separate analysis from brainstorming;
- how to get clear answers from the texts you use;
- how to avoid being dictated to by the authors you read.

Over the last five chapters we have seen how important it is to interpret carefully the meaning and implications of questions. Learning to do this well means we're better able to see the structure our essays should adopt in order to produce a full and relevant answer to the question. What's more, we're less likely to overlook the significant, though subtle, issues that might be hidden in the question. Almost inevitably, when we overlook the importance of doing this well, we end up with essays that not only are confusing and poorly organised, but miss the point.

In this lies the importance of the three-step technique. It develops those skills you need in order to use your analytical abilities effectively. Once you've used it two or three times, you'll be confident that you can interpret any question whose meaning and implications depend upon a perceptive analysis of its concepts. But, as we saw, there are other reasons why these skills and abilities are so important. If we overlook them we're likely to disqualify ourselves from the highest marks on offer. Examiners are likely to assume that we simply haven't developed that thoughtful, reflective ability to question the assumptions we make when we use language.

▶ Analysis and brainstorming: two different things

What all of this amounts to is the importance of 'staking your claim' as early as possible, indeed as soon as you get the question. This involves two things: first, as we've seen, thinking through *your* analysis of the concepts and implications of the question, and second, writing down *your own* ideas on the question. It's now time to turn to the second of these: brainstorming your own ideas. This means that you empty your mind on the subject, without the aid of books. As quickly as possible you track the flow of your ideas as you note what you know about the subject and what you think might be relevant to the question.

You might be tempted to think this sounds strikingly similar to what we've just done; so much so that you're tempted to assume that brainstorming is just a part of the process of analysis. After all, they both involve your own ideas, which you get down on paper as quickly as you can without the aid of books. But they are, in fact, quite different, and if you allow yourself to merge the two, skimping on one, you will almost certainly have problems.

In analysis you're unwrapping what's already there. It may be buried deep, but by a process of introspection, through which you examine the different ways you use a concept such as authority or advertisement, you come to see more clearly the contours of the concept, its essential characteristics.

In contrast, with brainstorming you are going beyond the concept: this is synthesis, rather than analysis. You are pulling together ideas, arguments and evidence that you think may have a bearing on the question's implications that you have already revealed through your analysis. So, whereas analysis is a convergent activity, brainstorming is divergent, synthesising material from different sources. If you like, one activity is centripetal, the other centrifugal. Confuse the two and you'll do neither well.

▶ The importance of brainstorming

If you overlook this distinction and merge the two activities, you're likely to struggle with two problems. First, if you abandon analysis too soon and embark on brainstorming, your focus will shift away from the implications of the question and the concepts it contains. Consequently, you're likely to find that you don't have the guidelines to direct your brainstorming into profitable areas. You will find a lot less material and much of what you do unearth you will no doubt discover later that you cannot use, because it's irrelevant.

On the other hand, if you analyse without brainstorming you'll fail to arm yourself with *your* ideas and what *you know* about the topic. As a result, almost certainly two things will happen:

1 **The authors you read for your research will dictate to you**
Without your own ideas to protect you, it will be difficult, at times impossible, for you to resist the pull of their ideas and the persuasiveness of their arguments. As a result you'll find yourself accepting the case they develop and the judgements they make without evaluating them sufficiently, even copying large sections of the text into your own notes.

2 **And, equally serious, you will find it difficult to avoid including a great mass of material that is quite irrelevant to your purposes**
All of this material may have been relevant to the author's purposes when he or she wrote the book, but *their* purposes are rarely identical with *yours*. Nevertheless, having spent days amassing this large quantity of notes, it's most unlikely that you're going to find the detachment somewhere to decide that most of these notes are irrelevant to your essay and you've got to ditch them. You're more likely to convince yourself that they can 'be made' relevant, and you end up including them in a long, discursive, shapeless essay, in which the examiner frequently feels lost in a mass of irrelevant material.

So, brainstorming should be seen as distinct from analysis. It needs to be done straight after you've completed your analysis, which in turn needs to be done as soon as you have decided upon the question you're going to tackle. This will give your subconscious time to go away and riffle through your data banks for what it needs before you begin to set about your research.

> If you don't make clear *your own* ideas and *your* interpretation of the implications of the question, your thinking is likely to be hijacked by the author and his or her intentions. If you don't ask your author clear questions you are not likely to get the clear, relevant answers you want.

▶ Empty your mind

Now that you've analysed the implications, use this to empty your mind on the question. Most of us are all too eager to convince ourselves that we know nothing about a subject and, therefore, we have no choice but to skip this stage and go straight into the books. But no matter what the subject, I have never found a group of students, despite all their declarations of ignorance and all their howls of protest, who were not able to put together a useful structure of ideas that would help them to decide as they read what's relevant to the essay and what's not.

Once we tap into our own knowledge and experience, we can all come up with ideas and a standard by which to judge the author's point of view, which will liberate us from being poor helpless victims of what we read. We all have ideas and experience that allow us to negotiate with texts, evaluating the author's opinions, while we select what we want to use and discard the rest.

Throughout this stage, although you're constantly checking your ideas for relevance, don't worry if your mind flows to unexpected areas and topics as the ideas come tumbling out. The important point is to get the ideas onto the page and to let the mind's natural creativity and self-organisation run its course, until you've emptied your mind. Later you can edit the ideas, discarding those that are not strictly relevant to the question.

Practice exercise 4
Empty your mind

Taking the advertising question, empty your mind on the subject, using the analysis you've already created as your basic structure, but not restricting yourself to that if you think there are other ideas that are connected.

The most important point to remember is not to put unnecessary brakes on your mind; allow it to run freely over the issues, making connections, analysing issues and arguments, and pulling ideas and evidence together. Therefore, don't worry too much about relevance at this stage.

Although it is bound to be different, the structure that results from brainstorming is likely to be similar to the structure outlined on

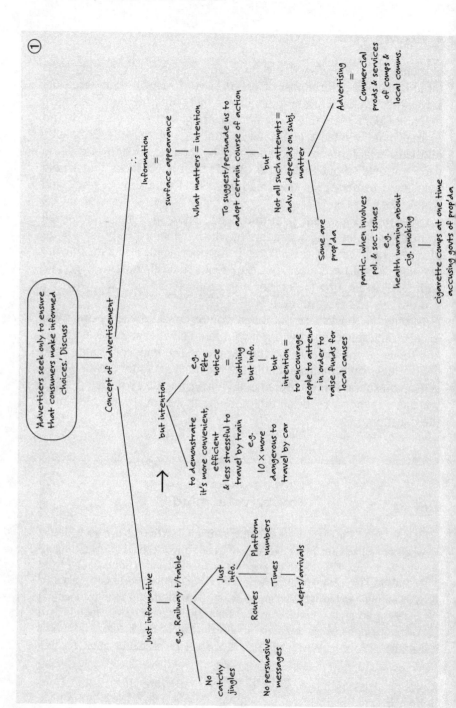

①

'Advertisers seek only to ensure that consumers make informed choices.' Discuss

Concept of advertisement

Just informative

e.g. Railway t/table

No catchy jingles

No persuasive messages

Just info.
— Platform numbers
— Routes
— Times
— depts/arrivals

but intention

to demonstrate it's more convenient, efficient & less stressful to travel by train

e.g. 10 × more dangerous to travel by car

e.g. Fête notice = nothing but info.

but intention = to encourage people to attend — in order to raise funds for local causes

∴ Information = surface appearance

What matters = intention

To suggest/persuade us to adopt certain course of action

but Not all such attempts = adv. — depends on subj. matter

Some are prop'da

partic. when involves pol. & soc. issues

e.g. health warning about cig. smoking

cigarette comps at one time accusing govts of prop'da

Advertising = Commercial prods & services of comps & local comns.

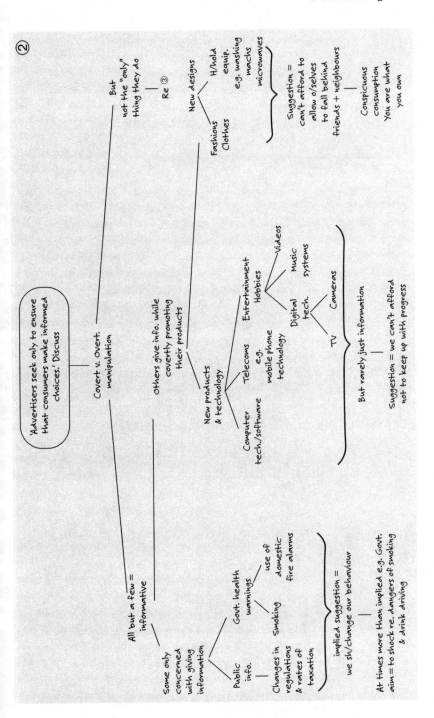

②

'Advertisers seek only to ensure that consumers make informed choices.' Discuss

Covert v. overt. manipulation

But not the "only" thing they do
Re ③

All but a few = informative

Some only concerned with giving information

Public info.

Govt. health warnings

Smoking

use of domestic fire alarms

Changes in regulations & rates of taxation

implied suggestion = we sh/change our behaviour

At times more than implied e.g. Govt. aim = to shock re. dangers of smoking & drink driving

Others give info. while covertly promoting their products

New products & technology

Computer tech./software

Telecoms

e.g. mobile phone technology

Entertainment

Hobbies

videos

Music systems

Digital tech.

Cameras

TV

But rarely just information

Suggestion = we can't afford not to keep up with progress

New designs

Fashions

Clothes

H/hold equip.

e.g. washing machs

microwaves

Suggestion = can't afford to allow o/selves to fall behind friends + neighbours

Conspicuous consumption
You are what you own

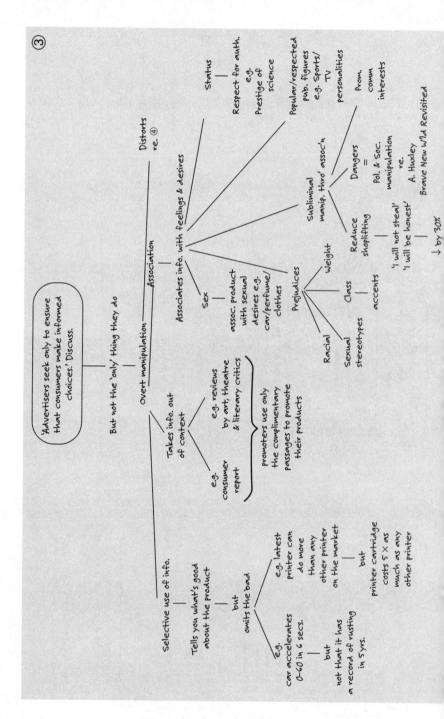

③

'Advertisers seek only to ensure that consumers make informed choices.' Discuss.

But not the 'only' thing they do

Overt manipulation — **Association** — Distorts re. ④

Overt manipulation

Takes info. out of context

e.g. reviews by art, theatre & literary critics

e.g. consumer report

promoters use only the complimentary passages to promote their products

Selective use of info.

Tells you what's good about the product

but omits the bad

e.g. latest printer can do more than any other printer on the market

but printer cartridge costs 5 × as much as any other printer

e.g. car accelerates 0–60 in 6 secs.

but not that it has a record of rusting in 5 yrs.

Association

Associates info. with feelings & desires

Status

Respect for auth. e.g. Prestige of science

Popular/respected pub. figures e.g. Sports/ TV personalities

Prom. comm interests

Sex

assoc. product with sexual desires e.g. car/perfume/ clothes

Subliminal manip. thro' assoc'n

Dangers = Pol. & Soc. manipulation re. A. Huxley Brave New w'ld Revisited

Prejudices

Weight

Class accents

Racial

Sexual stereotypes

Reduce shoplifting

'I will not steal' 'I will be honest'

↓ by 30%

④

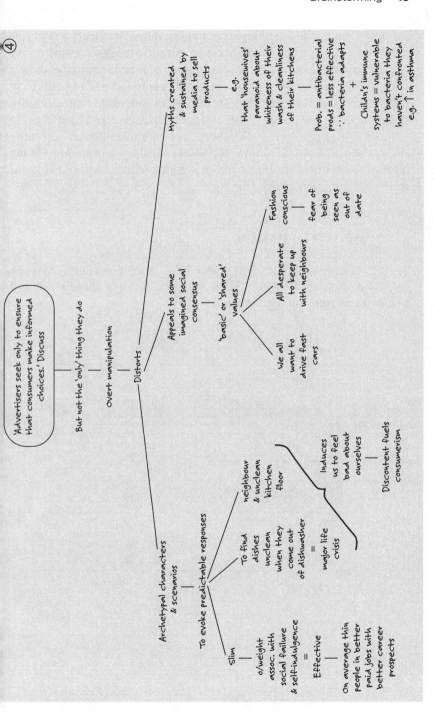

'Advertisers seek only to ensure that consumers make informed choices.' Discuss

But not the 'only' thing they do

Overt manipulation

Distorts

Appeals to some imagined social consensus

'basic' or 'shared' values

- We all want to drive fast cars
- All desperate to keep up with neighbours
- Fashion conscious
  - fear of being seen as out of date

Myths created & sustained by media to sell products

e.g.
that 'housewives' paranoid about whiteness of their wash & cleanliness of their kitchens

Prob. = antibacterial prods = less effective ∴ bacteria adapts
+
Child's immune systems = vulnerable to bacteria they haven't confronted e.g. ↑ in asthma

Archetypal characters & scenarios

To evoke predictable responses

Slim
- o/weight assoc. with social failure & self-indulgence = Effective
- On average thin people in better paid jobs with better career prospects

- To find dishes unclean when they come out of dishwasher = major life crisis

neighbour & unclean kitchen floor

Induces us to feel bad about ourselves

Discontent fuels consumerism

pp. 46–9. You might use different examples, different evidence, and you might have thought of different points, but the overall structure, based on the principal issues the question raises, will be broadly the same.

Of course, not everything in these notes will find its way into your final essay: they simply may not be strictly relevant. Brainstorming depends upon your ability to follow your ideas and record them quickly without close attention to relevance. Your internal editor will exert his or her influence later. For now, the key is to allow your mind to make all the connections, contrasts and extensions of ideas without slowing it up with concerns about relevance.

▶ In the next chapter

In the next chapter you will learn how greater flexibility in your approach to note-taking will help you catch more of these ideas and use more of your mind's potential.

7 Flexibility

In this chapter you will learn:

- how to use your skills more flexibly to get the best out of your abilities;
- how to capture more of your most creative ideas;
- how to make better use of your mind's potential in your essays.

At this point it's worth making the first of a number of concerted appeals for flexibility in your pattern of study.

We're all concerned with getting the best out of our abilities. Indeed most of us have abilities we haven't even used before. In order to get at these, you've probably experimented with different ways of planning your essays to find a method that suits you. But the key to it is to be flexible. Choose note-taking, planning and reading strategies that are appropriate for the job you have to do. This way you will find the right key that will unlock your abilities. Don't just stick to one strategy that you've always used even though you know it isn't always as much help as you would like it to be.

For example, if you were on holiday and your car broke down in an unfamiliar region of the country, and you decided to look in the *Yellow Pages* for the phone number of a local mechanic, it would not be the most effective reading strategy to begin at page one and read word-for-word through the rest of the book. Obviously, you would scan the pages for the right information. This is sensible, but when we tackle similar tasks in our studies we tend to stick to the familiar, reliable method of word-for-word reading, that we've always used for every task we're set.

▶ Pattern notes

The same applies to our note-taking and planning techniques. One of the most effective methods for the brainstorming stage is the method known as 'pattern notes', as shown in the examples so far. Rather than starting at the top of the page and working down in a linear form in sentences or lists, you start from the centre with the title of the essay and branch out with your analysis of concepts or other ideas as they form in your mind.

The advantage of this method is that it allows you to be much more creative, because it leaves the mind as free as possible to analyse concepts, make connections and contrasts, and to pursue trains of thought. As you're restricted to using just single words or simple phrases, you're not trapped in the unnecessary task of constructing complete sentences. Most of us are familiar with the frustration of trying to catch the wealth of ideas the mind throws up, while at the same time struggling to write down the sentences they're entangled in. As a result we see exciting ideas come and go without ever being able to record them quickly enough.

The point is that the mind can work so much faster than we can write, so we need a system that can catch all the ideas it can throw up, and give us the freedom to put them into whatever order or form appears to be right. The conventional linear strategy of taking notes restricts us in both of these ways. Not only does it tie us down to constructing complete sentences, or at least meaningful phrases, which means we lose the ideas as we struggle to find the words, but even more important, we're forced to deal with the ideas in sequence, in one particular order, so that if any ideas come to us out of that sequence, we must discard them and hope we can pick them up later. Sadly, that hope is more often forlorn: when we try to recall the ideas, we just can't.

The same is true when we take linear notes from the books we read. Most of us find that once we've taken the notes we're trapped within the order in which the author has dealt with the ideas and we've noted them. It's not impossible, but it's difficult to escape from this. By contrast, pattern notes give us complete freedom over the final order of our ideas.

It's probably best explained by comparing it to the instructions you might get from somebody if you were to ask them the way to a particular road. They would give you a linear list of instructions (e.g. 'First, go to the end of the road, then turn right. When you get to the traffic lights, etc.'). This forces you to follow identically the route they would take themselves. If you don't, you're lost. By contrast, pattern notes are like a copy of a map or the *A to Z* of a large city: you can see clearly the various routes you can take, so you can make your own choices.

Freeing the mind to work more imaginatively

Indeed, those who advocate pattern notes argue that the brain just doesn't work in a linear manner and that conventional ways of planning and taking notes are, therefore, not the most useful. They force the mind to operate in artificial ways, thereby releasing only a small fraction of its potential. If the brain works best within the clusters of key concepts in an interlinked and integrated manner in the way we've already seen, it makes sense to structure our notes and our word relations in the same way, rather than in the traditional linear manner.

This is borne out by those students who've adopted the method as an integral part of their pattern of study. Some of my most exciting and rewarding experiences as a tutor have come from seeing students use this method. For most of them this is the first time they realise that education can be an exciting business in which they have a valuable and significant role to play in producing their own insights and perceptions seen only by them in their own unique way.

By leaving them as free as possible to write down their own ideas as they come to them, it injects more creativity into their work. It also gives their own ideas greater prominence, so that when they come to research them they're better prepared to evaluate and select from what they read.

Indeed the flexibility of this strategy is almost unlimited. You can go on adding connections and new ideas as and when they occur to you. So, unlike many other systems, rather than stunting your abilities, it gives the mind the freedom to work more imaginatively, creating new analyses, seeing unexpected connections and contrasts, and synthesising ideas from different sources.

Better for unstructured situations

It's particularly useful when we have to work in unstructured situations, unlike linear notes, which work well in the structured tasks like taking notes from a book. For example, pattern notes are useful when we're trying to make notes from recall and the ideas come tumbling out thick and fast. The same is true of taking notes during a class discussion, where ideas might be thrown about quite rapidly and, unlike those in a book, you have no control over them. You can't go back to get something down you may have missed, as you can in your book by re-reading a difficult passage. Therefore you need a note-taking strategy that is fast and flexible.

But perhaps its most notable advantage over the traditional methods of note-taking lies in tackling the more creative tasks, like interpreting questions and planning essays. Not only does it allow you to keep up with the ideas as they come at you rapidly from all angles without any apparent predictability, but it also enables you to work on several lines of discussion simultaneously. Then, once the pattern is completed, all the ideas are readily available and all you need to do is to make a decision as to the final order in which to develop the arguments.

In one study, undergraduates at Oxford University, who began to use these techniques, were able to complete their essays in a third of the time they usually took, while at the same time receiving higher marks.

▶ Brainstorming and flexibility

This appeal for greater flexibility to get the most out of our abilities applies just as much to brainstorming as it does to the note-taking strategy we use to catch our ideas. Of all the things we need to do to produce an essay that will earn the highest marks, this is probably the one we are most likely to dispense with as we rush forward, impatient to get on with our reading.

But ideas come from many different sources, and they only come to the mind that is prepared to receive them. Almost everyone has had the experience of looking up an unfamiliar word in a dictionary, and then, in the days and weeks that follow, seeing and hearing the word everywhere – on advertising hoardings, in newspapers and magazines, on the radio and television, even from friends. But this is not because it is simply being used more frequently by people, it's just that we've prepared our minds to notice it.

The same applies to ideas: once we have prepared our minds we begin to pick up, from a range of different sources, ideas and evidence that we can then use in our writing. This explains why it's so import-ant to carry a notebook with you, so you can record the ideas whenever they come, from whatever source, rather than allow them to disappear into the ether.

In this context it's worth re-emphasising that ideas are organic: they grow and develop through time. If at an early stage you have allowed these ideas to come tumbling out onto the page, the subconscious will go away to riffle through your data banks for more ideas and evidence, making connections and analysing your arguments and concepts in ways that you just hadn't suspected when you set out to think about the issues. As a result, when you next come to look at your ideas, you'll be surprised by just how far they have developed.

And each time you work on them you set the mind a new set of problems to go away and solve, which develops your ideas still further. Consequently, by the time you've finished your interpretation, research and planning, and you begin to write the first draft, you have come a very long way indeed. Your ideas are more developed, subtler and far better supported by evidence, than they were when you first started out.

Assignment 2
Brainstorming a question

Take the question you worked on in the first assignment. You've already underlined the key words and concepts in the question and you've analysed what you think are its main implications. Now brainstorm the question, getting all your ideas down as quickly as possible in pattern-note form.

Give yourself a time limit, say 30 minutes, to get it all down. Then put it aside. After a day or so, come back to it and add any ideas you've come up with since. Some ideas may push themselves into your conscious mind before that, so note them, don't lose them.

Now that you've brainstormed the question you've not only tapped into ideas that are genuinely your own, but by clarifying what you know and what questions you want your books and articles to answer, you are less likely to waste time taking mounds of irrelevant, unusable notes. But the success of this depends upon using the appropriate skills for the job, rather than tying yourself inflexibly to a way of working that prevents you from using your mind's potential to process your ideas imaginatively.

▶ In the next chapter

Nevertheless, there is still one last thing you need to be sure about before you launch into your research. You must be clear about the range of abilities the examiner wants to see you use.

8 Using the Right Ability

In this chapter you will learn:

- how to make sure we answer the question using the abilities the examiner wants to assess;
- how to interpret accurately the 'instructional verbs' in questions.

So far we have seen how important it is to interpret the question carefully, because it tells us the structure our essay should adopt for us to deal relevantly with all the issues it raises. With this clear in our mind we can avoid taking masses of irrelevant notes, which are likely to find their way into our essays, making them irrelevant, shapeless and confusing.

But we also made it clear at the beginning that there is one other thing that the question tells us: the range of abilities the examiner wants to see us use. This is normally made clear through what is known as 'instructional verbs'. Given below is a list of short definitions of those most frequently found in questions, which should help you avoid the common problems that arise when you overlook or misinterpret them.

▶ Instructional verbs

Analyse   Separate an argument, a theory, or a claim into its elements or component parts; to trace the causes of a particular event; to reveal the general principles underlying phenomena.

Compare   Look for similarities and differences between two or more things, problems or arguments. Perhaps, although not always, reach a conclusion about which you think is preferable.

Contrast   Set in opposition to each other two or more things, problems or arguments in order to identify clearly their differences and their individual characteristics.

Criticise   Identify the weaknesses of certain theories, opinions or claims, and give your judgement about their merit. Support your judgements with a discussion of the evidence and the reasoning involved.

Define   Outline the precise meaning of a word or phrase. In some cases it may be necessary or desirable to examine different possible, or often used, definitions.

Describe   Give a detailed or graphic account, keeping to the facts or to the impressions that an event had upon you. In history this entails giving a narrative account of the events in the time sequence they occurred.

Discuss   Investigate or examine by argument; sift through the arguments and the evidence used to support them, giving reasons for and against both sides; examine the implications. It means playing devil's advocate by arguing not just for the side of the argument that you support, but for the side with which you may have little sympathy.

Evaluate   Make an appraisal of the worth of something, an argument or a set of beliefs, in the light of their truth or usefulness. This does involve making your own value judgements, but not just naked opinion: they must be backed up by argument and justification.

Explain   Make plain; interpret and account for the occurrence of a particular event by giving the causes. Unlike the verb 'to describe', this does not mean that it is sufficient to describe what happened by giving a narrative of the events. To explain an event is to give the reasons why it occurred, usually involving an analysis of the causes.

Illustrate   Explain or clarify something by the use of diagrams, figures or concrete examples.

Interpret   Reveal what you believe to be the meaning or significance of something; to make sense of something that might otherwise be unclear, or about which there may be more than one opinion. So usually this involves giving your own judgement.

Justify   Show adequate grounds for a decision or a conclusion by supporting it with sufficient evidence and argument; answer the main objections that are likely to be made to it.

Outline   Give the main features or the general principles of a subject, omitting minor details and emphasising its structure and arrangement.

Relate   This usually means one of two things. In some questions it means narrate a sequence of events – outline the story of a particular incident. Alternatively, it can mean show how certain things are connected or affect each other, or show to what extent they are alike.

Review   Examine closely a subject or a case that has been put forward for a certain proposal or argument. Usually, although not always, this means concluding with your own judgement as to the strength of the case. However, if it involves examining just a subject or a topic, and not an argument or a proposal, it will mean just examining in some detail all the aspects of the topic.

State   Outline briefly and clearly the facts of the situation or a side of an argument. This doesn't call for argument or discussion, just the presentation of the facts or the arguments. Equally it doesn't call for a judgement from you, just reportage.

Summarise   Give a clear and concise account of the principal points of a problem or an argument, omitting the details, evidence and examples that may have been given to support the argument or illustrate the problem.

Trace   Outline the stages in the development of a particular issue or the history of a topic.

Practice exercise   5
Instructional verbs

Gather together as many past examination papers for your course as you can, at least enough to give you a representative sample.

For each paper, list the questions in three columns: those that ask for a descriptive and factual answer (the 'what', 'how' and 'describe' type of question); those that ask for an analytical answer (the 'outline', 'analyse', 'compare' and 'contrast' type of question); and those that ask you for a discussion of the issues (the 'criticise', 'evaluate' and 'discuss' type of question).

Once you've done this, calculate the percentage of each type of question on each paper.

▶ **In the next chapter**

On the face of it this should be the end of a simple story: get the instructional verbs right and we won't make the mistake of answering the question in the wrong way. However, although this is right, it doesn't go far enough. Unless we acknowledge the difference in the assumptions about the nature of education at this level, in sharp contrast with what has gone before, we're unlikely to change the way we work. Instead, we'll just tack a few new techniques and skills onto our existing pattern of study and then quietly abandon them when we realise they don't fit within the way we work. In turn, this will deprive us of those skills we need to access and develop the abilities that are assessed at this level.

9 The Range of Abilities

In this chapter you will learn:

- that university education is less preoccupied with learning and recalling the facts, than with developing the skills and abilities that are crucial to your subject;
- the importance of adjusting to a different style of learning at university;
- about the range of abilities the essay is designed to assess.

It's at this point that most of our problems in studying begin. Although we will talk about this again later when we come to the writing stage, it's worth confronting it twice, so important is the problem.

Most students at university are handicapped in one form or another by the restricted notion of education they bring with them. Unfortunately, we spend most of our time in schools believing that education is largely about 'knowing things', that a clever person is one who can remember a vast number of isolated facts. If you spend, say, 13 years in compulsory education from the age of 5 to 18, during at least 11 of these you come to believe that education is largely, if not solely, concerned with learning the facts of every subject you study, dispensed by the authorities of education, the teachers and the textbooks.

This perception of education is reinforced not just by the syllabuses we study, the examinations we take and the teaching styles of some of our teachers, but by a whole range of social and cultural conventions, not least the ever popular TV quiz show, in which contestants are asked to recall isolated items of information.

▶ A passive style of learning

The result is that we all assume a passive style of learning. We sit silently in class absorbing the truths, the right answers that we come to believe should be our paramount concern. The teacher dictates while we silently note. The best student, then, is one who is quiet, who patiently and uncritically records word-for-word all that the teacher says. He or she is not there to question, to discuss or to challenge, but to absorb the teacher's statements, to imitate authority and to reproduce it accurately without alteration. They know success in the examination depends upon how effectively they can trade the facts for marks. And that's all there is to it.

But if that were the case the last thing we would be setting as a form of assessment would be essays, because they are notoriously unreliable. They assess a wide range of abilities – to analyse, to criticise, to discuss, to synthesise ideas, to construct consistent arguments, to use evidence, to evaluate, as well as to remember the facts. However, the more abilities you try to assess, the less reliable that form of assessment is for any one ability alone. And, despite all our attempts to reduce the subjective element in marking, most markers would acknowledge that it's impossible to remove it entirely from essay marking.

Other forms of assessment that target just one ability, however, have a much better record. For example, the most reliable form of assessment, the multiple choice question paper, boasts 100 per cent reliability. Using this we are guaranteed that each student's paper will be assessed with absolute objectivity and all will be judged on exactly the same criteria. Indeed, for marking purposes the human element can be removed entirely with computerised answer sheets.

It follows, then, that if we were really assessing our ability to recall the facts, as so many of us have come to believe, the essay would be the very last form of assessment we would use. Far better to use the reliable, though restricted, multiple choice question paper. Here we know we have absolute objectivity, albeit at the cost of assessing only a restricted range of abilities.

▶ Challenging authority

However, as most of us come to realise, we're not just assessing our ability to recall what we've heard in class or read in our books. After years of compulsory education in which we believe that our main task as students is to learn the facts and reproduce uncritically what the authorities say in each subject, we reach university and we're suddenly expected to challenge the opinions we hear, to analyse, discuss, and have opinions of our own.

Not surprisingly, most students find it difficult to make sense of this. They have learnt that if they use their study skills in a particular way it will bring success. After all, that's exactly what has happened so far in their education. Therefore, understandably, they continue to back what they believe to be a winner: they continue to take notes in the same way, to read in the same way and to write essays in the same way.

However, they face different examinations, with different assumptions about the nature of learning, requiring a different pattern of study. Unless this is explained to them, they will continue to get poor marks for their essays. And they will have no idea why, when all they're doing is just what they've done successfully in all their work before. Confused and dispirited, many will go through the whole course believing that while they might have been up to taking the examinations at school, they're just not up to these at university. Whereas, in fact, it is not that they lack the abilities, or the motivation, or even the capacity to understand, but just that they lack the right skills to unlock their potential.

▶ The cognitive domains

It should be clear, then, that by setting essays as a mode of assessment, particularly in university courses, our aim is not just to assess the limited ability to understand and recall, but to assess a much broader range of abilities. All syllabuses are written in the context of six 'cognitive domains' – six intellectual abilities. Listing them from the simplest to the most complex they are as follows:

1 Recall
2 Comprehension
3 Application
4 Analysis
5 Synthesis
6 Evaluation

While many of us find it difficult to shake off the belief that examinations are set exclusively to assess our recall and understanding (abilities 1 and 2), most syllabuses at universities are designed largely to assess abilities 4, 5 and 6. The questions set use instructional verbs like 'Discuss', 'Criticise', 'Analyse' and 'Evaluate', to assess our abilities to analyse difficult concepts and arguments, to synthesise ideas and evidence drawn from a range of different sources, to construct consistent arguments, and to discuss and evaluate the ideas and arguments of others.

These are not the 'What', 'How' and 'Describe' questions that would be more appropriate for assessing our ability to recall information. This would assume that there are right answers, whereas in fact there are none at this level. As one tutor at the University of Oxford makes clear in the guidance he gives to his students:

> It is never a question of coming to the 'right' answer (though you can expect a tutor to defend his or her position if it differs from yours) but rather of demonstrating that you understand what the issue is about and that you can produce a well-reasoned, balanced and critical argument concerning it.[1]

Practice exercise 6
Syllabus objectives

Get a copy of the syllabus for each of the courses you're taking. Then, underline the passages that describe the syllabus objectives. For this exercise ignore the description of the course content, the topics the course will be covering. You're interested just in the abilities that the course sets out to develop, which will be assessed in the examination.

See if you can assess what proportion of the marks in the examination will be awarded for the recall of knowledge and for the other abilities. Some syllabuses will give the actual percentages, others are not so helpful. If this is the case, then ask your tutor. Ultimately, of course, the best guide is the type of question that's set on the examination paper. So, again, look at past papers.

Even so, we still have to show that we understand and can recall the facts, the core knowledge at the heart of the subject. But for most syllabuses that employ essays as a mode of assessment this comprises as little as 30–40 per cent of the mark. Examiners want to see us use our abilities, so even though we may come to a conclusion that the examiner disagrees with, this should not affect our mark, because we're not working with a syllabus that assumes there are indisputable right answers that have to be traded for marks. Examiners should be more concerned with the way we have analysed the issues, discussed them, played devil's advocate, used evidence to support our arguments, and come to a measured evaluation that's backed up by our discussion.

In the Sociology Department at the University of Harvard, students on one first year course are left in no doubt that the course's main objective is to develop a particular range of abilities and skills that are central to sociology as a discipline:

> This course is intended to help students to develop an understanding of and ability to do social science analysis – to appreciate what a research problem is, how to pose it, what alternative answers might be, how to evaluate relevant evidence, and generally to understand the logic of establishing knowledge about how society works. . . . The emphasis in the course is on developing writing skills, the ability to formulate and design research projects, and the ability to critically evaluate empirical work in the social sciences.[2]

As this shows, most university departments now realise that you don't learn how to think like a scientist or a historian by simply learning scientific or historical facts. In literature courses, recognition of this has led universities to allow students to take their set texts into the examination room. This has largely done away with that horrifying, yet futile, annual spectacle of thousands of candidates frantically memorising huge tracts of text for the exam, all of which they will certainly forget within three weeks of taking it.

▶ In the next chapter

With this in mind, we have to create a new pattern of study in line with these changed assumptions. In the next chapter we will look at the importance of this and what we can do to bring it about.

Notes

1 Eric Eve, *A Guide for Perplexed Students, 4: Tutorial Essays* (Oxford: University of Oxford, 2000), pp. 3–4.
   Available at: http://www.hmc.ox.ac.uk/
2 Mary Waters, *Sociology, 128: Paradigms of Social Inquiry* (Cambridge, Mass.: University of Harvard, 2000).

10 Changing our Pattern of Study

In this chapter you will learn:

- about the causes of many of our most common study skills problems;
- about the need to change our pattern of study.

In the light of these changed assumptions about the purpose of learning tasks like essay writing, it should be obvious that we now need a new pattern of study – we need to use our study skills differently, more appropriately for the tasks we're set. If we don't, if we retain the assumption that education is exclusively about 'knowing things', then certain things will follow. We will be cursed with the sort of problems of which most of us are all too aware.

▶ Common problems

Note-taking

In our note-taking we will continue to argue, quite reasonably on these misplaced assumptions, that when we take notes in tutorials, seminars and lectures, or from the source material we use for research, we cannot leave anything out, because these are the facts, the right answers, and if we omit them we will not have all the facts we need to pass the examination. As a result we take vast quantities of verbatim notes. Even worse, they're unstructured, because all we're doing is recording them accurately – we're not processing them in any way for fear of getting them wrong.

Consequently, we're left with masses of unusable notes, most of them irrelevant to the questions we're going to have to answer in the examination. This presents us with the most daunting of problems, which leaves even the most resourceful student dispirited when it comes to revising from them for the examination. In effect, those students with a will of steel will revise by starting from page 1 and continuing until they have gone through them all. In the end their grasp of the subject is likely to be confused, with little structure and organisation. But this is only the fate of a few. The more reckless majority will decide to ditch half their notes, gambling that what they've covered will come up in the exam.

Reading

But now consider the impact of these assumptions on other areas of our pattern of study. Quite reasonably we will argue that when we come to read books and articles we cannot exercise any flexibility by adopting different, more appropriate reading strategies, like skimming and scanning, for the different types of passages and texts we have to read. We argue that the text must be read word-for-word, otherwise we might miss something vital.

Remember, under these assumptions we believe that these are the facts in the passage before us. If we fail to read it carefully we are likely to miss a vital fact that we will need to trade for marks in the exam. Reading, then, becomes a slow, time-consuming activity. Along with note-taking it takes up nearly all of our study time. Consequently, we never have sufficient time to read around our subject, to make comparisons with what others are saying, and to explore our understanding.

Writing

Much the same goes for our essay writing. No matter how many times we might be told by our tutor that we must try to put things in our own words, this makes no sense if we accept the assumption that education is dominated by authorities, and our job is just to understand and recall the facts.

We argue, again quite reasonably, that here is the text, the authority, the source of right answers, so if we were to spend time putting it into our own words, rather than copy passages from it accurately, we would be changing what is already right. We would be making it less right, in effect we would be getting it wrong. So, far better to plagiarise the text and put large chunks directly into our own work. And no matter how many times students are told not to plagiarise, because this is literary theft, a form of cheating that constitutes just about the most serious offence in academic writing, they still continue to do it, because they're convinced that these are the facts and their role is to trade them for marks, if they're to succeed.

▶ Plagiarism

In fact plagiarism illustrates the point we've been making in this chapter perfectly. As we've seen, one of the causes of it is this belief that exams are passed as a result of giving right answers. But unfortunately all too often the solution to plagiarism reflects the same assumption, thereby compounding the original problem. We argue that the only way to avoid plagiarism is to give a reference for every idea quoted, paraphrased or borrowed in any way. In other words, students come to realise that to get good marks they must continue to trade for marks as many right answers as possible, only now in the form of references.

Worse still, they are given the impression that there is nothing new in education. It reduces academic work to the far less significant exercise of just recycling received opinion. There is no room for originality, or at least you are not required to produce it. All that's asked is that you show evidence of hard work by breaking up every paragraph with five or six references to works from which you have derived your ideas. The only challenge this presents for most students is how they can throw as many references in as possible at minimum cost. Inevitably they gather the impression that education is more concerned with *what* they think than *how* they think.

One mature student explains the problem in his student magazine,

> In my opinion the most important purpose of higher education is to teach the student how to think in a sophisticated manner. Sadly . . . universities . . . cannot resist the temptation to teach the student what to think as well – not the best way to produce enquiring and innovative minds.
>
> There seems to be a tradition . . . that an opinion is somehow more valid if someone has said it before: I can see a justification for this, in that if an opinion has been in the public domain it has been subject to public scrutiny, but I suspect that the motivation has more to do with the 'hero-innovator' notion: if the person who has said it is important enough it must be right.
>
> When I write essays I am required not only to give facts and ideas, but to quote exactly where I found them: if I simply thought of them myself

does that mean they are not valid? Generally, I feel a strong pressure to reflect back the opinions and prejudices of the course team: maybe this is not justified, but that's how it feels. I am reminded of what Henry Beeching wrote in the 19th century concerning the Master of Balliol:

'I am Master of this College: What I don't know isn't knowledge.'[1]

Of course, most students know that they should be eschewing this assumption that their paramount concern is to impress the examiner by exchanging facts, in the form of references, for marks. But plagiarism seems vague and all-encompassing: like the medieval crime of witchcraft, just about anything seems to qualify. Inevitably, then, they play it safe and give a reference for anything that might seem to deserve it: out of fear they are driven into this regressive, primitive form of learning. In Chapter 30 we will look at the problem of plagiarism and how you can avoid it without just becoming a recycler of what others have said.

▶ Creating a new pattern of study

In the next chapter we will set about creating a new, more flexible pattern of study that will equip you to tackle the different challenges presented by essay writing at university. But the success of this will depend upon how much you're willing to accept the need to change.

We only ever really learn when we have a genuine need. If we retain the assumption that education is exclusively about knowing things, there will be no need to change. The new flexibility and skills in reading, note-taking and writing will only be tacked on to our present pattern of study as we go about studying in the way we've always studied. And in time, of course, they will be silently dropped, because in the light of our unchanged assumptions, they are irrelevant.

It's worth reminding ourselves that the real joy and challenge of education lies not in how much we can remember, but in what we learn to do with our minds. Out of this come students who can genuinely think for themselves, capable of real innovation that pushes back the frontiers of knowledge. As B. F. Skinner describes it, education is that which 'survives when what has been learnt has been forgotten'.[2]

Assignment 3
Planning your research

When you were given the essay question you are working on you were no doubt also given a reading list by your tutor, composed of books and journal articles. You won't have to read every text on the list, so before you begin your research you will need to prioritise them. First, categorise them into those whose approach is general and those that are specific. Then consider, in each of these categories, which appears to be the most useful. Some may appear too general, others too specific. In some cases you will need to skim and scan the texts before you're sure. In the next stage you will be shown how to do this.

However, now that you know the meaning and implications of the question, you will know what you're looking for. Generally tutors try to indicate the pages you will find most helpful, but this is not always possible. For most questions it helps to begin with the more general text and move to the specific, but this will depend upon your prior knowledge of the topic. Either way, you will still have to narrow down the specific sections you need to read. In the next stage you will be shown ways of doing this.

The same applies to the journal articles. Your interpretation and brainstorming of the question will have given you a much clearer idea of the specific issues raised and where you need to devote more of your time. In most cases, of course, we're not lucky enough to find that the author of an article is examining exactly the issue we need to think about. So, again, you will have to prioritise and be selective about the sections that are most useful.

▷ The next stage

Now you should be clearer about what the question is getting at and what you want from the texts you're about to read. You will also know the range of abilities the examiner wants to see you use when you come to answer the question. As you move into the research stage this should be reflected in your pattern of study – in the way you use your skills, like reading and note-taking.

In the next stage you will learn how to use these skills to ensure you do more than just recall what you've read and imitate your authors. You will be shown how to use your skills to process ideas in more complex and sophisticated ways. You will learn how to analyse a passage and extract the structure from what you read, and how to criticise and discuss the ideas and opinions of authors, rather than just reproduce them accurately. As a result you will be better equipped to produce ideas that are genuinely your own.

Notes

1 Lem Ibbotson, 'Teach us how, not what, to think', *Sesame*, August/September 2000 (The Open University).
2 B. F. Skinner, 'Education in 1984', *New Scientist*, 21 May 1964, p. 484.

Stage 2
Research

INTRODUCTION

We have now reached the point where we can confidently set about our research. We've interpreted the meaning and implications of the question, in the course of which we've analysed the key concepts involved. From there we've brainstormed the question using our interpretation as our key structure. As a result, we now know two things: what questions we want answered from our research; and what we already know about the topic. The latter is important if we are to graft the ideas we come across onto our own understanding and make them our own. Only in this way will we be able to use these ideas skilfully and persuasively when we come to write.

Lastly, we've identified clearly the range of abilities the examiner wants to see us use. Otherwise, as we saw, there is a danger that we will assume the question is largely about demonstrating that we understand and can recall the facts about the topic in the question, rather than showing we can use the higher cognitive skills to analyse its implications, synthesise arguments and evidence from different sources, discuss and argue consistently, and criticise and evaluate the ideas we use.

This means that we must reorganise our pattern of study. Otherwise we will continue to use our skills, like note-taking and reading, in the way we have always used them: to meet the demands of questions that test the simpler cognitive skills. In effect, if we don't reorganise it, we will be preparing ourselves for the wrong exams: for those we have already taken, rather than for those we are about to take. In this stage, therefore, we will examine the three key skills in research (reading, note-taking and organisation), showing how we can reorganise our pattern of study to meet the newer demands of the higher cognitive skills.

▶ Reading

To use these skills effectively in our reading we will see that it's important to read purposefully: to be clear about why we're reading a particular passage so that we can select the most appropriate reading strategy. Many of us get into the habit of reading every passage word-for-word, regardless of our purpose in reading it, when in fact it might be more efficient to skim or scan it. Adopting a more flexible approach to our reading in this way frees up more of our time, so that we can read around our subject and take on board more ideas and information.

It also gives us more time to process the ideas. We will see how important this is if we are to avoid becoming just 'surface-level processors', reading passively without analysing and structuring what we read, or criticising and evaluating the arguments presented. We will examine the techniques involved in analysing a passage to extract its structure, so that we can recall the arguments, ideas and evidence more effectively. We will also learn the different ways we can improve our ability to criticise and evaluate the arguments we read. In this way we can become 'deep-level processors', actively processing what we read and generating more of our own ideas.

▶ Note-taking

Many of the same issues resurface when we consider note-taking. As with reading, we will see that it's important not to tie ourselves to one strategy of note-taking irrespective of the job we have to do. We will see that for different forms of processing there are the most appropriate strategies of note-taking: linear notes for analysis and structure, and pattern notes for criticism and evaluation. Cultivating flexibility in our pattern of study helps us choose the most effective strategy and, as a result, get the most out of our intellectual abilities.

But our problems in note-taking don't end there. The best notes help us structure our own thoughts, so we can recall and use them quickly and accurately, particularly under timed conditions. In this lie many of the most common problems in note-taking, particularly the habit of taking too many notes that obscure the structure, making it difficult to recall. We will exam ways of avoiding this by creating clear uncluttered notes that help us recall even the most complex structures accurately. Given this, and the simple techniques of consolidating notes, we will see how revision for the exam can become a more manageable, less daunting task.

Finally, if our notes are going to help us recall the ideas, arguments and evidence we read, as well as help us to criticise and evaluate an author's arguments, they must be a reflection of our own thinking. We will examine the reasons why many students find it difficult to have ideas of their own, when they read and take notes from their sources, and how this affects their concentration while they work.

▶ Organisation

Needless to say, if we are to make all these changes successfully, we will have to make sure we organise our work in the most effective way. In the final chapters of this stage we will look at how to reorganise our retrieval system to tap into our own ideas and to pick up material wherever and whenever it appears. We will also examine the way we organise our time and the problems that can arise if we fail to do it effectively. Indeed, if we ignore either of these, we make it difficult for ourselves to get the most out of our abilities and to process our ideas well. Even though most of us routinely ignore it, organisation is the one aspect of our pattern of study that can produce almost immediate improvements in our work.

11 Reading Purposefully

In this chapter you will learn:

- how to use your time more effectively by reading only what you need to read;
- about the importance of being clear about your purpose in reading the text in order to select the right reading strategy;
- how to read more efficiently with more flexible techniques.

Having got our own ideas down on paper, the concepts analysed, and a clear idea of what we're looking for, we are now in a position to begin our research, confident that we can identify what's relevant and what's not.

▶ Knowing what you're looking for

But before you hit the books, a warning! It's all too easy to pick up a pile of books that appear vaguely useful and browse among them. This might be enjoyable, and you might learn something, but it will hardly help you get your essay written. Now that you've interpreted the question and you've brainstormed the issues, you have a number of questions and topics you want to pursue. You are now in a position to ask clear questions as you read the books and the other materials you've decided to use in your research.

Nevertheless, before you begin you need to pin down exactly the sections of each book that are relevant to your research. Very few of the books you use will you read from cover to cover. With this in mind, you need to consult the contents and index pages in order to locate those pages that deal with the questions and issues you're interested in.

For most books this is all you will need to do. However, there are those books that have very misleading chapter titles, which tell you very little about the content of each chapter. The same books may also have a short and unhelpful index. In this case you'll find it helpful to read the first paragraph of each chapter, where the authors explain what they will be doing in this chapter, and then the last paragraph, where they explain how they've done it.

Failing this, and this will be rare indeed, you can *skim* each page, picking up a general impression of the contents of each chapter. Alternatively, if you know the specific problem you want the book to address, you can *scan* each page swiftly, looking for those key-words through which you can find the answers. It's surprising just how effective both of these strategies can be, but they will only work well if you've already pinned down the issues clearly in the interpretation stage.

In a nutshell

Check:

- the contents page;
- the index;
- chapter headings;
- the first and last chapters;
- summaries at the end of the chapters and at the end of the book;
- the first and last paragraphs in each chapter.
- **Skim** the text for a general impression of the contents, key ideas and structure.
- **Scan** for keywords.

Through this process you should be able to answer a number of important questions which will determine exactly how you use the text:

1 Is it relevant?
2 If so, what sections?
3 What approach does it take?
   - Is it too difficult?
   - Or too technical?

This underlines again the importance of flexibility in the way we approach our work. We have three different reading strategies to choose from, each one appropriate to a different type of job.

1   We can read carefully **word-for-word** when we're reading a text or a passage we know is of central importance to our work, from which we want to extract in our notes the detailed structure of the main points and subsections.

2   In contrast, when we just want to pick up the general impression of the contents, the key ideas and the broad structure of a text or an article, then we would do better to **skim** it.

3   And, if we're just looking for an answer to a specific question, say a date, a name, a set of figures, or what the writer says about a certain subject, then we need to **scan** it.

The key is flexibility and, in turn, the key to this is to read with a clear purpose in mind, so you can choose the most appropriate strategy.

Practice exercise   7
Reading purposefully

Faced with the following situations, decide which reading strategy would best suit your purpose.

1   You're given a 50-page report the night before a conference you're attending. Do you skim, scan, or read word-for-word?

2   You're attending a press conference held by the head of state of a country which has a very poor record on human rights. To prepare yourself you refer to a detailed report on the country's judicial system compiled by Amnesty International. In particular you want to know how many political prisoners are at present detained without trial and the length of time they've been in custody. Do you skim, scan, or read word-for-word?

Continued

3   You've been asked to take over the job of secretary at your local cricket club, because of the sudden illness of the current secretary. You've got to compile an agenda for the next meeting by reading the minutes of the last meeting. Do you skim, scan, or read word-for-word?

4   After ordering it some months ago you receive a copy of the latest novel by your favourite author. You start reading it on the train going to work. Do you skim, scan, or read word-for-word?

5   You're studying at a university on a scholarship grant. But the terms of the grant are changing next year, which might mean you no longer qualify. You've just received a copy of the new regulations. Do you skim, scan, or read word-for-word?

Now compare your answers with those below.

Answers

1   Skim to get the general impression of the contents.
2   Scan to see what Amnesty says about political prisoners and their detention.
3   Skim to identify those things that were discussed at the last meeting and were to be raised again at this meeting.
4   Not wanting to miss anything, you read word-for-word.
5   You read them carefully word-for-word, like you would a legal document, until you are completely clear one way or the other whether you qualify.

▶ In the next chapter

We can all see the common-sense of scanning the Yellow Pages in search of the telephone number for a mechanic when our car has broken down; but in our academic work it seems much more difficult to use the same common-sense judgement. With many of us, as we've already seen, the most likely reason is that we still harbour the belief that to pass an exam we must accumulate as many right answers as possible, and the only way of doing this is to use just one reading strategy: read every passage word-for-word. This, in turn, affects the quality and depth at which we process the ideas we read, as we'll see in the next chapter.

12 Processing the Ideas

In this chapter you will learn:

- how to improve your recall of what you read;
- how to read analytically, to take the structure out of a passage;
- how to read critically.

Ultimately, the quality of the work we produce will depend upon the quality of our internal processing of the ideas we read. There are 'surface-level processors', who read passively, that is without actively analysing and structuring what they read, and without criticising and evaluating the arguments, evidence and ideas the author presents. In most cases this sort of student will have poor recall of what they read, and in general they will be restricted to just 'describing' the ideas.

If the question asks them to 'evaluate', or 'assess critically' a certain claim, they will, more often than not, find themselves answering the question inappropriately, employing the lower ability range, in which they merely 'describe' an argument, or 'outline' a particular case. As we have seen, this is a mistake that derives from overlooking the importance of the instructional verbs. But more often than not it has its origin in a reading habit that drives students into the lower ability range, when they least want to be there.

▶ Multiple readings

To avoid this problem, and to ensure that you're able to do 'deep-level processing', it may be necessary to accept that you need to do two or three readings of the text, particularly if it is technical and closely argued.

Reading for comprehension

In your first reading you might aim just for the lower ability range, for comprehension, just to understand the author's arguments. It may be a subject you've never read about before, or it may include a number of unfamiliar technical terms that you need to think about carefully each time they are used.

Reading for analysis and structure

In the next reading you should be able to analyse the passage into sections and subsections, so that you can see how you're going to organise it in your notes. If the text is not too difficult you may be able to accomplish both of these tasks (comprehension and analysis) in one reading, but always err on the cautious side, don't rush it. Remember, now that you've identified just those few pages that you have to read, rather than the whole book, you can spend more time processing the ideas well.

Reading for criticism and evaluation

The third reading involves criticising and evaluating your authors' arguments. It's clear that in this and the second reading our processing is a lot more active. While in the second we're analysing the passage to take out the structure, in this, the third, we're maintaining a dialogue with the authors, through which we're able to criticise and evaluate their arguments. To help you in this, keep the following sorts of questions in mind as you read.

- Are the arguments consistent or are they contradictory?
- Are they relevant (i.e. do the authors use arguments they know you'll agree with, but which are not relevant to the point they're making)?
- Do they use the same words to mean different things at different stages of the argument (what's known as the fallacy of equivocation)?
- Are there underlying assumptions that they haven't justified?
- Can you detect bias in the argument?
- Do they favour one side of the argument, giving little attention to the side for which they seem to have least sympathy? For example, do they give only those reasons that support their case, omitting those that don't (the fallacy of special pleading)?
- Is the evidence they use relevant?

- Is it strong enough to support their arguments?
- Do they use untypical examples, which they know you will have to agree with, in order to support a difficult or extreme case (what's known as the fallacy of the straw man)?
- Do they draw conclusions from statistics and examples which can't adequately support them?

This sounds like a lot to remember, and it is, so don't try to carry this list along with you as you read. Just remind yourself of it before you begin to criticise and evaluate the text. Having done this two or three times you will find more and more of it sticks and you won't need reminding. Then, after you've finished the passage, go through the list again and check with what you can recall of the text. These are the sort of questions you will be asking in Stage 5 (Revision) about your own essay before you hand it in. So it's a good idea to develop your skills by practising on somebody else first.

One last caution – don't rush into this. You will have to give yourself some breathing space between the second reading and this final evaluative reading. Your mind will need sufficient time to process all the material, preferably overnight, in order for you to see the issues clearly and objectively. If you were to attempt to criticise and evaluate the author's ideas straight after reading them for the structure, your own ideas would be so assimilated into the author's, that you would be left with no room to criticise and assess them. You would probably find very little to disagree with the author about.

Assignment 4
Reading for analysis and structure

Read the following passage, first for comprehension, and then for analysis and structure. Leave it for a few hours, even a day or so, then go back to it to take out the structure in normal linear notes. If you're unsure about how to do this, read the first part of Chapter 13.

But remember, your aim is to take out the hierarchy of points, the main sections and the way they break down into subsections. Cut out as much unnecessary detail as you can. Where there are examples or explanations, and you think you might need reminding of them, briefly note them in one or two words to act as a trigger for your memory, and nothing

Continued

more. Choose words or succinct phrases that you know will make the connections to the information you want.

Keep in mind that the most important part of this exercise is to have a clear, uncluttered model of the passage. You will not achieve this if you allow yourself to be tempted into noting unnecessary detail. Your mind will have self-organised in the interval between reading and noting, producing a very clear structure of the passage in your subconscious, so you must develop the skills to tap into this to get an accurate picture of it clearly and simply on paper.

You won't do this if you continually tell yourself that you must note this and this and this, otherwise you're bound to forget them. Don't make it difficult for your mind by doubting its capacity to remember details that don't need to be noted.

Passage

Understanding Totalitarianism

In the 1930s writers and historians struggled to come to terms with a system of government that seemed to have no precedent in history. Unlike liberal democracies, totalitarianism appeared to have no fixed characteristics, everything was in flux. The most one could say about the regimes in the Soviet Union and Nazi Germany was that they possessed certain 'contours',[1] to use Leonard Schapiro's description. Three of these are worth examining.

The most obvious one to observers in the 1930s was the leader, who appeared to dominate everything. Although he was the leader of a state composed of the usual institutions of government, he successfully subjugated these to his own personal will. Aware that those who wielded power through these institutions could pose a real threat to his authority, he side-stepped them, setting up an alternative structure staffed by his own supporters who owed their position to his patronage. With their future prospects in his pocket their loyalty was beyond question.

The same strategy was used to influence the relationship between the leader and his party. On the face of it the leader owed everything to the party, after all it had brought him to power. But it also posed a serious challenge to his authority. It was respected by its members as the guardian of the ideology to which the leader was ultimately accountable. Therefore, like the state, the party had to be subjugated to the will of the leader, until the ideology became whatever the leader said it was.

But to achieve both of these the leader had to appeal over the heads of the party and the state to the people directly. For this he needed to generate a charismatic authority built on the power of his own personality. In an age of mass communication this offered a source of authority that far exceeded the more usual sources that lay in tradition or in the institutions of government. But it needed a vast propaganda machine that would project the leader not only as the benevolent father of his people, but as an infallible leader whose judgement could not be challenged, what Koestler describes in *Darkness at Noon* as the 'infallible pointsman'.[2]

What's more, the leader had to demonstrate to his people that he was virtually omnipotent, omniscient, and omnipresent – all-powerful, all-knowing and ever-present, respectively. In the Soviet Union the economic and industrial progress achieved in each successive five-year plan suggested that anything was possible under his leadership. He seemed to be not only benevolent, but infinitely wise and knowledgeable on just about any subject – history, art, literature, architecture, philosophy, military theory, any subject on which people could have an opinion. He also appeared to be ever-present, using air travel to be in two or three places on the same day. His picture was always there on massive hoardings and in every government office.

Yet perhaps the most important source of his charismatic authority and the most convincing evidence of his infallibility lay in the fact that he had survived the internecine struggles for power within his own party, outmanoeuvring his opponents, who could also lay claim to being the rightful guardians of the ideology. Indeed, at times the ruthlessness with which he dispatched his opponents seemed to be evidence in itself of his charismatic infallibility. In one night on 30 June 1934 Hitler removed Ernst Röhm, his most dangerous rival, and his followers in the SA, and with it earned the respect not just of big business and the army, but, one suspects, of the people too. In the same ruthless manner Stalin removed the threats of Trotsky, Kamenev, Zinoviev and finally Bukharin.

Nevertheless, for the leader to maintain his monopoly of power in the long term, more was needed than just respect for his personality. Control had to be exerted not just over people's political convictions, but over their private moral beliefs and opinions too. Intolerant of all dissent, a moral consensus was created and artificially imposed on the people, claiming to sum up all the values it believed were valid. No values were irrelevant or beyond its total grasp. In this way, unlike in liberal democracies, the distinction between public and private was effectively destroyed. What was generally regarded as private and moral was also public and political.

Censorship and intimidation penetrated the most personal recesses of private life, effectively destroying the distinction between public and private. One of the most popular jokes in Moscow in the 1930s concerned a hostess who had invited ten of her closest friends for a dinner party. Aware of her moral and political obligations to the state, she submitted the names to the secret police for their approval, fully expecting the list to be returned with two names added – the secret police needed their observers to be present to record who said what to whom. But to her dismay the list was returned unamended – there was no need to add two of their own. Unknown to her they were already there, among her own trusted friends.

Propaganda assailed individuals on the streets, from the radio, and in their newspapers, while indoctrination shaped the values of the future generation in schools, with the leader dictating the books that could be read, the content of lessons and the teachers who would teach them. Likewise, all independent institutions, like the church or professional bodies, capable of throwing doubt on the consensus, were suppressed.

The only writing and artistic expression that was allowed had to conform to the officially approved form. In the Soviet Union many of those who were the most creative influences in the 1920s, responding to the challenge of revolutionary art by developing new styles and artistic forms, rapidly became enemies of the people, perishing in the Gulag or falling silent. In their place emerged new controls on the form that literature and the arts could take. A. A. Zhdarnov, in his famous speech at the First Soviet Writers' Congress in 1934, outlined the task facing writers in the new revolutionary state and the method of 'socialist realism'[3] that all writers were to adopt.

Nevertheless, this sort of control over the private moral side of people's lives could only be maintained by keeping everything around them moving – by creating an atmosphere in which people were uncertain, fearful and suspicious of everyone else. This is the third 'contour', that of mass mobilisation. Unlike liberal democracies, where, during times of emergencies like wars, there is a temporary mass mobilisation of effort to achieve the ultimate goal of defending the nation successfully, in totalitarian regimes this is permanent, what Hannah Arendt describes as 'permanent impermanence'.[4]

She argues that totalitarian leaders were driven by 'perpetual motion mania' to keep everything around them in a process of constant change and uncertainty to secure and enhance their power. In this way the leader could guarantee uncritical acceptance of his policies and the sacrifices he demanded from his people, particularly in terms of their lost individual rights – their right to free speech, to information, freedom of the press, freedom of movement, and their freedom from arbitrary arrest.

To achieve this, two types of ultimate goal were used as the justification for mass mobilisation. The first, the achievement of certain ideal goals, like social equality or rapid industrialisation, was used to justify the worsening economic and social conditions. The leader argued that if there were to be jobs for all, free education and health care, and improvements in living standards, sacrifices had to be made – present consumption had to be cut to invest in the future. With everyone working to achieve such noble ideals, uncritical acceptance of the leader's policies was virtually guaranteed.

But probably the most popular pretext was national defence. This could take two forms: against the external and the internal aggressor. The external aggressor in turn could be defensive or expansionist. In either case it was frequently fictitious. The nation, it was argued, faced a serious threat to its survival from a foreign power, although this could change with the most bewildering about-turns, as occurred in 1939 when Soviet Russia signed the non-aggression pact with Nazi Germany.

However, this one example illustrates equally well the expansionist ambitions that lie behind such pretexts, in that the 1939 pact also divided Poland between the two totalitarian regimes. The justification here was the supposed international plot to weaken the nation by creating internal pressures that would ultimately lead to its break-up. The only effective remedy, it was argued, was an expansionist policy.

For example, the Nazi Government in Germany in the 1930s frequently used the Treaty of Versailles as evidence of an international conspiracy to contain Germany, when the rapidly rising German population needed more, not less, territory in which to expand. This was the policy of 'Lebensraum', which provided the pretext for mass mobilisation and the series of diplomatic and military initiatives to push back the frontiers of Germany – the demilitarisation of the Rhineland in 1936, the annexation of Austria in 1938, the Sudetenland in 1938, the rest of Czechoslovakia (Bohemia and Moravia) in 1939, and finally Poland in 1939.

Like that of the external aggressor, the pretext of the internal aggressor could be equally fictitious. People were constantly reminded that the nation was under continual threat from the ruthless activities of counter-revolutionaries within the state, who were dedicated to forcing them into slavery, into the servitude of other nations. Their agents were supposed to be everywhere – working on the next bench in the factory, sitting next to you in the works' canteen, or living in the apartment opposite.

With these three contours the totalitarian leader could keep everything around him moving, in a state of constant uncertainty, leaving people more willing to depend blindly on the leader's supposed infallibility. In this way he could avoid being trapped within the fixed rules and systems of accountability of institutional government which would have ensured the regular use of power and authority. Consequently, under these conditions, to talk about the state is fundamentally misleading: there *was* no state. As Schapiro says about the term 'totalitarian state', this is a contradiction in terms. Indeed, given these three contours it's doubtful whether we are justified in describing this as a 'system' of government at all.

Answer

Understanding Totalitarianism

3 contours – everything in flux

A   The Leader

    1.   Leader & the state

        Leader subjugates the state

        (a)   posed a real threat to his authority
        (b)   alternative structure – his own supporters

2. Leader & the party

   Subjugated the party – ideology = whatever the leader says
   it is

   (a) owed his rise to power to the party
   (b) party = guardian of the ideology

3. Charismatic authority

   (a) vast propaganda machine
       - 'infallible pointsman' (Koestler)
   (b) omnipotent, omniscient, omnipresent
       (i) all-powerful
              e.g. five-year plans
       (ii) all-knowing – on any subject
       (iii) ever-present
              e.g. air travel & hoardings
   (c) outmanoeuvred opponents
              e.g. Hitler v. Ernst Röhm
                   Stalin v. Trotsky, Kamenev, Zinoviev & Bukharin

B Control over private morality

No distinction between public & private – what is private & moral
= public & political.
  e.g. Moscow joke, 1930s

1. propaganda
   - on streets/radio/newspapers

2. Indoctrination in schools
   - textbooks/lessons/teachers

3. Suppression of independent institutions
       e.g. churches/professional bodies

4. Writing/artistic expression = in the approved form
       e.g. Zhdarnov – First Soviet Writers' Congress 1934 –
            'socialist realism'

C   Mass mobilisation

Atmosphere of uncertainty & suspicion – 'permanent impermanence' (Hannah Arendt)
Therefore, uncritical acceptance of leader's policies + sacrifices he
demanded.

2 types of ultimate goal:

1.   Ideal goals
      e.g.   social equality, rapid industrialisation

2.   National defence – frequently fictitious

     (a)   external:
            (i)   defensive
                   e.g.   1939 Nazi/Soviet non-aggression pact
            (ii) expansionist
                   –   international plot to weaken the nation through
                        internal pressure
                        e.g.   Treaty of Versailles & 'Lebensraum' –
                        German expansion in 1930s
     (b)   internal:
            –   supposed threat from counter-revolutionaries who
                 were thought to be everywhere

D   Result =

1.   No fixed rules & systems of accountability

2.   No state – Totalitarian state = contradiction in terms

3.   No 'system' of government at all

Your notes may not contain as much detail as there is in these, but you
shouldn't be discouraged by that. Your primary aim in this exercise was
to create notes that reflect your understanding of the main structure
of the passage as clearly as possible. Therefore, if you've been able to
extract the three 'contours' along with some of the hierarchy of
sub-points, then you've done well.

As you know now, this is not an easy exercise. It will take a few more attempts at different passages to get it right, but you will see quite dramatic improvements in a short time as long as you remain clear about what you're trying to achieve. While you were reading the passage your mind self-organised to produce a structure out of what you read. Your main goal, then, is to reproduce this in your notes.

▶ In the next chapter

Having done this, you should then be able to recall the structure accurately as long as the main points are triggered off by memorable key words. In the next chapter we will examine ways to improve this and other aspects of our note-taking.

Notes

1 Leonard Schapiro, *Totalitarianism* (New York: Praeger Press, 1972).
2 Arthur Koestler, *Darkness at Noon* (Harmondsworth: Penguin, 1947).
3 A. A. Zhdarnov, *On Literature, Music and Philosophy* (London: Lawrence & Wishart, 1950).
4 Hannah Arendt, *The Origins of Totalitarianism* (London: Allen and Unwin, 1966).

13 Note-taking for Analysis and Structure

In this chapter you will learn:

- how to increase your flexibility in note-taking to make better use of all your intellectual abilities;
- how to choose the most appropriate strategy for the different levels at which we process ideas: comprehension, analysis and criticism;
- how to use linear notes to produce clear, uncluttered structures of the passages you read.

▶ Choosing the right note-taking strategy

By now, no doubt, you will have realised that for each of these different levels of processing (analysis/structure, and criticism/evaluation) there is the most appropriate note-taking strategy.

Of course, this should come as no surprise. It endorses what we've said a number of times already, that flexibility and choosing the most appropriate strategy is the key to effective essay writing. For example, we have already found in the interpretation stage that pattern notes are the most effective strategy for generating and recording the flow of ideas, when we brainstorm a question. And the same is true here: pattern and linear notes are each appropriate for different types of processing.

Nevertheless, there will always be a text or an article which we're using that seems to fall between two strategies, neither of which alone seems to do the job we want to do. On these occasions I find myself taking the highly structured linear notes first, and then creating a set of pattern notes to give me a broad overview of the issues involved. In this way you can get around the problem of seeing nothing but detail; of not being able to see the wood for the trees.

But for most of the jobs we have to do, the choice is clear: linear notes for analysis and structure; and pattern notes for criticism and evaluation.

▶ Note-taking for analysis and structure

As we've already discovered, our aim here is to identify and extract the hierarchy of ideas, a process which involves selecting and rejecting material according to its relevance and importance.

Although by now this sounds obvious, it's surprising how many students neglect it or just do it badly. As with most study skills, few of us are ever shown how best to structure our thoughts on paper. Yet there are simple systems we can all learn. Some students never get beyond the list of isolated points, devoid of all structure. Or, worse still, they rely on the endless sequence of descriptive paragraphs, in which a structure hides buried beneath a plethora of words.

This makes it difficult to process ideas even at the simplest level. Without clear structures we struggle just to recall much more than unrelated scraps of information. As a result students do less well in exams than they could have expected, all because they haven't learnt the skills involved in organising and structuring their understanding. They sit down to revision with a near hopeless task facing them – mounds of notes, without a structure in sight, beyond the loose list of points.

This could be described as the parable of two mental filing systems. One student uses a large brown box, into which she throws all her scraps of paper without any systematic order. Then, when she's confronted with a question in the exam, she plunges her hand deep into the box in the despairing hope that she might find something useful. Sadly, all that she's likely to come up with is something that's, at best, trivial or marginally relevant, but which she's forced to make the most of, because it's all she's got.

On the other hand there is the student who files all of her ideas systematically into a mental filing cabinet, knowing that, when she's presented with a question, she can retrieve from her mind a structure of interlinked relevant arguments backed by quotations and evidence, from which she can develop her ideas confidently. And most of us are quite capable of doing this with considerable skill, if only we know how to do it.

▶ **Linear notes**

This is, perhaps, the most familiar and widely used note-taking strategy, because it adapts well to most needs. As we've already seen, at university the exams we prepare ourselves for are designed to assess more than just our comprehension, so notes in the form of a series of short descriptive paragraphs, and even the list, are of little real value. Exams at this level are concerned with a wider range of abilities, including our abilities to discuss, criticise and synthesise arguments and ideas from a variety of sources, to draw connections and contrasts, to evaluate and so on. To do all this requires a much more sophisticated and adaptable strategy that responds well to each new demand. It should promote our abilities, not stunt them by trapping us within a straitjacket.

Linear notes are particularly good at analytical tasks, recording the structure of arguments and passages. As you develop the structure, with each step or indentation you indicate a further breakdown of the argument into subsections. These in turn can be broken down into further subsections. In this way you can represent even the most complex argument in a structure that's quite easy to understand. Equally important, with clearly defined keywords, highlighted in capital letters or in different colours, it's easy to recall the clusters of ideas and information that these keywords trigger of.

In most cases it looks something like the following:

A Heading

   1. *Sub-heading*
      (a)
      (b)
      (c)
         (i)
         (ii)
         (iii)
            e.g.
      (d)

   2. *Sub-heading*
      (a)
         (i)
         (ii)
         (iii)

(b)

(c)

B   Heading

1.   *Sub-heading*
     (a)
     (b)
         (i)
         (ii)
     (c)
         (i)
         (ii)
                    e.g.
     (d)

2.   *Sub-heading*

3.   *Sub-heading*
     (a)
     (b)
     (c)

The set of linear notes below is taken from a course that examines the rise of the dictators in Europe in the 1920s and 1930s.

Factors Promoting the Rise of Nazism

A   Humiliation of Germany

1.   The Treaty of Versailles betrayed Wilson's ideals

2.   Allies wanted:

     (a)   to weaken Germany – so it wouldn't threaten peace again
     (b)   revenge – punish Germany – reparations:
           •   humiliation extended with incidents in 1920s:
               (i)   Dec. 1922 Non-payment – French & Belgian troops cross into Ruhr
               (ii) 1924 Dawes Plan – reparations renegotiated
               (iii) 1929 Young Plan – reps renegotiated, payments to continue until 1988

B   Economy in Ruins

1.   Broken by War

2.   Damaged by reparations

3.   Economic slump in Europe
     - inflation in Germany reached its height when Govt printed money to pay strikers resisting French occupation of Ruhr

     Effects:
     (a)   Middle-class savings wiped out – sold possessions at low prices
     (b)   Young, old & sick suffered most
           e.g.   Berlin – 31% of children with diseases related to malnutrition
           – 8.2% had rickets
     (c)   Discontented flocked to Nazism – re. Hitler's confidence in staging the Munich Putsch in 1923

C   Weakness of Weimar Republic

- didn't appear to be working, therefore Hitler's propaganda all the more effective & appeared that only effective govt = autocratic govt

- no party could get a majority:

1.   Proportional representation:

     (a)   extreme parties survived – gave representation to all parties, even the smallest

     (b)   large number of parties – therefore difficult for one to obtain overall majority
           e.g.   even Hitler in July 1932 landslide only obtained little more than third of the seats

(c)   coalitions – every govt had to be a coalition:
- (i)   survival depended less on vigorous policies, than on readiness of coalition members to agree
- (ii)   average life of a cabinet under Weimar = less 8 mths

(d)   rule by second-rate politicians:
- (i)   rare for govts to be defeated outright
    - in most cases reshuffled because ministers of one member party disagreed with rest & walked out
- (ii)   party leaders gen. preferred not to compromise themselves by accepting office – unless Chancellor or key ministries – therefore most portfolios taken by second-rate politicians

(e)   same politicians remained at centre of politics despite reshuffles & shifts in public opinion:
- (i)   had each cabinet change included complete turnover no minister wld have time to get to know the job
- (ii)   regular practice for new Chancellor to persuade some ministers to stay on – therefore tempted to appoint technocrats, rather than statesmen

(f)   compromise rather than policies:
- (i)   difference between cabinets = little
- (ii)   leadership largely with Centre Party – little preconceived policy, exc. trad. defence of catholic & federalist interest
- (iii)   most observers concluded it had little real value to offer country

(g)   Weimar pols = constant change in govts – little change in policies:
- (i)   policy = whatever minimum policy members of coaltn wld accept – therefore unlikely to inspire loyalty
- (ii)   real test = Depression – failed – few were prepared to defend it

2. Article 48:
    • Constn gave President powers to rule by decree – therefore democracy abandoned from 1930 in preference for presidential rule by decree

As you can see, the structure is clear and concise. At a moment's glance you can pick out the main points and their supporting arguments and evidence, commit them to memory and then test yourself that you can recall the structure.

▶ In the next chapter

In the next chapter we will look at ways of organising your notes, so that you can make this structure as clear as possible and retrieve your ideas accurately and quickly whenever you need them.

14 Remembering your Notes

In this chapter you will learn:

- the techniques for producing clear notes that you can recall accurately;
- how to avoid the most common problems in note-taking;
- how to organise and consolidate your notes.

The key to good note-taking is to make the structure clear. The mind remembers structures, not lists nor paragraphs of continuous prose. So, keep it free and uncluttered. Don't convince yourself that unless you include this one fact you'll never remember it. You will. The structure will act as a net bringing to the surface of your mind more than you ever thought you could remember. But it has to be a good net – well constructed, with clear logical connections and free of all unnecessary material.

▶ Creating a clear structure

Here are a number of things you can do to make sure your structure works:

1 **Keywords** Choose sharp, memorable words to key off the points in your structure. In the notes on the Rise of Nazism the three main points are not difficult to remember, particularly with keywords, like 'Humiliation', 'Ruins' and the alliteration of 'Weakness of Weimar'. But you need other words to key off the subsections, although you don't need them for every step and every subsection in the notes.

Keying off the main points and the principal subsections will trigger off the rest. Don't doubt yourself on this, it will – try it.

So just choose sharp, memorable words for the principal subsections, words like 'Treaty of Versailles', 'Allies', 'Weaken Germany', 'Revenge', 'Reparations', 'Economic slump', 'Middle class', 'Discontented' and so on. They don't have to be snappy and bright, just memorable.

2 **Capitalisation**   Having chosen your keywords they must stand out, so you can see at a glance the structure of your notes. It's no good having a structure if it can't be seen beneath the undergrowth of words. Some people choose to put all their keywords into capitals.

3 **Colour**   If you don't think this is sufficiently prominent, put your keywords in different colours. This doesn't have to be too fussy – you're not creating a piece of modern art – but it's not too much of a bureaucratic task to get into the habit of working with two pens of different colours, one for picking out the keywords and the other for the rest. You will be surprised just how well this works. It's not unusual to come across people who can still visualise accurately in their mind's eye pages of notes they took when they were studying for their school-leaving exams many years ago.

4 **Gaps**   If the structure is to stand out, your notes must not appear too crowded. To avoid this, leave plenty of gaps between your points. This also gives you the opportunity to add other related things as you come across them in your reading, although you need to do this in such a way as to avoid overcrowding.

5 **Abbreviations**   Most of us use these, indeed we all tend to create our own personalised abbreviations for those words we seem to use most often. Even so, it's still surprising how many students look with open-mouthed astonishment when you list the standard abbreviations, like the following:

Therefore	$\therefore$
Because	$\because$
Leads to	$\rightarrow$
Increase/decrease	$\uparrow\downarrow$
Greater than/smaller then	$><$

Would/should	wld/shld
Would be, should be	w/be, sh/be
Equivalent	=
Not	≠
Parallel	llel

Nevertheless, as your tutors have no doubt told you, although these abbreviations are indispensable in compiling clear, concise notes, they shouldn't find their way into the final draft of your essay.

▶ Being brief

If you've left sufficient time between reading the text the first time for comprehension, and then reading it for structure, you're more likely to have a clear, uncluttered set of notes free from all unnecessary material. You'll certainly be free of that most time-consuming of activities, taking notes on notes, which many of us are forced to do because our notes are not concise enough in the first place.

Unfortunately, there are many students, even at university, who convince themselves that this is a valuable thing to do; that it's a way of learning their notes if they rewrite them more concisely. They seem to believe that by committing their notes to paper, they're committing them to their minds, whereas, in fact, they're doing anything but that.

Taking notes can be a pleasant substitute for thinking. It's something we can do on auto-pilot. In fact it can be one of the most relaxing parts of our pattern of study. While we are placing few demands on our mind, it can go off to consider more pleasant things, like the plans for the weekend, or reminiscences about last year's holiday.

This underlines the main problem in note-taking: most of us find it difficult to be brief. While we have our minds on auto-pilot we're able to convince ourselves that almost every point, however insignificant, is vitally important to our future understanding. Not surprisingly then, we end up omitting very little, obscuring the structure so that when we come to revision we have to start taking notes on our own notes.

▶ Notes must be a record of our understanding

But there's another reason that's more difficult to tackle. Most of us, at times, doubt our ability to remember details, so we allow ourselves to be seduced into recording things that 'might' be useful in the future. Inevitably, this results in masses of notes that obscure the main structure, which, as we've seen, is the only means by which we can recall them in the first place.

To avoid this we need to remind ourselves constantly of two things: first, that almost certainly we have better memories than we think; and secondly, that we're not producing encyclopaedic accounts of the subject, in which we record every known fact. To be of any use, notes should be an accurate record of *our* understanding, of *our* thinking, not someone else's.

We can easily lose sight of this when we try to take notes while we're reading the text for the first time or straight after we've read it. We lose our objectivity: all we can see is the author's ideas and opinions, not our own. We need to give our minds time to digest the ideas and self-organise. You will find that if you leave time between reading and noting, your mind will have created its own structures out of the ideas it has taken from the text.

Then, after we've allowed our minds sufficient time to do this, we need to organise ourselves to tap into it, to get our own understanding down on paper, without using the text. Otherwise the author will hijack our thinking and we'll simply copy from the text without thought. Remember, you can always go back to check on details afterwards.

Practice exercise 8
Note-taking for analysis and structure

Take a chapter from one of the books you're using for the essay you're working on in the assignments. Read it through, first, for comprehension. Then, a day or so later, read it again, this time for analysis and structure. Leave it a few hours for your mind to self-organise. Then, take a blank sheet of paper and try writing the broad structure of what you can recall of the main points that interest you from the chapter.

Don't be tempted to go back to the text, even if it's just to check up on an isolated fact. And give yourself up to an hour trying to recall the structure. Normally you won't need this amount of time, but for this exercise give yourself plenty of time to do it thoroughly.

You will be pleasantly surprised by the complex structure of interconnected points you've been able to produce unaided. You will never again

Continued

be entirely convinced when you try to tell yourself that you cannot trust your memory. You'll find that what your mind has given you is a clear, uncluttered structure around which you can build a fuller set of notes, if you need to.

But if you do decide to fill this out with more detail, always remind yourself not to clutter and obstruct your view of the structure with unnecessary detail. Remember, notes are of little use if they're not a record of *your* understanding of the subject.

▶ Reading an author's structure

In most passages it's quite easy to see the author's plan, the structure he or she has created, but not in all. In the most difficult cases you will need to interpret and translate what the author says into terms and structures that make sense for you. In effect, *you* will need to give the passage the sort of structure that will help you recall the points. Here we're reminded of the familiar advice from all our tutors, 'Put it into your own words.' And, of course, this is exactly what you need to do with this sort of text.

But more important is to go a little further and graft it onto your own thinking: make the ideas your own. At this point the ideas become universal; they are yours as well as the author's, leaving you in no danger of plagiarism. Just take the essence of the idea, stripped of all the phrases and sentences that are distinctive of the author. Put it into your own words; but don't worry if the author has found a crisp, memorable word that you know you'll never forget. Use it. Remember, ideas are universal, they're the currency of learning; it's the way we explain and develop those ideas in the passages we write that isn't.

However, even the most difficult and poorly organised author is likely to leave you a trail of literal symbols that indicate the structure he or she is following. We're all familiar with these, although we don't always pay as much heed to them as we should. The introductory and con-cluding sentences often indicate the main points of the passage. Here you're likely to find the memorable keyword that will trigger off in your mind a whole cluster of ideas.

Once you get into the body of the text, words like 'first' and 'finally' act as pointers to the structure, indicating the number of points that are to be, or have been, made. Others, that introduce illustrative material, like 'for example' and 'for instance', indicate that you need not take close and detailed notes from what's to come. A word, a brief phrase or sentence, should be enough to remind you of the example when you want it.

▶ Consolidating your notes

All of this means you're better able to take out a clear structure from what you read. But, if structure is one of the main features of good note-taking, then, as we've said a number of times already, flexibility is the other.

There are few things worse during revision than finding your notes on a particular topic are spread throughout your file in different places, because each time you've taken notes your organisation hasn't allowed you to change or to add to those you already have. As a result you have different packets of notes on the same subject spread throughout your file, none of them related, and all of them taking a slightly different approach to the subject.

Few things can be more confusing and frustrating. At just that moment when you want to get down to some organised revision for the exam, you realise you've got to re-organise your notes. You have to take notes on all the notes you have, so that you end up with the one integrated package of notes you should have had in the first place.

It's worth reminding yourself that notes are only the raw material, they're not fixed in stone as soon as they're written. You add to them, adapt and reshape them, as your ideas change, and as you read and see more. They must be able to adapt continually to the changes in your understanding of the subject. You must, then, have a note-taking strategy that is flexible enough to record these changes, while leaving you with one coherent set of notes.

To create this flexibility in your note-taking use a loose-leaf file, so you can slip into your notes at the appropriate place new notes that expand or adapt what you already have. Use an index-card system, broken up into the topics on your course, to record isolated quotations, statistics and examples (see below, Chapter 16). Spread your notes out on the page, leaving enough space between each section, so you can add new material as it arises. And, for the same reason, write just on one side of the paper, so you always have a blank sheet opposite your notes on which you can enter new information.

▶ In the next chapter

With these techniques and the flexibility they bring to your study you can, with more confidence, note your own responses to the ideas and arguments you read, as we'll see in the next chapter.

15 Note-taking for Criticism and Evaluation

In this chapter you will learn:

- a four-step technique for criticising and evaluating arguments;
- how to take notes that allow you to record your own criticisms and evaluations of the passage;
- how to improve your concentration.

Obviously, our ability to discuss and criticise the implications of arguments depends first on the skills needed to lay bare their structure: to isolate clearly the points for and against, so that we can enter into the discussion more confidently. But we also need a note-taking strategy that will allow us to go one step further and record our own arguments and criticisms in the body of the notes.

Unfortunately, many of us never get to the stage of being able to criticise and evaluate an author's arguments, because we're handicapped by note-taking skills which condemn us to many hours of patient toil, taking irrelevant, verbatim notes. A large part of the reason for this lies in our willingness to omit the interpretation stage, and the pattern notes we should have made there in response to two questions:

- What issues does the question raise that need to be researched and examined in the essay?
- What do I know and think about the issues raised?

In effect, by ignoring these questions we've failed to preview any passage we're likely to read when we undertake our research. As a result we're going in blind. We have little idea of the important issues raised by the question and, consequently, we don't really know what we're looking for.

▶ No standard by which to judge the author's ideas

Equally important, because we haven't declared what *we* know and think about the issues, we have no way of grafting onto our own understanding the ideas we're about to read and consider. Not surprisingly, then, they will always appear to be somebody else's. And, because of this, the most we'll be able to recall are mere scraps of what we've read without any consistent organisation to them. However, perhaps the most serious consequence is that we'll have nothing to judge the author's ideas against. We'll be in no position to criticise and evaluate the arguments.

Having read the passage we're likely to be so thoroughly convinced by the author's arguments that we find little to criticise. Then, when we go on to read another text by another author, who presents views conflicting with the first, we're likely to find we're equally convinced by these arguments. Lost between the two, we find it almost impossible to discuss the merits of either. Having failed to establish where we stand, we have nothing to argue with. Consequently, we're left just to imitate and reproduce uncritically what we read.

▶ Poor concentration

This also goes a long way towards explaining why many of us find it so difficult to concentrate on our work for all but relatively short periods. Because we're asking the mind to do relatively simple things, just translating the words on the page and copying them into our notes, it's under-utilised, so it looks around for more interesting pursuits. It looks forward to the party at the weekend or back at last summer's holiday. It can do all this and still cope with the trivial tasks we set it. The only problem is that when we get to the bottom of the page, or after we've spent two hours taking notes, we struggle to recall a word of it. We've read it, but we haven't processed it beyond copying the words.

There are, therefore, very good reasons why we should, at all times, attempt to escape this tendency towards passive, surface-level processing. Splitting up our reading and note-taking into the three levels of processing helps, but so does a more flexible note-taking strategy that will allow us to inject more of our own ideas and criticisms into the structure of the notes.

Therefore experiment, particularly with your pattern notes. If you still feel that linear notes are more appropriate for a particular piece of work, set time aside later to sit down with a blank sheet of paper and tap into your own ideas and criticisms, which will have been self-organising in your own mind since you finished reading. As you know, it won't take long. The ideas will come tumbling out and you will be surprised at just how good they are and how much you have to say about it.

▶ Playing devil's advocate

Even so, there are many students who still believe they don't see as much to criticise in a passage as other students do. If this is your problem, the following four-step technique will help you think more critically about what you read.

An argument may be weak or fallacious for one of three reasons: that the authors have misstated the facts (material fallacies); that they have wrongly used words (verbal fallacies); or that they have drawn the wrong inferences (logical fallacies). In Chapter 12, I listed ten of the most common fallacies, to guide you in what to look for. To help you use these more systematically, try working through the following steps:

Step 1: Are there exceptions?
When authors make claims that are important to their arguments, even though you might agree with them, play devil's advocate: ask yourself, are there exceptions to these?

For example, an author might argue that 'All criminals come from socially deprived backgrounds.' However, you can probably think of convicted criminals that you've read about in the newspapers, who, on the contrary, come from quite privileged backgrounds.

Step 2: If there are exceptions, are they general or specific?

2.1 Specific exceptions If they are specific, then while an author can still retain his or her claim, you've found sufficient grounds to justify qualifying the claim in order to take account of the special cases you've uncovered.

To return to our example, if the exceptions were just limited to one or two individuals from privileged backgrounds, the author would have to qualify the original claim.

2.2 General exceptions   However, if you have found a general category of exceptions, then you will have to move on to Steps 3 and 4.

Say you've discovered that most white-collar and computer crime is, in fact, committed by criminals with university degrees. In this case the objection cannot be dealt with so easily: you will have to ask the following questions.

Step 3: Is the claim too strong?

If you have found a general category of exceptions you must first ask yourself, does this make the original claim too strong: more than the evidence can support? If it does, then your author cannot maintain his or her claim. They must either reign it in, qualifying it in general terms, or abandon it altogether.

In our case the evidence can't support the claim, so, if the author wants to maintain it, she must qualify it by excluding all white-collar and computer crime. However, this might weaken and restrict it so much that it might be wiser to abandon it altogether, particularly when it leads you to suspect that you could probably find other groups, too, if you looked hard enough.

Step 4: Does it account for only part of the case?

Alternatively, if it can't be qualified, and there is sufficient merit in the argument to warrant not abandoning it, then the only thing you can do is to extend the claim to cover the general category of cases that is currently excluded. However, if this is possible, it is quite likely to lead to conclusions your authors either didn't see in the first place, or wouldn't agree with on the basis of their argument so far.

You might, for example, agree with the claim our author has made, although you question the notion that it is the 'socially' deprived that is the source of crime. You might argue that there are others responsible for crime, who are deprived in different ways. They may never have been socially deprived, but they may not have had a stable father-figure in their lives: there may have been a family breakdown, or they may have been moved from one boarding school to another without ever being able to establish long-lasting paternal relations.

So, in this case the claim may be worth holding on to, but only in the extended form to cover this new category of deprivation. However, this may lead the author either to conclusions she didn't foresee, or in a direction which doesn't serve the main purpose of her argument, which may have been to establish the claim that all crime can be identified with a particular social class.

Whichever is the outcome, whether you step off at Steps 2, 3 or 4, you will have discovered for yourself that you have well thought out reasons for criticising and discussing the authors' arguments. Try it in the following exercise.

Practice exercise 9
Note-taking for criticism and evaluation

Read the following passage carefully for comprehension. Then, after you've read it a second time, take the structure out of it in pattern notes. Now go through each of the steps above, asking yourself the questions about the principal claims made in the passage. You may not come up with much at this stage, but at least you've set your subconscious mind thinking about the issues. Then leave it for a day or two.

When you come back to it, go through the steps again, critically assessing the author's arguments. Your aim is to map out your reactions in pattern notes. So allow your mind to range free and fast over the issues. Remember, you're trying to tap into your mind's self-organised structures, so fluency and quick responses, as the ideas come flowing out, are important to get it all down in a structured form without losing any of it.

After you've completed this, compare it with the answer given below.

Passage

A Carnivore's Credo

This may be the age of enlightened sympathy for all animals, but certain facts are unassailable. We are at the end of a long evolutionary process that has produced a human society for whom meat-eating is natural. Indeed man's superiority is built on exploiting inferior species, who lack our intellectual and moral capabilities: they cannot think, make decisions, or communicate.

The loudest and most successful critic of this view over recent years has been Peter Singer, whose book, *Animal Liberation*, has achieved cult status since its publication in 1975. Singer criticises meat-eating because he claims it is based on the arbitrary moral distinction of species: whereas we wouldn't condone eating humans, we do accept eating non-human animals. This, he argues, ranks alongside other arbitrary moral distinctions which we are only too ready to condemn, like sex or race. These, we believe, are irrelevant to moral judgements. We condemn racism and sexism, and any other form of discrimination not based on relevant moral distinctions, like the practice of treating people differently because they have lower intelligence.

The only non-arbitrary moral distinction, he argues, is sentience, the capacity to suffer. This is a prerequisite for having interests. While there is no moral responsibility if we kick a stone, there is if we kick a mouse. So, anything that can suffer, that can experience enjoyment and happiness, has interests in avoiding pain and, therefore, deserves moral consideration.

However, as R. G. Frey points out in his article 'Pains, Interests, and Vegetarianism',[1] it is not the case that the capacity to suffer is a prerequisite of having interests – it is not, as this suggests, a necessary condition. In fact, he argues, we still speak of people having interests even when they can feel no pain at all.

His first example is of a soldier friend, who suffered extensive spinal, head and nervous injuries while serving in Vietnam. He is conscious, but cannot feel pain, yet still he has interests. Indeed his interests in being cared for are now greater because of his injuries. What's more he has interests in the care of his wife and children, and in protecting his good name. These interests continue to exist even though he can feel no pain and even though he may not know his good name might be harmed.

His second example is that of Karen Quinlan, a comatose patient, who cannot feel pain, yet who, again, clearly has interests. For example, as Frey points out, if a photographer entered her room and photographed her, her interests in maintaining her privacy would have been invaded; whereas Singer would argue, because she can feel no pain, she has no interests. In fact, as individuals we all seem to have interests, like privacy, that have nothing to do with our capacity to feel pain.

Given these arguments, it would seem that humans are distinct from animals in non-arbitrary ways, that may be difficult to pin down, but are no less real.

Answer

In this passage most, if not all, the criticisms relate to verbal, rather than material and logical, fallacies. We're entitled to ask, 'Is this what we mean when we use this concept, or do we mean more than this, or less?' Take Frey's criticism of Singer's argument and the cases that he raises to make his point.

Step 1: Are there exceptions?

When Frey uses the concept of 'pain', are there exceptions to this; types of pain that he doesn't include within his concept? In other words, is there just more to it than this? In the case of his friend, the Vietnam soldier, he appears to use 'pain' in a narrow sense, meaning just physical pain. Yet his friend is, of course, also capable of feeling emotional pain, anguish, insecurity, fear, for himself, his family and his good name. So, according to Singer's principle, he does have interests, because he can feel pain of this type.

Step 2: If there are exceptions, are they general or specific?

In this case they are general, not specific, so we cannot qualify Frey's case to acknowledge special cases. We are driven, then, to consider Steps 3 or 4.

Step 4: Does it account for only part of the case?

It's not that the claim is too strong and can be reigned in (as in Step 3), but that it's too narrow: it only accounts for a limited range of types of pain. If you were then to extend Frey's claim to cover the general category of cases that is currently excluded, this would amount to conceding the argument to Singer.

By the same process you can arrive at all the other criticisms in the answer below. As you gain confidence with this technique you will be able to adapt it to your needs and apply it to every question that asks you to criticise, discuss and evaluate arguments. For example, select one of the books you prioritised on your reading list for the essay you've chosen to write in these assignments, and complete the following assignment.

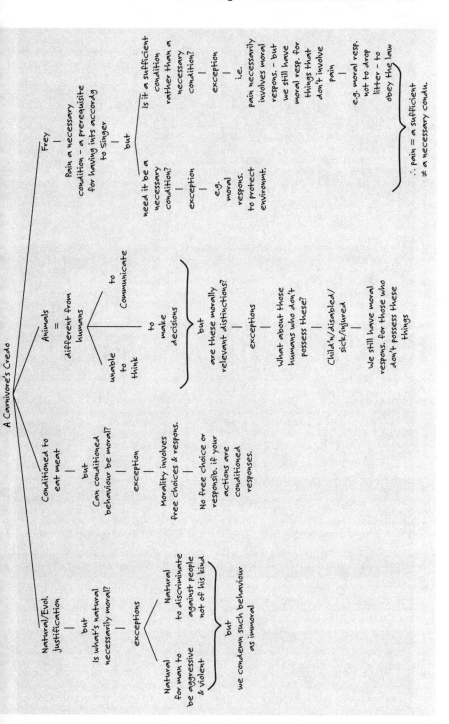

A Carnivore's Credo

Natural/Evol. justification
- but
- Is what's natural necessarily moral?
- exceptions
  - Natural for man to be aggressive & violent
  - Natural to discriminate against people not of his kind
  - but
  - we condemn such behaviour as immoral

Conditioned to eat meat
- but
- Can conditioned behaviour be moral?
- exception
- Morality involves free choices & respons.
- No free choice or responsib. if your actions are conditioned responses.

Animals = different from humans
- unable to think
- to communicate
- to make decisions
- but are these morally relevant distinctions?
- exceptions
- What about those humans who don't possess these?
- Child'n/disabled/ sick/injured
- We still have moral respons. for those who don't possess these things

Frey
- Pain a necessary condition — a prerequisite for having ints accord'g to Singer
- but
  - need it be a necessary condition?
    - exception
    - e.g. moral respons. to protect environmt.
  - Is it a sufficient condition rather than a necessary condition?
    - exception
    - i.e. pain necessarily involves moral respons. – but we still have moral resp. for things that don't involve pain
    - e.g. moral resp. not to drop litter – to obey the law

∴ pain = a sufficient ≠ a necessary condn.

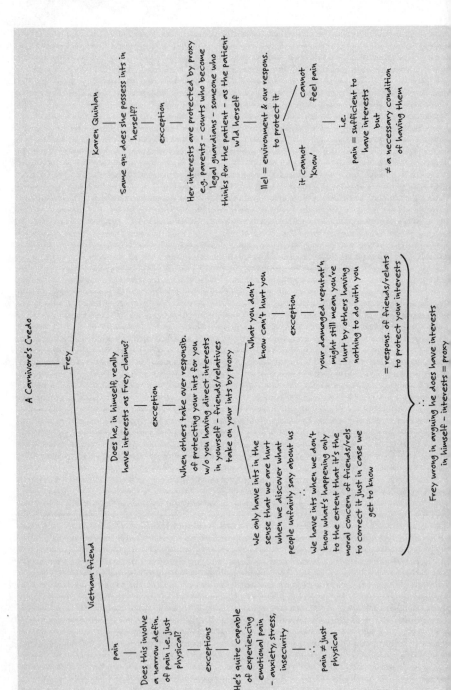

A Carnivore's Credo

Vietnam friend

pain

Does this involve a narrow defin. of pain i.e. just physical?

exceptions

He's quite capable of experiencing emotional pain – anxiety, stress, insecurity

∴ pain ≠ just physical

Frey

Does he, in himself, really have interests as Frey claims?

exception

When others take over responsib. of protecting your ints for you w/o you having direct interests in yourself – friends/relatives take on your ints by proxy

We only have ints in the sense that we are hurt when we discover what people unfairly say about us

∴
We have ints when we don't know what's happening only to the extent that it's the moral concern of friends/rels to correct it just in case we get to know

What you don't know can't hurt you

exception

your damaged reputat'n might still mean you've hurt by others having nothing to do with you

= respons. of friends/relats to protect your interests

∴ Frey wrong in arguing he does have interests in himself – interests = proxy

Karen Quinlan

Same qu: does she possess ints in herself?

exception

Her interests are protected by proxy e.g. parents – courts who become legal guardians – someone who thinks for the patient – as the patient w/d herself

llel = environment & our respons. to protect it

it cannot 'know'

cannot feel pain

i.e.
pain = sufficient to have interests but
≠ a necessary condition of having them

Assignment 5
Note-taking for criticism and evaluation

In this assignment select a chapter that you plan to read for your essay. Read it through first for comprehension. Then, after a day or so, take a blank sheet of paper and try to recall the broad structure of the chapter.

After you've done this, go over each point in the structure, critically assessing the argument in the way we have in this chapter. Map out your reactions in pattern notes, allowing yourself to explore quite freely your reactions to the arguments the author has made. If you appear to be going off the point at times, don't worry. Try to exhaust your ideas on an issue before you move on to another. But if an idea comes up out of place, note it, don't rely on picking it up later. Give yourself licence to analyse points thoroughly, to make contrasts, and to bring in other evidence you've come across elsewhere, that you think has a bearing on the issues raised.

Remember you are trying to get your mind's natural self-organisation down on paper. It's there, if only you can tap into it. To do that, you must allow it to pick up top speed. At this point it's more likely to make connections, to draw contrasts and comparisons, and to use items of information, evidence and examples, that you might never have thought of.

▶ In the next chapter

You should be pleasantly surprised by the number of interesting ideas, criticisms, and examples that you were able to produce from your own resources. This will make your essay not only more interesting, but also more fluent and persuasive, because these are genuinely your own ideas. In the next chapter we will look at ways of organising your work, so that you can generate more of your own ideas and insights, and use them more effectively.

Note
1 R. G. Frey, 'Pain, Interests, and Vegetarianism', in his *Interests and Rights: The Case Against Animals* (Oxford: Clarendon Press, 1980), ch. XI.

16 Organising your Retrieval System

In this chapter you will learn:

- how to create an effective retrieval system to catch more of your own ideas and insights;
- the importance of using a journal and a notebook;
- how to gather material by using a card-index and a project box.

If we are to generate and use more of our own ideas and insights, we will have to spend some time organising an effective research strategy. The key to this is to have a retrieval system that is sufficiently adaptable to catch the material *whenever* and *wherever* it shows itself, and then provide us with a means of accessing it easily whenever we want it.

To create such a system isn't difficult, but it means going beyond the normal loose-leaf folder, a few wallet files and a reliable source of A4 paper. It calls for a thoughtful approach, a little imagination and, above all, flexibility. As we've already seen with our reading and note-taking, inflexibility in the way we use our skills can trap us within the confines of low-level work. We're forced into surface-level processing, dependent on the ideas that our tutors and texts can give us.

The same goes for our retrieval system too. Unless we choose and organise its various components thoughtfully, we're likely to lose most of our best ideas, and produce work that is predictable and imitative of the ideas we've been given. To put it simply, our system should promote, not frustrate the quality of our work. This is not an unimportant part of our pattern of study, and its influence is never neutral. Get it right and we can find ourselves with an abundance of insightful ideas that are genuinely our own. Get it wrong and our work struggles to rise above the mundane and imitative.

▶ The usual sources

Most of us are used to using the obvious sources of material, like the booklists and references provided by the tutors of courses. But you can go further than this and uncover texts and articles of your own by checking the bibliographies of the recommended texts. Certain texts will be common throughout each bibliography, which is often a good indication of those that are the most useful and respected in the field. But check the date of the publication. If you're looking at a text published in 1964 and its bibliography is recommending another text published in 1944, you might find that other texts have been published since, that have superseded it. However, don't be surprised if this is not the case: there are still the classic, highly respected, indispensable texts in most subject areas.

Beyond bibliographies, probably the most under-used resources are libraries and their staff. The local library, and particularly college and university libraries, are more than just a source of books: they collect and classify information from a wide range of sources. Most take an impressive range of journals, newspapers and periodicals, along with government reports on a range of topics. Of course, in addition, most have computer terminals that can give you access to the Internet and to other information stored on disk. You can find a number of encyclopaedias on disk, along with thesauruses and dictionaries such as *Chambers*. Many libraries also have large stocks of video recordings of educational material.

▶ The richest source is found in your own mind

For most of us this just about covers the range of sources available to us. But it ignores one of the richest sources of ideas and evidence, mainly because we're not accustomed to recognise it as such. Each day we talk to friends and acquaintances, we listen to the radio and watch TV, or we just sit thinking as we drive home in our cars, or on a bus or train. On all of these occasions our minds are taking in ideas and processing them into complex, self-organised structures. This is rich material, that we ignore at our own cost. Just because it doesn't come from an authoritative book or article, or from a knowledgeable tutor, doesn't mean it's not full of insights that the mind will feed on to produce interesting and useful structures of ideas.

Take those moments in the day when we're alone with our thoughts without any interruptions from friends, the TV, the radio, or a book we ought to read. It's just us and our ideas in the car as we drive home, or in a bus, or on a train. On most of these occasions it's difficult in retrospect to recall exactly what we were thinking at the time. This in itself is not always a bad thing. Such moments of reverie are the time when the mind can process the material it's taken in during the day, and organise it into structures for us to use if we have the will to access it.

But on other occasions, rather than whiling away this valuable time with just empty static in your head, it's useful just to set yourself a topic to think about and sort out as you sit there – in fact more useful than most students ever imagine. It's the time when you can do some serious thinking for yourself, not in response to someone else, a book or a tutor, but responding to your own ideas and your own original insights. You will be surprised at the results, maybe not immediately, although that's quite likely to occur, but certainly a few days later when all sorts of ideas, insights and structures will appear in your mind and you'll wonder where you picked them up from.

Some students, who have deliberately set about adopting this strategy whenever they're alone, tell me they plan whole essays in their head. Others describe how they've given themselves a difficult problem to sort out or a complicated argument that they've never really understood before. And, without the usual distractions around them, such as their books and other sources of reference they've come to rely on whenever they want to solve a problem, they've sorted it out on their own terms. Or, failing that, they've at least discovered for the first time what the problem was.

But it's not just these quiet moments that are a rich source of material and insights. When we discuss topics with friends we find ourselves using what we've read in books and articles, in the course of which we produce interesting ideas and arguments without any conscious prompting. Each day as we read the newspapers we are quite likely to come across new evidence for something we've been studying, or interesting quotations that would support an argument we're planning to use in an essay. And, of course, there are those really special moments when we have a sudden dramatic insight, when we suddenly see something that's been troubling us for some time, clear and in sharp focus for the first time.

► Carry a notebook

On all of these occasions we need to have our retrieval system well worked out. In particular, we need to have with us at all times a small notebook in which we can note our sudden insights, or just work out our arguments and plans on paper. This represents the internal monologue we have with ourselves on the subjects we're studying. You may say, of course, 'Well, as soon as I leave the classroom I don't think about the subject again, until the next lesson, or until I have to do work on it.' But not only is this unwise for obvious reasons, it's also most unlikely. This internal monologue may be buried deep, but it's still there. Although for some it's louder than for others, we all need to cultivate a system for tapping into it, so we can make the best use of its insights and then switch it off so we can get on with other things.

The point is that the most thoughtful and creative insights come to us not in the customary learning situations, such as lessons or as we work at our essays, but when we're off guard. And if we fail to live with this internal monologue and organise ourselves to use it, we'll lose a wealth of ideas and insights, which are essentially *ours*. You can always follow these up later with further research, but if you fail to record them the moment they occur, you will almost certainly forget them. Even if you're able to recover a small fragment of them sometime later, the most valuable part, the insight, the form that the idea took in the first place that forced it to the surface, will be lost to you forever. And it's this that made it vivid and clear for you and will, in turn, make it vivid and clear for others too.

► Keeping a journal

Nevertheless, this is not the only way in which you can tap into more of your own thoughts. Probably the most useful method is to set up your own journal, either manually or in a computer file, in which you give yourself the opportunity of writing, say, two or three times each week for at least half an hour each time.

Unlike a conventional diary where you describe the events that have occurred in your life, a journal gives you the opportunity of writing exclusively about your ideas and their development. For most of us, opportunities to write in this free, unconstrained manner are rare: we're usually working with books, or with our notes, so the ideas that are genuinely ours, untainted by what we're reading or referring to, rarely reach the surface of our consciousness, although they're always there.

▶ Index-card systems

To make the system complete, back up the notebook and the journal with an index-card system divided into sections for each topic on the syllabus. Whenever we come across an interesting idea, an isolated statistic, or a useful quotation, it's very difficult to know exactly what to do with it. Do you write it up on a sheet of paper? But if you do, where are you going to file it? And it's all too easy to lose just one sheet. To cope with this we need a simple, flexible system that we can use to catch all those isolated items that we would otherwise lose or not know what to do with. The card system fulfils this role perfectly.

Using just one card for each item (a quotation, an idea, an argument, or a set of figures), you have a retrieval system that makes it very easy to find what you want whenever you want it, particularly when you come to revise for an examination, or set about the research for an essay. Once you've worked with a card system for a few months, you'll wonder how you ever lived without one.

Equally important, most students find a card system frees them from the authors they read when they come to write the essay. First, because they are restricted, by the limited space, to noting only the ideas they need, they avoid getting trapped within the complex web of the author's arguments. And secondly, because they can sort and shuffle the cards, they can take each idea in the order *they* want to, and not in the order their authors presented them.

You will also find a good card system will help you avoid the temptation to plagiarise. Not only is this unacceptable, because, in effect, it's 'literary theft', but it will unbalance your writing. It will break up the flow of *your* words and ideas, and make it increasingly difficult for you to keep control of your structure and, therefore, the relevance of your arguments. Even more important, it will make it difficult for you to develop your own ideas. Once you've accepted an author's statement as the undisputed authority, you're left with no good reason to discuss or challenge it.

A card system gives you the opportunity to record your sources accurately at the top of each card, and with the limited space it forces you to put the ideas into your own words. If the phrase or section in the text is so telling that no summary in your own words will capture the idea, then you're restricted to recording only short quotations of a sentence or two, which must be chosen with much greater care.

▶ The project box

Finally, you might borrow an idea from professional writers. It's not unusual for writers to use a project box or file for the job they're working on. Into this they will put anything that comes to hand which might be useful in the future when they get around to organising the piece they've planned to write. You can do the same. Take a file, or even an actual box, that you can use for the essay you're going to have to write, or the topic you're about to study, and whenever you come across something that might be useful, drop it in. It may be an article taken from a newspaper or magazine; it may be notes taken from a TV programme; it may be anything that just stimulates an idea that you might otherwise forget.

This has all sorts of advantages. On a practical level, the very fact of having a box or file of this kind will in itself generate material that we would not otherwise have noticed. Knowing that we have something into which we can throw material of all different kinds is all the encouragement most of us need to set about noticing and collecting it wherever we can find it.

But equally important, it prepares the mind not just to recognise material when we see it, but to work on the ideas continuously; to see the essay as a developing project to be worked on even when we're not consciously thinking about it. We learn to regard our work as more like open-ended, ongoing projects, that we can't just switch off as soon as we leave the seminar or tutorial, or put down a book. It encourages us to develop our ideas over time and beyond the normal confines of study.

▶ In the next chapter

Nevertheless, if this retrieval system is to work, we will have to organise our time more effectively. In the next chapter we will examine the simple things we can do to make sure we have enough time not just to catch our own ideas and develop our thinking and writing skills, but also to relax.

17 Organising your Time

In this chapter you will learn:

- how to minimise the stress of studying;
- how to organise your time to make better use of your thinking and writing skills;
- how to get more done in less time;
- about the importance of planning to relax as well as to work.

Although our new retrieval system means that we will have to organise our time more effectively, it doesn't necessarily mean that we will have to find more time. It's just that we will need to work in a more predictable, routine way, so that we can find regular time slots in our week to do these things that will so improve our thinking and writing.

▶ Why plan?

'Why', you might ask, 'do I need to plan my time, when I always get my work done on time anyway?' It's a good question that we ought not to dismiss cheaply. The simple answer is that, although we might believe we don't plan and don't really need to, the fact is we all do it anyway, one way or another. We might not sit down, draw up a piece of paper and write down the times we plan to do things, but we still do it in our minds. We have a rough idea what work we're supposed to be doing at various times throughout the week. You might even be a list maker: someone who sits down once a week to compile a comprehensive list of those things that need to be done in the following week and then sets about to work their way through it as best they can.

For some people this works perfectly well, but for most of us it doesn't. Under this system we find ourselves leaving tasks to the last minute, giving ourselves insufficient time to do the jobs we have to do, or just doing things at the most inappropriate times, when we don't do that sort of work very well. What's more, without a timetable we have to remind and constantly nag ourselves to get on and do things that have to be done. This is tiring, it saps energy, and for many it can be quite depressing, taking all the joy out of learning. Indeed it can even result in seriously harmful stress.

Nevertheless, we all seem to accept this as a normal part of study, even though it's quite avoidable. If we were to plan our work, so that we did things in a repetitive, regular manner, it would become merely routine, relieving us of the responsibility of nagging ourselves constantly to do things. We could set aside the same time each week to tackle certain tasks, and the nagging stress, that makes study an intolerable burden for many, would largely disappear.

▶ The right time for the right task

Avoiding stress is not the only gain that comes from planning. Equally significant, we learn more about ourselves as learners, particularly about the times when we work best. We all have some idea of when we seem to have most concentration and when we're most productive. Some people prefer to work late, into the early hours of the morning, when there are no distractions. Others prefer an early start, so they can get a couple of hours work in before breakfast. It's quiet, they argue, and the normal cares and concerns of the day haven't yet asserted themselves and hijacked their thinking.

These might seem to be just personal preferences, but they will affect the quality of our work. They are decisions we have to think about carefully as we plan how best to use our time. There are some tasks, such as reading, that call for the highest levels of concentration. At one time or another most of us have found ourselves sitting in a library after a heavy lunch, trying to read a chapter of a book. After struggling for an hour or two we realise we can't remember a thing we've read. Either that, or the effort of trying to force ourselves to do something at the worst possible time, leaves us slumped over the book in a deep sleep.

A few years ago one British university decided to conduct research on this: what's known as the 'post-lunch dip'. They found it to be so debilitating that it compares with heavy drinking, with its effects lasting as long as a few days as the body recovers. Under these circumstances business people probably should not be making important decisions that affect the lives of others, nor should people be operating dangerous equipment. But, by the same token, we should not be attempting to read, or do other things that call for the highest levels of concentration. After a heavy lunch the body has to divert energy into digestion, leaving less for other functions. And, as our body temperature rises, we begin to feel sleepy, so we find it almost impossible to concentrate on what we're doing.

Other tasks, particularly the more creative, demand just as much concentration. Analysing, brainstorming and planning questions all involve synthesising ideas and evidence from a range of sources. They call for tightly focused thinking to bring to the surface of our minds our ideas and the linkages between them. This is active deep-level processing, best done at those times when we know that our resources are not depleted, and there are few distractions to sabotage our thinking.

It's not difficult to see, then, that if we are to get the best out of our abilities we must find the right time for the right task. If we know that each week we have a certain amount of reading to do, it might be best to plot this in our weekly timetable on two or three mornings. The same might go for analysing, brainstorming and planning an essay. There are other times too when we know our concentration is likely to be unimpaired: late in the afternoon, in the evening, or late at night. Alternatively, some people try to postpone lunch as long as possible to give themselves four to five hours of good quality work in the morning.

Immanuel Kant, the great eighteenth-century German philosopher, preferred not to work at all in the afternoons. Of course, most of us are not so fortunate as to be able to give ourselves every afternoon off. But if we've plotted sessions in our timetable in which we can tackle the work that demands high levels of concentration, we can afford to use our afternoons for other, less demanding work. You might choose to tackle bureaucratic tasks like sorting out your notes, or writing up notes you may have taken in a lecture or seminar, which need to be rewritten. You might read the papers, or do your weekly survey of the magazines that tend to be useful, or go through the current journals in your subjects for articles that you should read later. You might even set aside an hour two or three times a week for writing your journal.

▶ Finding more time

Organising your time in this deliberate and careful way has one, almost unexpected, bonus. We're all inclined to believe that we already organise our time effectively and that we can't really get any more out of ourselves. We seem to work long hours, we make sacrifices to get the work done, and we never seem to have enough time to relax or to do those things that we enjoy most. So to ask us to plan more efficiently seems absurd: it cannot be done.

But once we settle down to write out our plan and force ourselves to design the best way of working, we are likely to find that there is more time to do things than we ever expected. It might be that without a clear, well designed plan in front of us, each time we get down to work we're more relaxed about what we have to do and the pace we need to work at. We have only a vague notion of how long a task should take, and we don't have a clear idea of what we've got to do after this, or what we're expecting to get done before the end of the day. Consequently, we tend to spend more time on the task than we need to.

This is one of the better illustrations of Parkinson's Law. The British historian, writer and political analyst Cecil Northcote Parkinson famously argued that, 'Work expands so as to fill the time available for its completion.'[1] In setting about our work, if we fail to make clear to ourselves what we want to achieve in a given time, we're likely to fall victims to this. Indeed, like a computer virus, it's likely to invade every activity in our pattern of study. And most students who are affected have no idea that they are.

What's more, those students who tend to be severely affected turn out to be the most hardworking and motivated. They will work prodigious hours, often getting exhausted, run-down and, in the end, extremely frustrated and depressed. It seems that no matter how much they put in there is never enough time just to do the work set, let alone read around the subject. They know they should do this, if they are to develop a comprehensive grasp of the issues, and not just a straight imitation of a major text, but despite all their good intentions, they just cannot find the time. Parents worry, understandably, that they seem to do nothing else but study and get run-down as a result.

And yet, as if to compound the problem, even with all their hard work they seem to do no better. Working such long unstructured hours they are rarely able to see the ideas objectively. They are simply too close to them. As a result they never successfully make them their own, or feel confident that they have any control over them. In class they struggle to explain the ideas they've read, whereas someone else who's done only a fraction of the work can bring reason and common sense to them. They can see the obvious questions to ask about them, they can identify the weaknesses in the author's arguments, and they can recall the organisational structure behind the passages they've read, all much better than the student who has spent hours reading the text and taking careful notes from it.

Of course it seems unfair that someone who has spent far fewer hours at work should get better marks. Our faith in the Protestant work ethic leads us to assume that those who work hardest get the highest rewards. Sadly this is more often not the case. It's the student who works hard within a well organised and effective timetable, who is most likely to get the best marks.

▶ Working hard means relaxing hard

There are, in fact, obvious reasons for this. Those who have worked without an organised timetable will know these all too well. As you sit down to work, time stretches ahead of you unstructured and without end. You don't know how long the task will take or what you will do afterwards. All you know is that the job's got to be done and you're there to do it until it's completed. This can depress even the most motivated student.

Faced with this daunting prospect we struggle to get down to work. We search for things to do, to lighten the burden and take our minds off our work. We suddenly find pencils that urgently need to be sharpened, or books which have been in the same position for years that urgently need to be rearranged. It can be anything just as long as it gives us some respite from our work. Even when we've got down to work, we still see time stretch out ahead without structure. So we search relentlessly for any distraction just to give us a break. Trivial things easily take hold of our concentration. We go missing from our work for five or ten minutes at a time. Obviously these are the breaks we should have planned. Without a plan, they come more frequently, taking up more time than we can afford.

In contrast, by planning not just our work but the times for relaxation too, we give ourselves clear goals and expectations. We have a certain amount of time in which to complete the work, after which we give ourselves a reward for hard work. We might arrange to have a coffee break with friends, or a session down at the gym or in the swimming pool. And, of course, at the same time we are free of that nagging conscience each time we have a break, telling us that we shouldn't be here, we should be back at work. With a well planned timetable we know that our time has been pre-planned, our relaxation as well as our work, and we have no need to worry because it's all under control.

Practice exercise   10
The personal weekly timetable

Before you organise your timetable it helps to have a clear idea of how you use your time at present. We need to know how well we do this and where we can make improvements.

Take a normal week and work in your usual way. On the timetable on p. 130 record accurately what you do in every hour. If you're working, record the subject and the activity – note-taking, reading, planning, and so on. If you're relaxing, record what you were doing. Record enough detail to give you an accurate picture of how you use your time.

At the end of the week, analyse the information you've recorded by counting up the hours you've devoted to studying, relaxation, social activities, travelling, sleep, meals and any other activity you may have recorded. It will also help if you break down the time spent studying into the subjects you study and into the activities of study, like note-taking and reading.

This will give you an accurate account of how you use your time. It will make clear to you where the problems are and what you need to do to solve them. Most students are shocked that they devote much less time to their work than they thought they did. They realise that there are demands on their time that cannot all be met if they are to complete their studies successfully. They also come to realise that the way they manage these competing demands at present is not the best way. They tend to go with the demand that is most pressing at that particular time, which in the long run may not work out to be the best way to apportion their time.

Personal Weekly Timetable

	MON.	TUES.	WED.	THURS.	FRI.	SAT.	SUN.
24.00–1.00							
1.00–2.00							
2.00–3.00							
3.00–4.00							
4.00–5.00							
5.00–6.00							
6.00–7.00							
7.00–8.00							
8.00–9.00							
9.00–10.00							
10.00–11.00							
11.00–12.00							
12.00–13.00							
13.00–14.00							
14.00–15.00							
15.00–16.00							
16.00–17.00							
17.00–18.00							
18.00–19.00							
19.00–20.00							
20.00–21.00							
21.00–22.00							
22.00–23.00							
23.00–24.00							

▶ In the next chapter

Once you've completed this you're in a better position to organise a timetable that gets the most out of your abilities and time. In the next chapter you will be taken step-by-step through the process of pre-paring such a timetable.

Note
1 Northcote C. Parkinson, *Parkinson's Law* (London: Helicon, 1958), p. 4.

18 Your Own Personal Timetable

In this chapter you will learn:

- how to plan your own personal timetable step by step;
- about the importance of giving your mind time to process the material you've read and develop ideas of your own;
- how to ensure you do the right job at the right time.

Now that you've got a clear idea of the way you use your time, you're more aware of the sort of adjustments you need to make. With this in mind you can now take another copy of the personal weekly timetable and this time compile what you believe is likely to be the best use of your time, which will ensure you get the most out of your abilities. You will need to keep in mind the points we've already made as you work your way through the following steps:

Step 1: Regular activities
The first step is to enter onto the timetable all the normal routine things you do each week – things like family commitments, meal times, the hours of sleep you normally need, regular social activities, the time you spend travelling each day, and so on. You can also enter your regular class times: the lectures, seminars and tutorials that you have to attend each week.

Step 2: How much study time?
Next you should ask yourself how many hours each day you're going to study. At present this might seem like asking you how long is a piece of string: you study as long as you have to. And there will be times when you have to go over your timetabled limit. But you do need to

set yourself boundaries, otherwise Parkinson's Law will take over and there will be no limits to the time you work. You'll use your time wastefully and experience all the frustration and stress we've already talked about.

As a general rule, set yourself around six hours of private study a day. On some days, when you have no classes, you might feel you're able to do more than this, say eight hours. But be careful: any more than six or eight hours and you'll find it difficult to recover for the next day. This doesn't just mean that you'll feel tired and jaded the next day, which, of course, is more than likely; but, equally important, your mind may not have been able to process successfully everything you gave it to do the day before. As a result, when you come to access it, you're likely to find a jumble of ideas, poorly organised, that you can't quite remember with the accuracy that you'd like to.

Step 3: Relaxation

For this reason relaxation needs to be planned just as carefully as work. Choose the times in the week when you will relax and the times when you will study. Remember that you're trying to create the right balance between work and relaxation, otherwise, as we've just seen, you won't leave your mind sufficient time to process everything. With this in mind, choose one day a week to have off from work, when you can have a complete break. You probably need to plan this day almost as much as you need to plan the rest of your timetable. You're working much harder, so you need to relax much harder too.

The same applies to rest periods throughout the week. If you can see that you have a long and tiring day, try to plan to do something in the evening that you'll find relaxing. You might belong to a club that you attend at that time each week, or you may have a regular date with a friend to go to the cinema or go out for dinner. This may be the time to plan the exercise that you might otherwise find difficult to squeeze in, perhaps at the local gym or swimming pool. But, like your day off, don't leave this unplanned: decide now what you're going to do at these times.

Step 4: Plotting the times

With all your other activities plotted onto your timetable you can now plot the times for your private study. The first step is to decide when you work best and at these times plot the work that calls for the highest levels of concentration – reading, analysing and brainstorming questions, planning, and writing the essay. As you do this, keep in mind the two most important reasons for planning your timetable: first, to plot each stage of essay writing so that you have sufficient time to develop the skills involved in each of these stages; and second, to allow your subconscious mind the time to process the material you've read, and develop ideas of your own.

Therefore, you will need a timetable that makes certain you'll be working on all five stages at the most suitable times, week in, week out. It must get you to work in a routine, predictable way. It might be that you are regularly set an essay every Friday to be handed in on the following Friday. Given this, you would plot on Saturday morning, say, an hour when you can interpret and brainstorm the question. With Sunday off, this gives your subconscious time to process the ideas and throw up new insights for you to pursue on Monday, when you get back to work. Monday and Tuesday, then, would be devoted to research. On Wednesday you could plan your essay, leaving it overnight so that you can add new ideas the following day before you start to write. On Thursday you write the essay, and then, on Friday you revise it and print it off to be handed in.

If you're set an essay every week, you will only need to work on one copy of the timetable. But you may be working on a two- or three-week cycle, in which case you'll need to be plotting your work on two or three copies. Either way, as long as this is a routine and settled way of working, you can plot each stage over your cycle and always know what you should be doing and when, confident that you're working at the best time and getting the most out of your abilities.

After you've done this, you will be ready to plot the other work you've got to do, bearing in mind that most of us are helped by having some variety in our working day. Taking notes, reading or writing for long periods can be very tiring. We need rest periods and changes of activity to maintain our efficiency levels. The same applies if you're working on just one of the subjects you're studying. It helps if you can create variety by working on more than one of your subjects each day. In this way you're better able to return to each subject with your ideas fully processed and a level of detachment that helps you see things more clearly.

Nevertheless, too much variety and too many changes of activities, can be confusing. It splinters and fragments our work, making it difficult to see all the contrasts and connections, and to develop the depth of understanding that comes from sustained work. So you will need to create the right balance between the activities and between the subjects you're studying to make each day both interesting and productive.

For the same reasons, try to give yourself sufficient time to process the ideas between each session on a particular subject or activity, so you can use the ideas convincingly. In effect you're timetabling not just to make sure you do everything you have to, but, more important, to ensure that you develop the best understanding of your subjects. This is a cumulative process, in which we build on what we've already achieved until we understand a topic well, and can recall and control the ideas confidently. It's likely to take a number of sessions of reading, note-taking and thinking until we're sure we have the ideas under our control.

In view of the importance of giving ourselves time to digest and process the ideas, try to divide up each study session into manageable periods of, say, two hours, with relaxation in between. This might be just a thirty-minute break while you have coffee with friends, but it will give your mind time to process and organise the ideas, helping you to see them with greater clarity and objectivity. As a result, you'll find that you're now able to criticise, discuss and evaluate the ideas you've read, rather than just absorb them uncritically. However, the break should not be too long, otherwise you'll waste time by having to go through the warming up stage again, as you re-read passages to get back into the ideas.

▶ Be specific

Finally, as you construct your timetable be as specific as possible. The timetables that work least well are those that are vague, that lack specific detail. If we are unsure about the time a task should take, Parkinson's Law will take over and we'll find we're working too long, having insufficient breaks and getting done only a fraction of what we could have done.

To avoid these problems be as specific as you can: about the number of hours you will work each week and each day; about the length of each session, so that you always work at your peak efficiency and you have enough breaks; and about the time each task should take you. Make sure you're clear about the subject you're going to be studying, and the activity of each study period – reading, note-taking, planning, writing and so on.

And, equally important, try to be specific about your relaxation. Don't underestimate the importance of giving yourself a clear goal to work to: a treat to enjoy at the end of your work as a reward for the hard work you've done. You'll be less likely to search for any diversion that will take you away from your studies to relieve the burden of unstructured hours of work. You will find yourself wasting less time urgently sharpening pencils or strolling along your bookshelves allowing your attention to be grabbed by just about anything that might be there.

What's more, plan to do something that marks a clear contrast with your work. If you've been reading for two hours, it may not be the best form of relaxation to give yourself an hour off to read a novel you're half way through, even though it might be thoroughly engrossing. It might be better to do some exercise, go for a run, or a swim, or just go for a walk. Or you might do something creative, like playing music, sketching, or painting. You might work on your car, or start building a bookcase in your study. The point is if you're working harder, you must play harder; and if this means that you plan your work, then you must plan your play too.

In a nutshell

- Decide how many hours each day you're going to study.
- Plan your relaxation – the right balance between work and relaxation.
- Decide when you work best – plot work that calls for the highest levels of concentration.
- Plot each of the five stages of essay writing.
- Make sure you have enough variety between the subjects and activities in each day – but don't fragment your work too much.
- Give yourself time between each session to process the ideas so you can use them convincingly.
- Divide each session into manageable periods of, say, two hours, with breaks in between.
- Be specific – about the time for study each day/week, the length of each session, the time a task should take, the subject and activity of each session, and relaxation.

Assignment 6
Plan your personal timetable

In this assignment take a copy of the personal timetable, or two or three copies, if you're working on a two- or three-week cycle. Work your way carefully through each of the four stages above, taking particular care to be as specific as you can about times and activities. When you've completed this, check it against the eight-point checklist above.

Then work with it, say for a month or two. You will find that some things won't work immediately, because you're having to adjust to working this way. Other things you will have to fine tune, because some jobs may be done better on other days or at different times. But don't make too many changes too soon. You will have to give it enough time for you to see a pattern emerging before you can think about the adjustments you might need to make.

Remember, in the long run the only reliable indicators of whether this is working are:

- whether you're getting your work done on time;
- whether you're getting better grades;
- whether you are able to use more of your own ideas and your abilities;
- and whether you're less stressed about your work.

▶ The next stage

Re-organising your pattern of study in the ways I've suggested in this stage can noticeably improve your work within a short time. The most immediate impact will be on your ability to process ideas actively and to access your own ideas, rather than simply reproducing those you find in your sources. Moreover, with a more sophisticated retrieval system you will find you have at your fingertips a wealth of interesting material for your essays. This, and a well-organised timetable, will give you more opportunity to develop those abilities that your syllabuses set out to assess.

As we've seen, a key element in this has been our organisation. And this is no less true of the next stage of essay writing: planning. Examiners regularly report that students lose marks not because they don't understand the subject, nor because they lack the ability, but because their poor organisation has resulted in essays that are irrelevant and confusing. And, like the organisation of our retrieval system and our time, the results of well organised planning can be almost immediate. Students accustomed to getting just average marks for their essays find themselves regularly getting marks that are two or three grades higher.

Stage 3
Planning

INTRODUCTION

As a result of what we did in the last stage, you should now have a wealth of material to work with. Moreover, you should feel more confident not just that you understand it well, but that you've successfully integrated it with your own ideas and made it your own. You've processed it thoroughly at all levels: for comprehension; for analysis and structure; and for criticism and evaluation. This should have left you with clearly structured notes taken from what you've read, which also record your own responses to the ideas in the form of criticism and evaluation.

What's more, you've now organised your retrieval system and your time to ensure that you catch the best material, including your own ideas, wherever and whenever it presents itself. You are, then, in a much better position to meet the demands of an essay that asks you to use the higher cognitive skills: to criticise, discuss and evaluate a claim or an argument. Given this, you can now move on to plan your essay; a stage that many regard as the most important, yet the most neglected. In this stage we will look not just at planning the essay, but at how this can improve your memory, your revision for the exam, and your exam technique.

▶ Planning the essay

Without a plan you will always struggle to produce your best work. The plan gives your essay a clear structure for examiners to follow as they navigate their way through ideas and arguments that are unfamiliar to them. Without this you're likely to lose them, and if they can't see why your arguments are relevant, or they can't see what you're doing and why, they cannot give you marks, no matter how good your work might be. Even your weakest arguments gain strength from planning. A carefully planned structure, which is clear, logical and relevant to the question, lends support to an argument that, on its own, might not be completely convincing.

In this stage we will look at the benefits of rehearsing your arguments in detail before you write, by planning an essay we interpreted and brainstormed in the first stage. In this way we are able to make sure that all of our arguments are relevant, that they are clearly and consistently argued, and that we have sufficient evidence to support them. It also reduces the risk of omitting some really important section or argument that is central to the issues raised by the essay.

What's more, by rehearsing your arguments in detail you will avoid the problem of trying to do the two most difficult things in writing, at the same time: pinning down your ideas clearly, and then summoning up the words and phrases that will convey them accurately.

To do this effectively we have to work through two stages: editing, and ordering the ideas. We will see that if the essay is to succeed we have to learn to be ruthless in cutting out irrelevant material that we may have worked hard to collect. Otherwise we will pass on problems to later stages and, if they're not dealt with there, they will seriously weaken the clarity and logical structure of our essay. They will cloud the structure with unnecessary distractions that weaken our arguments, and break up the logical sequence we've worked hard to create. The same applies to ordering our ideas, if we are to create logical coherence and give our essay more persuasive force.

▶ Planning for the examination

However, the value of planning stretches beyond this. The plans we produce for our essays provide the core of our revision material, making it much easier for us to recall the arguments and evidence we need to use in the exam. We will look at the ways in which we can improve our exam technique and our revision by planning the typical questions that are set on the topics on the syllabus; and we will look at how the memory works and what we can do to improve it.

19 Planning that Makes a Difference

In this chapter you will learn:

- how you can avoid losing the reader by planning carefully;
- how to strengthen your weakest arguments through planning;
- how to rehearse your arguments in detail before you write.

After completing the first two stages (interpretation and research), the plan of the essay should now be taking shape within your mind. In many cases it may not be very different from the original pattern notes you generated in the brainstorming session prior to the research.

▶ The importance of planning

Nevertheless, careful thoughtful planning, in which you rehearse your arguments in as much detail as you can muster, is vital. It will not only improve the structure of your essay, making it more coherent and logical, but it will make the business of writing a lot easier. Indeed, it is always possible to tell the difference between an essay that has been planned and one that hasn't.

Avoid losing your reader

Reading somebody else's work is like entering an unfamiliar city: you can get lost easily, you're dependent upon others to give you directions, and even worse, you really don't know why you're there in the first place, unless somebody else tells you. The plan of the essay, therefore, represents the city map, and the introduction and the 'topic sentence' at the beginning of each paragraph (Stage 4) are the writer's attempt to let readers know where they are being taken, which turnings they will be taking along the way, and why.

Without the plan and its clear development in the body of the essay, you will most certainly lose the examiners reading your work, and if they are lost they cannot give you marks, no matter how well argued your point is, or how skilfully it is supported by evidence. If they cannot see why a passage is relevant, they must ignore it. They are not expected to make great efforts on your behalf to try to make sense of your work, to fill in the gaps that you've left. They must accept it on face value, otherwise they could find themselves spending more time on your essay – making more allowances for what they thought you meant to say – than on the work of other students.

Examiners regularly report that students fail examinations, or just do badly, not because they don't know the subject, not because they haven't got the abilities, nor even because they lack the knowledge, but because they lose the reader, who is unable to discover why their work is relevant to the question. Almost always this comes down to the lack of planning.

The comments of one professor at Harvard are not untypical:

> One common problem is the meandering paper, one that wanders from one thinker to another, from summaries of concepts to counterarguments to restatements of the paper topic, without a clear plan or logical progression.[1]

Planning strengthens weaker points

In fact the benefits of this go even further. By providing your readers with a sequence of obvious logical steps, so they can follow your train of thought, you give yourself an invaluable safety net. In many cases a weak or poorly defined point will gain strength and precision from being a step in a clear logical argument.

We all experience this when we come across an unfamiliar word: in most cases we can deduce its meaning from the context in which it's used. Examiners are no different. When they read your essay and come across a set of phrases or explanations that seem unclear, if they are part of a set of arguments and points thoughtfully planned in a logical sequence, your meaning will probably be all too obvious. Your arguments will gain strength and clarity from the clear, well planned context in which they are developed.

Rehearsing the detail before you write

But it's not just a clear logical sequence that's created in planning: we're also able to sort out the main ideas and the important details we need in order to explain, illustrate and develop them. Doing so reduces the risk of omitting an important section or argument that is central to the issues raised by the essay.

Even so, it would be unwise to be so rigid that you cannot move away from your plan. Some new idea or relationship may occur to you and you might need to re-organise your material to include it. But be careful that this is really useful material for your argument, and not just irrelevant padding. Ultimately, the test of good planning comes when you rehearse your arguments in detailed note form before you write. At this point you make sure you've predicted what you need and you've rehearsed how you're going to use it, so there should be no last-minute changes.

Nevertheless, beyond the need to get high marks for your essay, planning has a still more important role to play: it's indispensable if you're to understand the subject. This is the opportunity to rehearse your arguments in note form so you can see how well you've understood the ideas.

It always surprises me to find how many students still choose not to plan, and therefore force themselves to do the two most difficult things in writing, both at the same time: that is, to summon up the ideas and plan the order in which they ought to be developed, and at the same time to search for the right words to convey them with just the right strength and nuance, in order to develop the argument in the direction they've chosen. This is a task that is virtually impossible for all but the most familiar subjects that we've written about many times before.

▶ Rehearsing your arguments in linear form

Rehearsing our ideas in the plan calls for different skills and techniques from those used in the brainstorming stage. As a result, some students feel more comfortable rehearsing their ideas in linear form, rather than the pattern-note form they used in the interpretation stage. Even so, in all the seminars I've run, in general, students appear to be equally divided between linear and pattern notes for the planning stage.

Nevertheless, there are clear differences between the two stages. Rehearsing ideas is a deliberate step-by-step process, unlike the imaginative flow of ideas in brainstorming, so if you feel more comfortable converting your pattern notes into the linear form prior to writing, this might make sense. But remember the importance of flexibility. Some assignments lend themselves more easily to pattern notes throughout, while others call for a combination of the two.

In the examination under timed conditions, when you want to capture the ideas quickly as they come tumbling out, pattern notes are clearly the most useful. But outside of that, when you're writing an essay on a subject for the first time and you're not pressed for time, you'll find the step-by-step patient rehearsal of your arguments in linear form gives you more control.

Practice exercise 11
Rehearsing your arguments in linear form

Question

'Advertisers seek only to ensure that consumers make informed choices.' *Discuss.*

In the interpretation stage you brainstormed this question in pattern-note form. With those notes in front of you convert them into linear notes, rehearsing your arguments in the sort of detail you would need if you were to write the essay.

Then compare your notes with those below. Your notes may not be quite so detailed, but it will give you a clear idea of the level of detail you need to aim for in order to answer most of the problems you're likely to face when you come to write.

Answer: linear plan – rehearsing the arguments

'Advertisers seek only to ensure that consumers make informed choices.' *Discuss.*

A Advertisement

  1. Just informative:

        e.g.   railway timetable

        (a)   no catchy jingles – 'Let the train take the strain'

    (b)   no persuasive messages – 'Children travel free'
    (c)   just information:
        (i)   routes
        (ii)   times – departures and arrivals
        (iii)   platform numbers

But intention = crucial characteristic:

        (i)   to demonstrate it's more convenient, efficient, and less stressful to travel by train
        (ii)   e.g. fête notice – nothing but information – but intention = to encourage people to attend, in order to raise funds for local causes

    2.   therefore, information = surface appearance

       •   what matters = intention – to suggest/persuade us to adopt certain course of action

B   Informative

  •   all but a few = informative

    1.   Some only concerned with giving information:

        e.g.   public information – changes in regulations & rates of taxation
              government warnings – smoking, use of domestic fire alarms

    2.   Others give information while covertly promoting their products:

       •   information about:

    (a)   New products & technology:
        (i)   computer tech. & software
        (ii)   telecommunications, e.g. mobile phones
        (iii)   entertainment/hobbies:

- digital tech. – TVs, cameras
- music systems
- video recorders

But rarely just information:
suggestion = we can't afford not to keep up with progress

    (b) New designs:
         e.g. fashions/clothes
              household equipment – washing machines, dishwashers, microwaves

Suggestion = we can't afford to allow o/selves to fall behind our friends & neighbours – comparisons/envy/ conspicuous consumption – you are what you own

C But not the 'only' thing they do:

- overt manipulation

1. Selective use of information:

- says what's good about the product, but omits the bad

    e.g. car accelerates 0–60 in 6 secs – but omits to tell you that it has a record of rusting in 5 years
    e.g. the latest printer that can do more than any other printer on the market – but omits to tell you that the print cartridge costs 5 times as much as any other printer

2. Uses information out of context:

- uses only those comments that appear to be in favour of the product in a report that is critical of it

    e.g. a critical report by a consumer association
    e.g. unfavourable comments of an art, literary or theatre critic ignored by promoters who comb through the article for isolated expressions of approval

3. Association:

    *   associates information about the product with strong feelings and desires

    (a) Sex – associates product with sexual desires
         e.g. cars – clothes – perfume – alcohol
    (b) Status – respect for authority
         e.g. prestige of science – laboratory coats worn by those promoting washing powders, vacuum cleaners, dishwashers, detergents
    (c) Popular/respected public figures
         e.g. sports-men & -women/TV personalities selling mobile phones, health drinks, clothes, deodorants, shampoos
    (d) Prejudices:
         (i)   sexual stereotypes
         (ii)   class – accents
         (iii) weight/size
         (iv)   race
    (e) Subliminal manipulation through association:
         (i)   to reduce shoplifting – messages like 'I will not steal,' 'I will be honest.'
                1970s experiment = 30% reduction in shoplifting
         (ii)   Dangers:
                a) political & social manipulation
                    re. Aldous Huxley, *Brave New World Revisited*
                b) promoting commercial interests
                    subconscious manipulation to buy unwanted products

4. Distorts:

    (a) archetypal characters & scenarios created to evoke predictable responses:
         (i)   that we all want to be slim – that large people are associated with social failure & self-indulgence
         (ii)   that we all believe that to find the dishes aren't clean when they come out of the dishwasher is a major life crisis
         (iii) that we all believe if our neighbour were to discover that our kitchen floor was not spotless this would

be a disgrace we would have to carry through the
rest of our lives

   (iv)   induces us to feel bad about ourselves – discontent
fuels consumerism

  (b) appeals made to some imagined social consensus – to
'basic' or 'shared' values:

   (i)   that we all want the fastest car on the road

   (ii) that we all want to keep up with the neighbours

  (iii) that we all worry endlessly about being seen out in
last year's fashions

  (c) myths created and sustained by the media to sell products

     e.g. that housewives are paranoid about the whiteness
of their wash and the cleanliness of their floors

▶ In the next chapter

Now that you've done this you will be aware not only of the
importance of working on your ideas in this sort of detail, but of the
problems it presents in first editing your ideas and then ordering them.
In the next chapter we will tackle these two problems in more detail.

Note

1 Michael Sandel, *Writing in Moral Reasoning, 22: Justice* (Cambridge, Mass.:
University of Harvard, 2000).

20 Editing and Ordering your Material

In this chapter you will learn:

- how to edit your material to create a structure in your essay that is clear and logical;
- how to order your ideas to develop arguments that are consistent and persuasive;
- how to make sure the examiners are left with the right impression of your work.

Planning your essays in this way involves routinely working through two quite distinct stages: editing, and ordering your material. Neither of them can be rushed: you must work through them carefully and deliberately.

Both call for what you might describe as the personality profile of a military planner: inexhaustible supplies of quiet patience matched by cool ruthlessness. There will be ideas, arguments and evidence with which you have developed a strong emotional bond, but you may have to cut them out and abandon them without a tear, if the essay is to succeed. However painful it is to realise that some of the material you've worked hard to collect is irrelevant to this essay, you cannot shirk the responsibility. If you do, you will pass on problems to later stages and, if they're not dealt with there, they will seriously weaken the clarity and logical structure of your essay.

▶ Editing

Unless you've spent enough time interpreting the question, editing the material you've collected can be a tortuous nightmare. We are all quite naturally reluctant to give up material that we've struggled hard to uncover and record, especially if it includes particularly interesting points that we know will impress our reader. It's not surprising, then, that without a clear criterion by which you can decide what's relevant and what's not, you will find it difficult, if not impossible, to resist using material that's not relevant.

This will have the effect of clouding the structure of your essay with unnecessary distractions that weaken your arguments, and break up the logical sequence you've worked hard to create. On the other hand, however, with a clear interpretation of the implications of the question, it is so much easier to be uncompromisingly ruthless with your material.

▶ Ordering

Although you don't have the same heart-wrenching problems of ditching material you've become attached to, you still need an iron will in ordering your ideas, if you're to avoid the same problem of being dictated to by your sources. It can simply be very difficult to abandon the order in which we recorded the notes in the first place.

Some people find that keeping their notes on index cards helps in sorting out and selecting their material: they can change the order of the cards, and their ideas, much more easily than if they are recorded on continuous sheets of paper in the order the notes were taken from the texts. Others use just one side of the paper and then cut the papers up and organise them. Both methods give you more control over your material. They free you from the sense of being dictated to by your sources.

In general it makes sense to arrange your ideas in ascending order: from the simplest to the most complex. Logically this makes sense, particularly if the clarity of your most complex arguments depends upon how convincingly you've used your simpler, more obvious arguments to build a basis for them. But it also makes psychological sense in that in dealing with the most subtle and impressive arguments at the end of the essay you leave your examiners with the impression that the whole of your essay was of that quality. Hopefully, you will have left them with a well developed, interesting argument to think over as they consider what mark to award you.

Practice exercise 12
Editing and ordering your material

Question

Are there any circumstances where the individual is justified in refusing to obey a law?

Interpret the question above as you did in the first stage: write a statement outlining as fully as you can the meaning and implications of the question. For this exercise you don't need to brainstorm the question as you are given, below, a set of notes to edit and then order into a plan for the essay; but your interpretation should give you a clear idea of what you expect to see as relevant to the question.

Once you've done this, go through the notes below, deciding what you think is relevant and what needs to be cut. Then, order what's left into a plan in linear-note form, indicating how you would tackle this essay.

After you've completed it, compare your plan with the one given below.

The notes

1   Outline the main types of law – common law – judicial precedent – statute law – conventions

2   Refusal justified when:

   (a) Government has no popular legitimacy – lacks majority support – authoritarian governments
        e.g.   South Africa/apartheid
   (b) Government is legitimate, but the majority tyrannises a minority
        e.g.   Germany – Nazi Government – 1935 Nuremberg Laws
        e.g.   USA – 1960s Civil Rights – segregation – M. L. King
   (c) Government extends its powers too far – restricting the liberties of the individual unnecessarily.

(d) There is a conflict between the legal and moral obligations of the individual. Question: Which takes precedence?

  e.g. moral obligation to help a friend by not turning him over to the police, who believe he has committed an offence

3 Give the reasons why Mahatma Gandhi deliberately broke the law in non-violent direct action to bring about the peaceful withdrawal of British power from India.

4 Problem = when government is legitimate and the law conflicts with individual conscience and principles, such as pacifism

  e.g. Quakers refusing to pay that proportion of their taxes that is spent on nuclear weapons

5 Danger = social breakdown – it allows individuals to pick and choose the laws they will obey and those they won't.

6 Describe the campaign of civil disobedience launched by the suffragettes in 1906 to get the vote for women.

7 Note the arguments put forward by A. V. Dicey for the importance of the Rule of Law in ensuring regular, non-arbitrary government.

8 The government should only restrict the freedom of individuals when their actions are likely to cause harm to others (John Stuart Mill):

(a) If you shout offensive racial remarks at people in public the government should intervene to restrict your doing this.

(b) You have freedom of speech but the government should restrict this freedom if you publish pornographic material that can be shown to cause people harm, e.g. rape, child abuse, etc.

(c) The government should intervene to prevent employers sacking staff for no reason at all without any hearing or compensation.

(d) The government is justified in restricting your freedom when your actions cause physical harm to others, e.g. passive smoking.

9   But should the government be free to intervene and restrict your freedom when your actions cause harm to yourself only, e.g. smoking, wearing crash helmets?

10 Give an account of the ideas of those who have made important contributions to the debate:
    Socrates
    Henry Thoreau
    Peter Kropotkin
    Martin Luther King
    John Rawls

The plan

Question

Are there any circumstances where the individual is justified in refusing to obey a law?

1   Problem: Government encroachment on our freedoms v. the danger of social breakdown if individuals are allowed to pick and choose the laws they will obey and those they won't

2   Government with no popular legitimacy – lacks majority support:
    Refusing to obey the law = justified
    • authoritarian governments, e.g. South Africa/apartheid

3   Government is legitimate:

    (a) But the majority tyrannises a minority:
         Refusing to obey the law = justified
         e.g. Germany – Nazi Government – 1935 Nuremberg Laws
         e.g. USA – 1960s Civil Rights – segregation – M. L. King.

    (b) Problem = when government is legitimate and the law conflicts with individual conscience and principles
         e.g. Quakers refusing to pay that proportion of their taxes that is spent on nuclear weapons, because of pacifist principles

4 Conscience/principles: Problem = Government extends its powers too far – restricting the liberties of the individual unnecessarily.

  (a) Extent of power 'harm' – Governments should only restrict the freedom of individuals when their actions are likely to cause harm to others (John Stuart Mill):
    (i) But should governments be free to intervene and restrict your freedom when your actions cause harm to yourself only, e.g. smoking, wearing crash helmets?
    (ii) Governments are justified in restricting your freedom when your actions cause physical harm to others, e.g. passive smoking.
    (iii) Justified if you cause psychological harm?
        e.g. If you shout offensive racial remarks at people in public?
    (iv) Moral harm? You have freedom of speech but the government is justified in restricting this if you publish pornographic material that can be shown to cause people harm, e.g. rape, child abuse.
    (v) Economic harm? The government is justified in restricting the freedom of employers to sack staff for no reason without any hearing or compensation.

  (b) Precedence – Question: Where there is a conflict between the legal and moral obligations of the individual, which takes precedence?
        e.g. moral obligation to help a friend by not turning him over to the police, who believe he has committed an offence

Editing

Of course, as you haven't made these notes yourself, you can only take them on face value: you cannot go beyond what's given, in the belief that if you search you may find something that's relevant. In fact, not being able to do this makes it easier for you to decide what's relevant and what's not.

We can all appreciate how difficult it might be for someone who has done the research, to dump material like that contained in items 3, 6 and 10. If you have slowly worked your way through passages that are very closely argued, taking out a lot of material that you thought might be useful, it will be hard to ditch it. It's not that it's irrelevant, but it has to be used with more discrimination than is proposed here, which appears to be a straightforward description of the material. Far better would be to select from the material, quotations and evidence that would support the arguments you want to make elsewhere in the essay.

In fact the same can be said for items 1 and 7, both of which again appear to be descriptions for the sake of description. It might be useful to know the different types of law and Dicey's arguments for the importance of regular, rather than arbitrary law, but you will have to make this case out: you will have to justify why you think this is relevant. For example, there may be different implications for the question depending on the type of law involved, although on the face of it this appears unlikely.

Ordering

Having edited the material, you are now left to order your ideas from the simple to the complex and, as in this case, from the peripheral issues to those that are central. It seems that the best strategy is to work from those situations in which there appears least doubt and very limited discussion as to whether disobedience is justified, to those cases where there is real doubt. In this way you will ensure that your essay delivers you at the point that gives you the opportunity to discuss all the important issues.

The obvious starting point, then, is with those governments who pass unjust laws or laws that lack the legitimacy of popular support. Few of us would not see some justification in the actions of those, like Steve Biko and Nelson Mandela, who refused to comply with laws passed as part of the apartheid policies of the South African government, which was supported by only a minority white population.

The more difficult case is that of a democratically legitimate government such as that in Germany during the Third Reich, which passed policies aimed at the minority Jewish population, denying them rights as citizens to practise their profession and to marry non-Jewish persons. Yet, again, few of us would have much difficulty in commending those who bravely refused to comply with the law, and rescued Jews who otherwise would have been sent to extermination camps.

So, perhaps the most difficult case that raises the issues we all have to consider is that of a legitimate government that is not tyrannising a minority, yet is passing laws that conflict with what we consider to be our moral obligations. In short, what should we do when our moral obligations conflict with our legal obligations?

This, in turn, appears to raise two distinct issues. The first can be described as the extent of government – the claim that a government can only rightfully restrict the freedoms of individuals when their actions do harm to others. Of course, this part of your discussion will turn on the various interpretations of the concept of 'harm': physical, psychological, moral, economic, etc. The second problem is that of precedence: when there is a conflict, which should take precedence, our moral or our legal obligations?

Assignment 7
Editing, ordering and rehearsing your arguments

First, edit your material, cutting out any ideas you think are irrelevant to the question. Be ruthless. Even though you may like some of the arguments, because you know they will impress the reader, or because they have the sort of impact you want, cut them out if they are not strictly relevant to the issues raised by the question.

Then, order your ideas, paying particular attention to ascendancy and fluency. Start with the weakest or the simplest argument, and move to the strongest. Try to envisage how you will move from one idea to the next. Think about the types of transition you will use to create fluency between paragraphs.

Once you've got the overall structure clear, move to the content of the essay. Your aim is to see clearly how you will develop your arguments: how you will analyse points and concepts, make contrasts and comparisons, synthesise ideas from different sources, extend arguments consistently, and illustrate and support your points with evidence. So, as you go through the plan try to get an accurate measure of each argument, the links between them, and the logical flow of the whole essay. You're trying to put yourself in the position of writing the essay without actually writing it. In this way you will confront all the problems now before you write – there will be no nasty surprises.

Finally, when you've finished, check that you've left nothing out: that you've answered the question relevantly and completely; that you haven't overlooked a major section or issue raised by the question; and that you haven't left important points vulnerable without sufficient evidence.

Now that you've completed two practice exercises, on editing and ordering your material, and on rehearsing your ideas in detail, it's time to do the same with the question you originally chose from one of your courses. You've interpreted this question and completed the research on it. In the following assignment, you are creating the plan from which you will write the essay.

▶ In the next chapter

In this assignment we've gone as close as we can to writing the essay without actually doing so. There are very few essays that don't benefit from this. If we fail to do it, there will always be unforeseen problems that slow down our writing and break up the flow of our words. Even more important, as we will see in the next two chapters, having rehearsed our arguments we will be left, for each question, with plans that will be invaluable in the exam, when we have to reproduce the arguments under timed conditions.

21 Planning for the Exam

In this chapter you will learn:

- about the importance of planning in the exam;
- how to prepare for the examination;
- how to structure your ideas to improve your memory;
- how mnemonics can help your recall.

▶ The importance of planning in the exam

If planning is vital for the writing of an essay you complete in your own time, it is even more important for your performance under timed conditions.

Some students claim they simply haven't got sufficient time in the exam to plan for five to ten minutes for each essay. Yet if you observe their behaviour during the exam it becomes clear they still have to plan, but in the least effective way. They will head straight into the essay without much deliberation, then they will stop at the end of the first paragraph to think about what they will do in the next paragraph. One to two minutes might pass before they head off again into their work, only to stop again for more thought to decide what they will do next. This happens, say, seven or eight times for each essay, amounting to twelve to fifteen minutes of planning on the run.

As a result they have, in fact, planned the essay, probably spending more time than they would have done if they had planned at the start. And, of course, they've planned in the worst possible way. Without much doubt, ideas will have come to them out of sequence, making little logical sense to the examiner. In turn this will have dissipated any fluency they might have created. In contrast, if they had planned at the start this would have left them free to write continuously and fluently, without interruption, until they had completed the question.

It's not difficult to see, therefore, that planning in the exam is vital to produce a well written and fluently argued piece of work. Only by preparing a plan can you maintain control over your material and present your ideas in a logical, concise and coherent manner, with support from well chosen, relevant evidence.

▶ Improving your memory for the exam

The advantages don't stop there. Not only does planning improve the quality of your writing and your discussion in the exam, but in terms of simple recall a plan is vital. As you probably know from your own experience, the mind only works in structures. Think how difficult it is to remember isolated items, like those things you've got to do throughout the day, or a quotation, or a few lines from a play. Presented with this sort of task, the mind attempts to create a structure, either out of the thing itself, like a telephone number you remember because you can see a descending or ascending structure within it, or by relating it to other structured information you already have.

Remembering telephone numbers

Descending	444332
	99877
Ascending	22344
	6788
Groups	553377
	881144
Bookends	683368
	532453
Arithmetic progressions:	
Even numbers	02468
Odd numbers	13579
Geometric progressions	24816
Mirror images	341143
Repeats	651651
	934934

Significant dates	1945
	1066
	1666
	1789
Sandwiches	650465
	91891

This explains why it is that those with the most active minds, those people who are genuinely interested in a subject, can remember a surprising amount of detail, over a wide range of topics. We all know friends who don't seem particularly bright in class, but who, if you get them on a subject they find really interesting, like baseball, cricket or football, can recall a staggering amount of detail: batting averages of players, how many times a particular team has won a particular trophy, who scored most goals or made the most runs in a season, and so on.

They can even analyse the most complex abstract concept, like a googly or a flipper in cricket – concepts that are as difficult to picture in your mind's eye and then analyse, as any scientific or academic concept, like a black hole or the conditions likely to bring about an economic recession. For example, *Chambers Dictionary* describes the googly as '. . . an off-breaking ball with an apparent leg-break action on the part of a right-arm bowler to a right-handed batsman, or conversely for a left-arm bowler'.

▶ Needs are the secret to learning and remembering

The point is that we only learn when we have a need to. It's easy to see, then, that those people who appear to know and remember a great deal are just good at creating needs. Our friend who might not do well in his college work, can show all the intellectual skills when it comes to cricket or baseball, because he's interested in these subjects and, therefore, he's better at creating needs in them. Once we've created these we become active, not passive, processors of ideas and information, and we begin to create structures out of what we know. Our minds then take over and begin to self-organise, generating more structures, which attach to those we first created. And before we know it we can recall a vast amount of material, that we never thought possible.

Just watch your friends' or your parents' faces when, in the middle of a discussion, you reproduce a structure of ideas you've created. Not only will you show that you can analyse the most difficult argument or concept, but you will demonstrate that you can remember a range of material from different sources, all of it relevant to a thoughtful, well constructed argument. And it will happen, almost without you realising, as a result of knowing just two things: how to create structures, and the need to create them.

To illustrate the point, take the following simple task.

Practice exercise   13
Remembering through structures

Here is a list of ten items you've got to purchase at the local supermarket. Look at them for about thirty seconds, committing them to memory. Then cover them and try to recall them.

carrots
yoghurt
tomatoes
beans
wine
butter
milk
gin
cheese
potatoes

Most students are able to recall six to eight items, but only those used to the most active form of processing get all ten. What most of these do is to process the list into a structure, something like the following:

1   Vegetables:
    (a)   carrots
    (b)   tomatoes
    (c)   beans
    (d)   potatoes

2 Dairy products:
    (a) yoghurt
    (b) butter
    (c) milk
    (d) cheese

3 Drinks:
    (a) wine
    (b) gin

With this, the mind has a much simpler job: instead of having to remember ten items it only has to remember three, knowing that once these have been recalled the rest will come without a problem. In fact this is no different from what you would have done normally if you were, indeed, shopping for these items. It would make obvious sense to group the items in this way so you could reduce the number of times you had to move between sections of the supermarket. You would know there were four things you needed to buy at the vegetable section, before you moved on to the next, and so on.

▶ Using mnemonics

The only alternative to this is to resort to some form of mnemonics, a deliberately created device to help you remember. Most of these consist of phrases created from the first letter of each word you want to remember. Some children are taught to remember the seven colours of the rainbow by learning the meaningless phrase: 'Richard of York gained battles in vain' – red, orange, yellow, green, blue, indigo and violet. But the better mnemonics are built on a rhyming or rhythmical phrase, particularly if this is well-known: a hymn, a popular song, an advertising jingle, or a well-known poem.

Nevertheless, this is just another way of structuring what you know – only, rather than create your own structure you borrow one. The least effective are those that create meaningless sentences, and therefore have no purchase on your own experience. If you've never studied English medieval history, a phrase concerning Richard of York fighting battles might be difficult for you to remember. In these cases you're forced to commit them to memory by repeating them to yourself over and over again. This is not only tedious, to say the least, but it also ignores the way the mind works naturally and effectively.

Memory is 'integrative': we remember things best if we can fit them into what we already know. We remember wholes, rather than isolated parts, so, if we're going to remember something, it must make sense in terms of what we already know. It must fit within the structures we've already created for ourselves, or within those that have already been created for us, as in advertising jingles or traditional songs. Although this may seem, at times, trivial and contrived, there's no doubt that there are occasions, when we're presented with an unstructured list that cannot be broken down into its own categories. In these circumstances a mnemonic may be the only answer.

But no matter what way you choose to help your memory, just remember: what we store in our mind is not isolated facts, but complex clusters of information and ideas, centred on some familiar keyword or concept. We may create these ourselves, or we may be forced to find them in a familiar jingle. But when we hear, read or recall them they trigger off the whole cluster. This explains why the structured note-taking techniques like pattern and linear notes are so effective. But if you can't generate your own structure, be prepared to use the rhyming jingle or a familiar line from a poem. They will certainly work better than a mere list or an unstructured summary.

▶ In the next chapter

Planning in this way makes our revision and the exams themselves so much simpler. In the next chapter we will look at what you can do to make sure that you're able to reproduce the same quality of essay within the exam as you can outside.

22 Revising for the Exam

In this chapter you will learn:

- how to use plans as your core revision material;
- how to take much of the stress out of revision and exams;
- how to plan in the exam.

▶ Planning the typical exam questions

Given what we said in the last chapter, that the mind only works in structures, it makes sense to prepare for the examination by planning all the typical questions that are set on each of the topics on the syllabus. Once you've done this, when revision comes around, all you need to do is commit them to memory, and test yourself to see if you can recall them within ten minutes under timed conditions as you will have to do in the exam.

The most well-organised tutors will give their students a course outline of all the topics on the course and then get them to list under each topic all the questions that have been set on each one. This will mean going back a number of years over past papers. In fact, it's more than likely that those tutors who teach a course year in, year out will have already done this for students. Each year all they will need to do is to bring the list up to date with the most recent questions.

When you analyse these lists into distinct types of question you will find that for each topic there are usually four or five typical questions that regularly appear. It's these that you need to plan. Your tutors will have their own plans for these and they will no doubt give you a copy when you've done yours, so that you can compare them and make adjustments if you need to.

▶ The plans become your core revision material

Once this is done you will find these plans represent the core material for your revision. In my revision classes we timetable well in advance the topics we will be revising on any given day in the run-up to the exam, so that everybody comes prepared with their revision done and their plans stored in their memories. Then we produce our lists of typical questions for that topic, from which I select a question and give the students ten minutes to produce a plan, in the same way they will have to in the exam. We all then take a blank sheet of paper and try to produce our pattern or linear note structures, whichever we've chosen as the right format for that question. Having completed that, we compare our results. Then we go through all the remaining typical questions on our lists in the same way.

As a result, revision takes on a far less daunting, less foreboding presence. In effect the students know that if there are, say, six topics that they know will come up on the paper, and there are four typical questions on each topic, then they have just 24 essay plans to commit to memory and recall under timed conditions. Most of them cope with this without any problem. Certainly it is much more manageable than the heaps of unstructured notes they might face otherwise.

To make revision even easier, throughout the year we have regular sessions of this. As we complete each topic on our syllabus, time will be set aside so that students can do timed essays and timed plans. As a result, by the end of the course they will have written or planned every typical essay question, under timed conditions. Most students will know them well, and have very little trouble recalling and writing them in the exam.

Even if you don't get in the exam exactly the question you've revised, your structured plans will enable you to recall all the material you need to answer the question. It may be that you get a hybrid question that calls upon you to select from more than one structure and then combine the relevant parts into a new plan. It's probably true to say that at least 80 per cent of success in any exam is due to organisation, and the major component of this is the structured plans you create throughout the course, and then commit to memory, so you can recall them in the exam.

Practice exercise   14
Typical questions

Take just one topic on your syllabus, preferably one that you've already covered, with which you're fairly familiar.

You've already collected some past papers. Usually, around ten is sufficient to identify the major issues and approaches to the topic, that form the basis for questions.

List all the questions that have appeared on the topic you've chosen, recording the date on which they appeared. You should now be able to see recurring types. Some may appear every year, others once every two years. But it should be clear that there are only a limited number of types of questions, say four or five.

If you find that you have many more than this, it may be because you don't realise that a question differently phrased is in fact the same as another. This is often the case. Sometimes it's not until you try to plan it that you realise it's taking the same pattern as another. Therefore, if in doubt, try planning those you're not sure of.

▶ **Planning in the exam**

Once you're in the exam the same principles apply: spend the first five to ten minutes writing down your plan. Don't get panicked into writing too soon, before you have exhausted all of your ideas and got them organised into a coherent, well structured plan, that answers the question with strict relevance.

Indeed, there are strong reasons for going even further than this. It makes very good sense to plan all the questions you have to do, before you pick up your pen to write the first one. Each time you plan an essay you set your subconscious mind tasks to undertake and questions to answer. Except in the strongest of questions, which you know exactly how you're going to answer, there are always arguments, points, evidence and examples that you can't remember exactly.

This is understandable: you're trying to brainstorm, to get the ideas down as quickly as possible as they come tumbling out. Therefore, unless it's a central issue that will shape the whole essay, you don't want to stop the flow just to make sure you've got every detail on one particular issue exactly right; you can always come back to that after the flow of ideas has stopped. But at that point you may find you can't recall all the details you wanted to use. Nevertheless, by identifying the problem in the planning stage you will have alerted your subconscious and, while you're writing another question, it will be busy unearthing what you need.

Let's say you're taking a three-hour exam in which you have to answer four essay questions, and you plan all four questions before you begin to write the first one. This will mean you will spend the first forty minutes of the exam planning. Then, if you write your strongest question first and your weakest last, it will mean that your mind will have 2 hours 25 minutes to riffle through your data banks and come up with those ideas, arguments and evidence that you weren't able to remember when you planned the weakest of your questions. Even with your strongest question your mind has 30 minutes, while you're planning the other questions, to find the few items that you couldn't recall.

The common-sense of this approach is clear to most of us who have ever taken exams. We've probably all had the experience of coming out of the examination centre with a friend, comparing what each of us did. As we go over it, all sorts of things suddenly spring into our minds, that we should have included but didn't. In this situation what's happening is that either we haven't planned at all, or we've planned each question just moments before we've written it. As a result, the mind has been set tasks to accomplish and questions to answer, but it has needed time for this, more than we have given it in the exam.

The sad irony is that over the next hour or so, as the mind comes up with what we asked it for, we'll recall a rich assortment of ideas, arguments and evidence, and we'll curse our luck for not being able to use it in the exam. But luck, in fact, had only a minor part to play in this familiar drama; the major part was played by organisation, or the lack of it.

One final point to remember about planning under timed conditions is that, in most systems, examiners will give you credit for a plan, if the essay is unfinished. In most examinations you cannot lose marks for a plan, however scrappy and indecipherable it may be. You can only gain marks. Therefore, if you run out of time half way through a question, a clearly structured plan of what you would have done will earn good marks.

Assignment 8
Revising and recalling plans

Now that you've planned your essay, the best test of whether it works, in so far as it's relevant, clearly structured and answers the question completely, is to try to recall it under timed conditions, as you will have to in the exam.

Spend fifteen minutes committing your plan to memory. Concentrate on the main structure. If you can recall the key points that make up this structure, you will be able to recall the detail within it, if your arguments are organised in a clear, logical manner, and they're relevant to the question.

After you've done this, put it aside for a day or so, but decide beforehand at what time you will come back to test yourself. Then, when you come back, take out a blank sheet of paper and give yourself ten minutes to reproduce the plan.

If the plan works, you will be able to recall, maybe not all of it, but at least the main structure. If you can't recall much at all, it may be due to technical reasons: the keywords that trigger off your arguments aren't crisp and sufficiently memorable, or perhaps the structure is buried beneath too much detail. Make the necessary changes and try again.

You will know when you've got it right: you will be able to recall with complete accuracy all of the structure and most of the detail. Having done this once successfully, you will know what will work in future.

▶ **The next stage**

As we'll see in the next stage, by planning in this way you can begin to write introductions, conclusions and paragraphs with complete confidence. It is impossible to write a good introduction to an essay if you don't know what you're introducing. The same can be said for developing your arguments from one paragraph to another. Without a clear idea of the structure of your arguments and how you plan to move consistently from one idea to another, you will be forced to do this at the very same time that you're searching for just the right word or expression to convey your ideas with complete accuracy. As a result you're likely to do neither very well.

Stage 4
Writing

INTRODUCTION

As you've seen already, by breaking down essay writing into its stages we have been able to isolate problems as they arise in each stage and concentrate our efforts on tackling them. In this stage you will see the same principle applied to breaking down the actual writing of the essay into the framework and content of essays.

▶ The framework

There are few of us who could confidently claim that we have never had problems with the structural features of essays: introductions, paragraphs and conclusions. At least part of the problem is a lack of planning, which leaves us with no clear idea of the structure and content of the essay. It's impossible to write a good introduction, if you don't know what you're introducing, and much the same can be said for paragraphs and conclusions.

Nevertheless, even with a good plan, most of us still have problems, because we're unsure what we're trying to achieve when we write introductions, paragraphs and conclusions. To cope with this, you will be shown a simple formula for each, which you can use as a model each time you write them.

With introductions you will be shown how to use your interpretation of the implications of the question and how to outline a map of the essay, to make sure you don't lose your readers as they try to follow your arguments and ideas. With paragraphs you'll be shown how to tie them into the introduction with clear topic sentences and transitions to create a taut, cohesive and tightly reasoned essay. You will also be shown how to develop your arguments in the body of the paragraph and support them with evidence. Similarly, with conclusions you'll be shown various ways of creating cohesion in your work by tying the conclusion to the introduction.

▶ The content

In the second half of this stage we will examine the problems we all experience with our style. These can be difficult to pin down, particularly when they're bound up with the other problems we've examined in previous stages. First we will look at the importance of simplicity, in particular the ways we can simplify our use of sentences and words, and what we can do to improve our writing skills to convey our ideas clearly and unambiguously.

You will be shown ways of avoiding heavy, unreadable prose and how to make your writing as light as your subject allows, more like talk in print. This is likely to result in not only a more enjoyable experience for the reader, but a memorable, effective piece of writing. By simplifying your writing in this way, you will also be less likely to lose your reader.

With sentences this calls for two things: keeping sentences relatively short, and, wherever it needs it, using a logical indicator to make clear what you're doing. We will see that the problem here is not just that we fail to use these indicators, believing that the reader can follow our train of thought without difficulty, but that they get lost in our sentences. You will also be shown ways of experimenting, using the rhythm of your words and punctuation to convey meaning. This helps to create a rhythm that is nearer to the spoken word, and the nearer we approach this the easier it is to understand what we've written.

With our use of words, similar problems tend to reappear. We're inclined to overcomplicate, using complex, even abstruse, language. This can give rise to all sorts of problems, not least the use of jargon and other words that are empty of real meaning. Ultimately, clear and effective writing depends upon thinking clearly. Language is the vehicle for ideas. If these are muddled and confused, then so too will be our language and style.

In addition to simplicity, we will also examine the other element of style, economy. We will look at the various ways we can improve our style, giving our writing greater clarity through a more economical use of language. We will also see how our use of evidence not only supports and illustrates our arguments, but makes our work more interesting and persuasive. All of this will be brought together in a practical way in the form of seven useful rules that we can use, day by day, to improve our style.

▶ Referencing and bibliographies

Finally, you will be shown how to avoid the danger of plagiarism by referencing the material you borrow. We will look at that most difficult of questions for most students: when do we need to cite sources and when don't we? You will be shown simple solutions that will help you avoid all the headaches this can entail. You will also be shown different methods of referencing and how to create a bibliography that is useful to both you and your reader.

23 Getting your Own Ideas Down

In this chapter you will learn:

- how to organise your work to allow yourself to write as freely as possible;
- about the importance of hanging a question over what you write;
- how to cope with thesis statements.

At last we have reached the stage at which many students think the process of producing essays begins. Writing the essay should be much easier now that you have completed the earlier stages. Because of this you're spared the nightmare we spoke of earlier – that of trying to do the two most difficult things in writing both at the same time. In other words, you no longer have to summon up your ideas and arrange them in a logical sequence and, at the same time, search for the right words that will convey the arguments accurately, at the right strength and with every subtle nuance accommodated.

▶ Write freely

However, you will still find there are advantages to be gained from splitting the actual writing into the two last stages: writing and revision. This helps you inject fluency into your writing, that may not otherwise be there. To do this you must keep your inner editor at bay. We all have one; some are more persistent than others. They will try to intervene whenever they can, but particularly when you start your work, or when you complete a significant section and sit back to bask in the glow of your achievement. At moments like these you will be tempted to read it all through to allow your editor to give his or her approval. Editors are persistent and, if you allow them to come in too early, they will overpower the artist.

To avoid this unwelcome intrusion allow yourself to write freely without too much concern for style. You need to tell yourself that it doesn't matter if you don't get the wording exactly right on the first attempt. The emphasis should be on allowing your thoughts to flow freely, while you follow your plan and develop your ideas. The key to success here is to remind yourself that the best writing reads as though it is talk in print. To help yourself, imagine you're talking to a group of friends who know about your subject, but have never seen it in exactly the way you do.

After this, when you move into the revision stage, you can clean up your work. Ideally, you should leave your first draft a few days. If you revise it straightaway, you may miss things that need to be changed. You may be so delighted to have got it out of the way, that your powers of self-criticism may have become blunted.

▶ Hang a question over what you write

Equally important, as you set about to write, it's worth reminding your-self that while you ought to have a point of view, you should avoid telling your readers what to think. Try to hang a question mark over it all. This way you allow your readers to think for themselves – to dis-cover for themselves the points and arguments you're making. As a result they will feel more involved, finding themselves just as commit-ted to the arguments you've made and the insights you've exposed as you are. You will have written an essay that not only avoids passivity in the reader, but is interesting and thought provoking.

▶ The thesis statement

However, advising students to hang a question over what they write can be confusing, particularly if their departments insist they write thesis statements. While most universities have a fairly broad and complex understanding of what they mean by a thesis statement, some insist on a more restricted interpretation, imposing a narrow range of expectations on students, who are told they *must* have a point of view, which *must* be stated in the introduction and then defended through-out the essay. As one university department puts it, 'form your own viewpoint and convince the reader that your viewpoint or perspective is credible'.[1] This doesn't appear to be a strategy designed to produce imaginative thinkers with minds capable of suspending judgement as they think beyond their own biases and preconceptions, so why adopt such a restricted and defensive strategy to essay writing?

As we've already seen, one answer, which makes this approach more understandable, is that many students come to university bringing with them a submissive attitude to authority, which encourages them to believe that to get good grades they must trade facts for marks and write the descriptive essay, even though they are asked to discuss and explore issues that have no right answers. At Harvard, students are warned, 'When you write an essay or research paper, you are never simply transferring information from one place to another, or showing that you have mastered a certain amount of material.'[2]

Therefore, to overcome this, students are told they must have an opinion of their own, which they must defend in their essays. However, this is just one side of academic work. The analogy of a hill will serve to make the point. One side, the more difficult inductive part, involves climbing the hill – analysing the problems and concepts involved, synthesising and discussing evidence and arguments from a range of sources, and finally, after careful measured thought, coming to your evaluation. The other side, the deductive part, going downhill, is far easier, because it is less open. Here you merely have to defend your view, drawing only upon the material you need to prove it. This is simpler, convergent, less imaginative. It uses a more limited range of abilities.

Predictably, then, when we emphasise just this one side, more often than not, opinion becomes the crude substitute for evaluation. We side-step the careful process of analysis, synthesis and discussion done in a context in which judgement is suspended. We merely declare an opinion, which we then set about to defend.

▶ A debate is not a discussion

In effect we abandon discussion in favour of the narrow intellectual demands of a debate. A discussion calls for an open, not a closed, mind. We suspend judgement, hanging a question over everything as we analyse the concepts and problems involved, explore the full weight of the evidence, empathise with others, synthesise ideas and evidence from different sources, and discuss conflicting arguments. In short, we play devil's advocate. As a tutor at Oxford makes plain, 'a good essay should always consider more than one point of view'.[3]

But as soon as we declare our opinion, the search for truth is ended. There is no need to play devil's advocate and no need to use this wide range of cognitive skills. It becomes a debate, in which we merely set out to defend our own opinion: a convergent, not a divergent, activity. Witness how one university department describes an essay: 'an essay has: an introduction which introduces your viewpoint (thesis or position), a body which develops and supports this viewpoint, and a conclusion which draws together the main lines of the argument to conclude that your viewpoint is correct'.[4] Everything is contained within the narrow confines of a simple objective: to convince the reader of a preconceived opinion.

▶ The courtroom analogy

Some departments even compare it to the adversarial process of a courtroom, telling their students to think like a lawyer presenting a case – decide on your opinion and then set about defending it. They are advised that everything in their essay should be directed towards establishing its validity. Time is spent spelling out the 'tactics' you should use to 'disarm' your opponent. If you come across something that conflicts with your case, you have no obligation to mention it. To do so would only weaken your case and strengthen your opponent's. And it's no business of yours to make your opponents' case for them.

Aware of how inconsistent this one-sided courtroom analogy is with academic work, some departments step back, arguing that the inclusion of opposing ideas actually strengthens your case. Yet, it's difficult to see how this could possibly be the case. A defence lawyer knows only too well that he or she would be foolish to mention something that conflicts with the defence they and their client have agreed upon, unless, that is, they can dismiss it convincingly in court and thereby influence the jury to their advantage. But then this amounts to no more than a rhetorical device: a deception achieved using the fallacy of the straw man (Chapter 12), which might work in a courtroom, but rarely in an academic essay.

The fact is that academic work is not adversarial in this sense of combative one-sided advocacy. It's a more open endeavour aimed not at winning a case, but at approximating to the truth by suspending your judgement and exploring all the issues and evidence available. It does not set out to win its case by withholding information that might damage it, nor by using rhetorical devices to manipulate the reader as a lawyer might seek to influence a jury. After all, as the *Greats Handbook* at Oxford advises, 'Examiners will notice if you try to fudge issues or sweep difficulties aside; it is much better to be candid about them, and to show that you appreciate the force of counter-arguments.'[5]

▶ How to cope with thesis statements

Nevertheless, not all universities adopt this narrow interpretation of thesis statements, and in this may lie a solution. Those who advocate them often maintain they are necessary, because this is the only way to give your essay a structure in which to develop a coherent argument. If this is all we are after, there might be less of a problem.

As we've already seen in Stages 1 and 3, you can come to a clear interpretation of the implications of the question, from which you develop a clearly structured plan of the essay, without that entailing a viewpoint that you must defend. Indeed, two students can have an identical structure and plan, yet come to quite different conclusions. Structure does not depend on having a preconceived opinion, just an interpretation of the implications of the question and a plan to go with it. In turn, as this means we have no need to set out to defend opinions which we have stated at the outset, we are free to suspend our judgement, on which all our higher cognitive skills depend. We need to be clear about this – unless we suspend our judgement as we write, we cannot and need not use these higher cognitive skills.

Take the following example of a thesis statement from the Writing Center at Harvard:

> Further analysis of Memorial Hall, and of the archival sources that describe the process of building it, suggests that the past may not be the central subject of the hall but only a medium. What message, then, does the building convey, and why are the fallen soldiers of such importance to the alumni who built it? Part of the answer, it seems, is that Memorial Hall is an educational tool, an attempt by the Harvard community of the 1870s to influence the future by shaping our memory of their times. The commemoration of those students and graduates who died for the Union during the Civil War is one aspect of this alumni message to the future, but it may not be the central idea.[6]

It gives structure, yet it suspends judgement and is not driven to prove one preconceived viewpoint. A question is hung over each sentence, with words like 'suggests', 'may not be' and 'it seems'. As this suggests, essays are far more complex than just the defending of a preconceived opinion, like a defence lawyer attempting to persuade a jury. Genuine discussion, and the higher cognitive skills that go with it, depend upon suspending judgement. As one tutor at the Writing Center at Harvard argues, 'An effective thesis cannot be answered with a simple "yes" or "no." A thesis is not a topic; nor is it a fact; nor is it an opinion.'[7]

So, if your department does require you to write thesis statements, just clarify for yourself: does this mean I am expected to announce my opinion and defend it in the essay; or am I expected just to give a clear indication of the map of my essay, while I suspend judgement and hang a question over the issues involved?

▶ In the next chapter

Structure, then, does not depend upon you announcing your opinion in the introduction. In the next chapter you will see that the most effective introductions do two things: analyse the implications of the question, and outline the map of the essay structure drawn from your plan.

Notes

1 Jan Regan, *Essay and Report Writing: What is Expected of You?* (Lismore: Southern Cross University, 2000), p. 1.

2 Kathy Duffin, *Overview of the Academic Essay* (Cambridge, Mass.: Writing Center at Harvard University, 1998), p. 1.

3 Eric Eve, *A Guide for Perplexed Students, 4: Tutorial Essays* (Oxford: University of Oxford, 2000), p. 3.
    Available at: http://www.hmc.ox.ac.uk/

4 Regan, *Essay and Report Writing*, p. 1.

5 *Greats Handbook* (Oxford: University of Oxford, 2000), p. 39.

6 Patricia Kain, *Beginning the Academic Essay* (Cambridge, Mass.: Writing Center at Harvard University, 1999), pp. 2–3.

7 Maxine Rodburg, *Developing a Thesis* (Cambridge, Mass.: Writing Center at Harvard University, 1999), p. 1.

24 Introductions

> In this chapter you will learn:
>
> - why so many of us struggle to write good introductions;
> - how to write introductions that leave the examiners with no doubts about what you're doing and why;
> - a simple formula for a good introduction.

There are very few students who wouldn't list introductions as one of the most difficult aspects of writing an essay. Much of this is due to the fact that most of us are unsure about what we should be doing in the introduction. If we don't know why we're doing something, what we're trying to achieve, we shouldn't be too surprised to find that we're not particularly good at it. But there's another reason why most of us are not good at writing introductions: we neglect stages 1 and 3 (interpretation and planning). If we have very little idea what we're going to be writing, it's difficult to do a good job of introducing it.

However, even with a clear interpretation of the question and a well structured plan it can be a problem, unless you set simple and clear objectives that you want your introduction to fulfil. These should include two things:

- the interpretation of the question (what is it getting at?); and
- the structure of your answer, the map the reader is going to follow.

▶ The interpretation of the question

The first question examiners are going to ask themselves as soon as they begin to read your essay, before they even consider anything else, is 'Has the writer seen the point of the question?' In two or three sentences you need to outline the main issues raised by the question, which you will have uncovered in the interpretation stage. This may involve identifying the main problem or set of problems at the heart of the question, or it may involve pointing to the central importance of one or two concepts, which need to be analysed. But this does not involve discussing these problems nor analysing the concepts in the introduction; it merely means you show the examiners that you have the ability to see the implications of the question and point them in the direction you intend to take them.

For example, in the question we discussed in Chapter 2 you might begin with the following introduction:

Question

> 'Authority amounts to no more than the possession of power.' *Discuss.*

> Most of us would no doubt agree that in the cases of police officers and government officials this claim is largely true: their authority does seem to derive exclusively from the power they have been given. Indeed, we acknowledge their authority because we are all too aware of the consequences of not doing so. But to accept that every case of authority amounts to no more than the claim that might is always right, threatens the very existence of modern democracy along with its goal of balancing order with accountability and justice. Either way, whatever we're prepared to believe depends upon our understanding of the two central concepts, power and authority.

By identifying the major issues in the first few sentences you establish the relevance of these, and the relevance of your essay in tackling them. This is what writers describe as the 'hot spot': the first sentence or two in which you sell the subject, making it clear that you've seen the problem the question is getting at, and you're aware of its importance.

▶ The structure of your answer

Having done this you then need to outline in the broadest of details the structure of your answer, the plan you're working from. You don't need to do this in the authority/power question, because you've already done it by pointing to the central importance of the analysis of the two concepts. Again this need not be in any great detail, but it must provide a map so that your examiners are at no time unsure which way you're going and where you're taking them. At Harvard students are told:

A good introduction is successful because it allows readers to prepare themselves mentally for the journey they will undergo as they follow your argument through the paper. Like a travel guide, it enables them to recognize and understand the major points of interest in your argument as they go by.[1]

Remember, lose the examiners and you lose marks, it's as simple as that. Your introduction should point them in the right direction, giving them a clear idea of what is to follow.

Practice exercise 15
Write an introduction

Take the advertising question we considered earlier:

'Advertisers seek only to ensure that consumers make informed choices.' *Discuss.*

Write an introduction that interprets the implications of the question and then outlines the map of your answer. When you've finished, compare your answer with the introduction below.

In this question our map might look something like the following:

Most advertising executives are willing to defend their profession by arguing that all they are doing is informing the public and in doing so protecting the democratic freedoms of individuals, in particular their freedom of choice. To a certain extent, of course, this is true: without advertising we would be less informed about new developments in technology, in fashion and in medical advances. Even government warnings about the dangers at work and in the home depend upon advertisements. But the key to this is the claim that this is the 'only' thing they do, when most of the public suspect their paramount concern is to manipulate consumers into buying products that they may not want or need.

This indicates what the reader should expect as the structure in the essay. One part will develop the view that advertisers are concerned with informing consumers. Then the structure will turn on the word 'only', leaving the writer, in the second half of the essay, to examine the way advertisers use information selectively and employ other devices to manipulate the consumer through appeals to sex, status and prejudices.

▶ A simple formula for introductions

The real value of writing introductions in this way lies in the fact that most of us benefit from having a simple structure, a formula, like this to work from. As a result we're likely to feel more confident about what we're doing when we write introductions. They'll present fewer problems and they'll focus the reader's attention on the issues we believe are the most relevant.

Nevertheless, you may find as your confidence grows that you want to do more with introductions. You may want to set the problem in the context of recent history, or you may want to endorse your analysis of the problem by quoting a respected authority.

For example, in the following question, which asks you to consider the inevitability of progress, you could begin with this:

Question

'You can't stop progress.' *Discuss critically with reference to one major technology.*

Looking back at the early years of the industrial revolution in Britain it's tempting to view opponents of progress, like the Luddites who smashed the machines they believed were threatening their way of life, as naïve and short-sighted. But in this we ought to be cautious; after all, theirs might not have been opposition to progress as such, but to just one account of it. It's worth wondering what makes *our* view of progress, with all its alienation at work, dissipated communities, rising crime, social disaffection and persistently high levels of poverty and homelessness, any better than that of the Luddites.

Today the problem is the same. Developing countries in the Third World can claim to have learnt from the mistakes of western industrialised countries. As a result their account of progress is quite different. So, while we might agree that 'you can't stop progress', there is no reason why we should accept the implication of this, that we have lost our freedom to choose. We may not be able to stop progress, but we can still choose the type of progress we want.

Doing more with introductions in this way carries with it the danger of obscuring the original intentions: to reveal the implications of the question and outline the map of your answer. In this case it was wise to split the introduction into two paragraphs to give us a chance of making the structure clearer in the second paragraph. But there are no hard and fast rules to this. Just keep in mind the simple structure on which you are weaving these improvisations and avoid allowing the introduction to become so long and complex that it obscures the simple intent that lies behind it.

▷ In the next chapter

The same advice applies equally to paragraphs. As we will see in the next chapter, they, too, have a simple formula.

Note

1 Julie Lynch and Jennifer Ritterhouse, *Writing at Harvard* (Cambridge, Mass.: Writing Center at Harvard University, 2000), Ch. 2, pp. 2–3.

25 Paragraphs

In this chapter you will learn:

- how to write paragraphs to produce a taut, well-argued essay;
- a simple formula for writing paragraphs;
- how to use 'topic sentences' and 'transitions';
- how to develop your arguments in paragraphs and support them with evidence.

▶ The main body of the essay

Having outlined in the introduction the broad map of what is to follow, as you write each paragraph you can now develop in your essay the tautness of a well planned, coherent piece of reasoning. Often essays fail because they read like a loose list of isolated points each dependent upon itself, and not supported by the context in which it is developed.

To avoid this, tie your paragraphs in with the major issues you identified in your introduction as being central to the question. You will be picking these issues up anyway as you follow the structure of your plan, but as you do so, make it clear to the reader that you are following the map you outlined in your introduction. In this way you not only maintain relevance throughout, but by tying each paragraph in with the introduction you create a cohesive piece of work. Its structure will be taut, giving the essay the feel of being well organised and tightly reasoned.

Of course, this doesn't mean you should announce clumsily that this is what you're doing, repeatedly making the same sort of reference to your introduction at the beginning of each paragraph. This would be tedious and the reader would begin to suspect that your concern was more for form than content. It can be done more subtly than this, as we'll see. But whichever way you do it, remember that in the first sentence of each paragraph, the 'topic sentence', the examiner needs to be informed about what you're doing in that paragraph, and why it's relevant to the issues you identified in your introduction.

Nevertheless, there is a qualification to this we need to mention. Not every paragraph needs to be tied in with the map in your introduction. Some of the major issues in the essay will take a number of paragraphs to develop. Therefore, in this case, you only need to tie in with the introduction the first paragraph of each major section. The paragraphs that follow will then have to be tied in with this paragraph to create fluency and cohesion.

This raises an important issue, as we'll see. In order to create a taut, coherent piece of work, each paragraph has to have a clear connection with the one that preceded it. To make sure of this you will need to have effective 'transitions' at the beginning of each paragraph to indicate to the examiners the course of your argument. From this they should be able to see that this is an extension of the previous paragraph, or that you're making a comparison, or that you're illustrating the point you've already made, and so on. In some paragraphs it will be obvious what you're doing and there will be no need to announce it, but if in doubt use a transition.

▶ A simple formula for paragraphs

As we've already seen with introductions, we do most things much more effectively if we know what we're doing and why. But for many students paragraphs are a complete mystery.

This shows up in their concern over the length of paragraphs. Some suspect that theirs are either too short or too long, while others confess that they decide to end one paragraph and begin another on a mere whim. In fact, although this may not appear too helpful, the best advice is simply to vary their length. It will make the essay more interesting to read and you'll be less inclined to send your readers off into a deep sleep as they follow the predictable rhythms of your writing.

Of course, ultimately the key to the length of paragraphs lies in the logic of the essay as a whole. In other words, keep to your structure and at all costs let the examiners see that, as they move from one paragraph to another, they're moving from one section within the structure to another. For the same reason, avoid long, ambling paragraphs that obscure the structure. In fact, this is not as difficult to avoid as it might seem. Long paragraphs, in which you lose the thread of what the writer's doing, are like the long, ambling essay: the product of writing without structure.

You can build this structure into each paragraph by keeping a simple formula for paragraphs in your mind. Although it would be arrogant to lay down the law on the structure of paragraphs, as it would be with introductions, it helps to have a simple formula, particularly when you're unsure of what you're doing. As for introductions, you can always use the formula as the basis for improvisation once you've grown in confidence using it.

Three parts

For this purpose remind yourself that there are three parts to a paragraph: the topic sentence; the development; and the evidence. This structure may not always be appropriate, you may need to adapt it, but if you remind yourself of each part, you will always be aware of the weaknesses you're allowing to appear in your essay when you omit one part. You'll be reminding yourself that if you do decide to leave one part out, you will have to address the problem later in the essay.

▶ 1 The topic sentence

The topic sentence, as its name implies, introduces the topic of the paragraph. But even more important, it establishes the topic's relevance by tying it in with one of the major issues in your plan, that you mapped out in your introduction. As we've already pointed out, by tying all the components tightly together in this way you create both relevance and tight cohesion within the essay.

For example, the paragraph after the introduction in the advertising essay might begin:

> As this suggests, at least part of the advertiser's role is to provide consumers and the public with information.

And, later in the essay, after you have examined the way advertisers manipulate through the selective use of information, you may go on to examine the other forms of manipulation by introducing it with the topic sentence:

However, advertisers have developed still more effective forms of manipulation, particularly in their exploitation of the sex, status and prejudices of the consumer.

As this illustrates, the topic sentence is important to establish the relevance of the paragraph you are about to write in the context of the paragraphs that have already been completed, and to indicate to your examiners which way you're now going to take them. To do this you need a 'transition' at the beginning of the sentence. This can be a short phrase, like 'As a result', or a single word, like 'Nevertheless'. In the examples above, we used 'As this suggests' and 'However'.

In effect these work as 'logical indicators': they indicate what you will be doing in the paragraph. You might be striking a contrast with what you've just done in the previous paragraph ('In contrast', 'However'). You may simply be extending the argument you've already developed in a slightly different way ('Moreover', 'Therefore'). Or you may want to strengthen your argument by developing a point that reinforces it from a different angle ('Similarly', 'Likewise').

In view of their importance, make sure your transitions do what you want them to do. Occasionally we find ourselves using weak transitions, which create only weak links and a weak essay structure. The worst are those we use for a list of points, words and phrases like 'Also', 'Another point is' and 'In addition'. These have their counterparts in subjects, like history, where we resort to time to order our ideas, which we introduce with transitions like 'After', 'Then' and 'The next'. When you find yourself using this sort of transition, just check to see what's happening in your essay. More often than not they will indicate that you're no longer discussing issues by developing a critical analysis. Instead, you've slipped into a description of the issues or into a narrative of the events.

The same warning about transitions doing real work applies to all those times when we've found ourselves pressing a transition into service to create fluency that simply isn't there in the first place. If we haven't planned carefully enough, establishing clear intellectual links between paragraphs, examiners will not be fooled if we try to paper over the disjointed paragraphs with carefully chosen transitions. It will always sound false and manufactured.

However, if your essay is clearly planned, not all of your paragraphs will need transitions. There are going to be some that are set in the context of a clearly sign-posted argument or analysis, and it's all too obvious what you're doing. Nevertheless, don't forget these are important directions for the examiners, who need to know which way you will be taking them as they try to navigate the unfamiliar terrain of your thinking. To take the city analogy again, they need to know at each intersection and every turning, which way you intend to go, otherwise you will leave them mystified and confused as to what you're doing, and they will be unable to award you marks, even though your work may be good. So, if in doubt use one.

Practice exercise   16
Write the topic sentence

Question

'Authority amounts to no more than the possession of power.' *Discuss.*

Look at the introduction we wrote for this question in the last chapter and our interpretation of it in Chapter 2. It's clear from the introduction that we are going to start by arguing that the proposition is true, if we take the concept of authority to imply someone 'in' authority. This section of the essay could be represented by the notes below.

As you can see, we could probably write this in two paragraphs. The first paragraph would deal with 'official authority', the sort given to people like the police and government officials. Taking this as our first paragraph after the introduction, write a topic sentence for it.

Once you've done this, compare your topic sentence with the one below.

The notes

Question

'Authority amounts to no more than the possession of power.' *Discuss.*

1.   Proposition = True if authority is taken to mean 'in' authority:

= authority amounts to the power to make things worse – to oblige people to comply with orders

(a)   Official authority – institutional power
    e.g.   the police
We accept this sort of power as authority, maybe because of
  (i)   our respect for the institution

      or, when this fails, e.g. an inner-city ethnic community
      feels unfairly targeted by the police,

  (ii)   because of our fear of the consequences

(b)   Unofficial authority – 'Might is Right'
    e.g.   the local gang leader
Their influence over the local community may be due to
  (i)   respect for individual leaders

      or

  (ii)   more likely it's due to fear of the consequences of going
      against their will, e.g. protection rackets

Answer

As this suggests, one way in which we understand the concept of authority is represented by the institutional power of officials like police officers, whose authority lies largely in their power to make things worse for us if we don't comply with their orders.

▶ 2   The development

Once you've established in the topic sentence the relevance of the topic you're going to be dealing with in the paragraph, the examiner can get down to assessing the quality of your work. It is here in the development that you show the examiner you are capable of the sort of intellectual processing that was called for in the question by the 'instructional verb' (see Chapter 8).

At this point it's worth reminding ourselves of the issues we raised when we first examined this. You'll remember we pointed out that all syllabuses are written in the context of six 'cognitive domains' – six intellectual abilities, ranging from the simplest, 'recall', to the more complex abilities, such as analysis, synthesis and evaluation.

Again, as we pointed out then, most of our problems, both in writing and in our study skills, begin here. We wrongly assume that education is exclusively concerned with the possession of knowledge, so we aim to produce evidence in our writing that we know a great deal, that we have good recall, the simplest cognitive domain. Whereas we should be exercising the more complex abilities to analyse, to criticise, to synthesise ideas and evidence, and to evaluate arguments.

All too often, even though the question might ask us to discuss, analyse or criticise, we assume the examiner merely wants evidence that we can understand the subject. With this in mind, as we set about researching the essay, we begin to take vast quantities of irrelevant, unstructured notes from texts, arguing that we cannot possibly leave any material out, because these are the facts and we are required to show evidence that we can recall them all. As a result, we lose sight of the implications of the question and our need to address them relevantly, preferring instead to put everything into our essays as long as they are facts. We assume the more facts we put in, relevant or not, the more marks we will earn.

Similarly, although we're told to put arguments in our own words, it's difficult to shake off the belief that, as the texts we use are the source of right answers, of indisputable facts, we can do nothing else but copy them with complete accuracy and without alteration, because to change anything would be to make it less than right. So we copy into our notes large chunks of them that we have neither structured nor processed in any way. As a result our notes assume the structure the author gives us, which might be quite inappropriate for our purposes in preparing to write this particular essay.

Passive surface-level processing

In other words we become passive 'surface-level processors': we neither exercise any judgement as to the relevance of the material, nor to the credibility of what is being said. We've ignored the instructions to operate in the higher cognitive domains, to evaluate the ideas critically, and instead we've settled for the simpler task of copying, reproducing and imitating what we've allowed ourselves to assume is the unquestioned authority, the source of right answers. Not surprisingly, then, in our writing we're inclined to plagiarise large sections, believing that to alter anything would be to make what is otherwise a right answer, less than right.

However, in universities the examinations we prepare ourselves for are not concerned with demonstrating recall or with reproducing faithfully what our authorities say. They're aimed at assessing the higher cognitive domains, where we synthesise ideas and analyse arguments critically. Rather than accept that there are authorities that are beyond question, this asks us to criticise and evaluate received ideas and opinions – to accept nothing on trust.

In this stage of essay writing, then, as we develop our arguments in the paragraph, it's important to remind ourselves that those who assess our essays are not concerned so much with right answers as they are with the abilities we use to reach our answer. Two essays can both receive the same high mark, even though they come to completely different answers. And, conversely, even though two essays may come to exactly the same conclusion, this doesn't mean they will be awarded the same mark: one might receive the lowest mark awarded, while the other the highest. And, of course, it's equally true that even though an examiner might agree with your conclusion, he or she may still award you low marks. It's not the conclusion you reach that matters so much as the way in which you reach it: the way you travel.

Travelling well
Given this, it should now be clear that in the development of the paragraph, examiners want to see you use these higher cognitive domains. They will want to see how well you travel from the simple description of the case, to an analysis of its implications, to the criticism of each one of these implications, to the evidence to support your view, and finally to your evaluation. In such a sequence you will have travelled far, and for this you will earn high marks.

Description → Analysis → Criticism → Evidence → Evaluation

Of course, it may not be possible to do all of this in one paragraph. After the analysis you may want to take up each implication as the subject for each subsequent paragraph.

Analysis → Implication → Criticism → Evidence
Implication → Criticism → Evidence
Implication → Criticism → Evidence

In this case, in one paragraph you would describe the implication, criticise it and show evidence for your view, before moving to the next implication in the next paragraph, where you would do the same, and so on. Then your evaluation may come two or three paragraphs later at the end of this section of your essay, when you've dealt with all the implications. Alternatively, it may come at the end of the essay, if this is more appropriate. As we will see when we examine the role of the conclusion, this is often the most appropriate stage in which to bring the various strands together and reach a measured evaluation based on the strength of the arguments and evidence you've considered in the essay as a whole.

▶ 3 The evidence

Given what we have just said about the development, the evidence should present few problems. Obviously, if the development of our argument is clear, the relevance of our evidence should be equally clear. We will have a much better idea of the sort of evidence we need, to support and illustrate our arguments in the paragraph.

The problems come when we revert to the assumptions that tell us the only thing worth anything in education is knowledge and facts. Then we can become obsessed with impressing the examiners with our knowledge by presenting a wealth of facts irrespective of whether they're relevant or not. The paragraph becomes overloaded, the facts are out of proportion with what they ought to be to support and illustrate our argument, and examiners become confused about what we're trying to do. They will assume that either they have missed something, or the structure of our essay has broken down.

Nevertheless, in virtue there can also be vice. There are some students who, realising that they should not be taking authorities on trust, that they should be analysing, criticising and evaluating them, jump from a statement of the problem in the topic sentence to evaluation, without any attempt to analyse and discuss the issues. As a result, because there has been no development, the evaluation is usually neither measured nor thoughtfully considered.

In effect they've convinced themselves that the only thing of any value is opinion – their opinion. As a result they fill up each paragraph with a series of unsupported claims, for which they provide neither analysis, nor argument, nor, in our present context, any evidence. In most examiners' minds this extreme of unsubstantiated opinion is probably worse than the other: blind acceptance and description of so-called right answers.

Practice exercise   17
Write the development and the evidence

Question

'Authority amounts to no more than the possession of power.'
Discuss.

Having written the topic sentence for the first paragraph after the introduction in the last practice exercise, now, with your topic sentence and
the notes for the plan in front of you, write the development and the evidence of the paragraph.
Once you've done this, compare it with the answer below.

Answer

Even so, stability in any society depends on there being a large proportion of the community willing to obey these orders because they
have respect for official institutions, like the police. When this fails
we may be left with a very volatile situation in which people feel
obliged to obey, simply out of fear for the consequences. For
example, if an ethnic community in an inner-city area feels that the
police are unfairly targeting them, in time they are likely to lose
respect for the institution and for the individual police officer, whose
only recourse thereafter is to implement the law by threats of force,
rather than by appeals to reason and justice.

▶ In the next chapter

If a large part of paragraph writing is about travelling well, conclusions
are about arriving in style. As we'll see in the next chapter, there are a
number of simple ways to ensure that your conclusion ties in with your
introduction, producing an essay that is cohesive, tightly argued and a
joy to read.

26 Conclusions

In this chapter you will learn:

- the most effective ways of writing thought-provoking conclusions;
- how to use conclusions to tie up your arguments into a cohesive, relevant essay;
- how to leave your readers with a sense of discovery, that they have read something worthwhile.

It's surprising how many people believe that the conclusion is for them the most difficult part of writing an essay, whereas it should be the easiest of the three parts. Having got your readers safely to this point without losing them or confusing them as to the relevance of your arguments, there is little you can do now to weaken your work.

However, there are still one or two problems that catch the unwary. Some students are convinced they must finish on an upbeat note, with a clear, firm declaration of their opinion. If the question asks for your opinion, they argue, you must give it. The problem with this is that such a declaration of opinion may just come completely out of the blue. The essay may be full of the most skilful analysis and discussion of the problems, leaving you with no clear grounds for absolute certainty one way or the other. Therefore, to make a clear statement of your opinion, showing no doubt or uncertainty, would be inappropriate.

The opinions you express in the conclusion must reflect the strength and balance of the arguments that have preceded them in the body of the essay. They must be carefully measured to match the discussion you have developed, and this may not allow for a firm declaration of certainty one way or the other. If you've genuinely discussed the issues and not just given a one-sided defence of your opinion, your conclusion might be pitched anywhere on a spectrum ranging from unqualified opposition to the proposition in the question, to qualified acceptance or denial, to outright support with no qualifications. In a genuine discussion it's all up for grabs.

It's well worth reminding yourself that firm, clear opinions have no particular value in themselves. Anyone can express their opinions, and almost everyone does. Down at your local bar you can find people with opinions on just about everything from the reasons why your local football team is doing badly this season to the ethical implications of human cloning. But you're not going to earn marks for your opinions. Marks are earned by developing your analysis and discussion of the issues, and then supporting them with relevant, well chosen evidence. Most of us down at the local bar are rarely so scrupulous in our attention to the quality of our arguments.

Of course, if you do want to make clear your own opinions and, on balance, they reflect the preceding discussion, then do so. Failing that, if you are genuinely undecided, give a tentative conclusion couched in the appropriate qualifications.

Pick up the theme raised in the introduction
Alternatively, you can summarise the main points in the essay, coming to a measured judgement of what you believe to be the most important issues the essay has raised. Or you could pick up the theme you raised in your introduction, reflecting on this in the light of what you've discussed since. Tying up the introduction with the conclusion in this way lends greater cohesion to your work – it is satisfying to the reader to know that you have come full circle and everything has found its appropriate place.

For example, the essay that examined the possibility of stopping progress began in the introduction by referring to the activities of the Luddites in the nineteenth century during the British industrial revolution. It suggested that in hindsight they might be viewed as naïve and short-sighted. Given this, you could conclude the essay by picking up this theme again. You might suggest that in the light of the discussion in the essay, rather than the Luddites, it might be more appropriate to accuse our own generation of naivety and short-sightedness in how we define and measure progress.

The wider implications or future trends
As this suggests, the best conclusion is one that is as thought-provoking as possible. As we've already seen, there are a number of ways of doing this. You could just re-state the theme of the essay, or you could summarise the main points of the arguments you've developed.

Alternatively, you may want to suggest the wider implications, or what you believe to be the future trends: you may want to tell the reader what you believe has to be done to solve the problems you've discussed, or predict what might happen if the problems are left unresolved. This might pick up on the broader issues that go beyond the limits of the essay, but which you have suggested in the introduction might become our ultimate concern.

Say, for example, you were writing an essay on the ethical implications involved in human cloning. In the introduction you might have pointed to the broader, long-term fears that we might be encouraging the development of a world in which children can be manufactured by parents according to their own ideal blueprints, rather like going along to a genetic supermarket to select the characteristics you most want in your children. In the conclusion, after your discussion, you may have decided that this really is a problem that needs to be faced now before it is too late, or you may want to conclude that the problem has been overstated. Either way, both would be appropriate as long as they don't go beyond the strength of the arguments and evidence you have presented.

Similarly, if you were discussing a literary text, you might suggest that the implications of the issues you've raised go beyond the scope of your essay. For example, if you were answering the question, 'How can the description of the need for distance at the beginning of chapter 19 of *Adam Bede* square with the novel's more general emphasis on novelistic sympathy?' (Harvard), you might suggest that a study of George Eliot's other novels, like *Silas Marner* and *Middlemarch*, would be interesting to see if this apparent contradiction runs throughout her work.

In a nutshell

You can do any of the following:

- give your opinions as long as they match the strength of your arguments;
- summarise the main points;
- pick up the theme of the introduction;
- suggest wider implications;
- predict future trends.

Example

The following example of an introduction and conclusion employs all of these devices in some measure. It is taken from a paper on organ donation and the effects that modern medical practices are having in discouraging potential donors from pledging their organs. The first two paragraphs present two contrasting anecdotes, while the third and fourth outline the theme of the paper, the problem it sets out to examine.

Introduction

On a cold, frosty morning, as the sun begins to rise above the lingering fog of night, a Chinese prisoner awaits his execution in a dark, damp cell that echoes with the reverberations of his own faltering heartbeat. Blindfolded, with his hands and legs bound as he kneels with bent head, he feels the cold steel of the gun at the back of his neck. The shot is fired and he loses consciousness, but he is not dead. He is rushed to the hospital ward, not to save his life, but to have his organs 'harvested'.

In another hospital, a world away in a small children's ward in South London, two parents clutching each other, worn down by years of struggle and tension, look anxiously on as their five-year-old son, Nicholas, is connected to a now-familiar machine that will do for him what his own kidneys cannot. Despairingly, they know he cannot struggle on indefinitely without a new kidney.

These horrifying scenes portray two sides of a problem that defies easy solution. Despite the shortage of donated organs and the despair of those who wait, most of us, out of fear and mistrust it seems, choose to have our bodies and all their life-saving organs either incinerated or buried to decompose beneath the ground. In Britain, a country with a population of 59 million, the number of donors fell to just 981 in 1995, and in Europe as a whole there were 15% fewer hearts and 14% fewer kidneys available to the Eurotransplant Foundation, that co-ordinates organ collection.

As a result the death toll of those who could wait no longer grows day by day. In the US each year over 3,000 patients die for the lack of organs, that is eight to ten a day, one every three hours. And all this tragic waste of life could be avoided. More than enough organs could be retrieved each year under the right conditions to satisfy the demand, if only we could find an effective and morally acceptable way to do it.

Conclusion

None of us like to think of our bodies as just collections of spare-parts, like old discarded automobiles. And we all probably realise that for each of us who refuses to carry a donor card, someone, some-where, pays the price. It may be the prisoner in his dark, damp cell, or five-year-old Nicholas, who can wait no longer. But as long as a doctor is free to omit treatment that might save our lives, to give up on us after only two minutes of resuscitation, and as long as the def-inition of death creeps under pressure for more organs, sadly this tragic death toll seems set to continue.

If you do nothing more in a conclusion, always try to achieve at least one thing: to wrap up the essay leaving your readers satisfied that they have read something worthwhile – leave them with a sense of discov-ery. Whether you use an idea that pulls everything together or extends it, or whether you tie up the essay by picking up an anecdote you've already used, let your readers participate, so that they feel they've been able to come to their own conclusion and have discovered something thought-provoking and interesting.

Assignment 9
The framework – introductions, conclusions and paragraphs

We've now reached the point where we're ready to write the essay. In the last stage you completed the plan of the essay you have chosen to work on. Now, with this in front of you, write the introduction to the essay, the conclusion and the two paragraphs that follow the introduc-tion. Once you've finished writing the whole essay, at the end of the book, you may find that you think a little differently about the issues and you want to change the conclusion, but for this exercise write it now, you can always change it later if you want to.

► In the next chapter

In this assignment you will have seen how much simpler essay writing can be if you have a clearly structured plan from which to write, and if you understand how the structural features of the essay work – introductions, paragraphs and conclusions. We can now turn, in the next two chapters, to all those problems that arise when we begin to develop the content of the essay.

27 Style – Simplicity

In this chapter you will learn:

- the three guiding principles for a better style;
- how to avoid heavy, unreadable prose;
- how to write sentences that avoid the danger of losing your reader;
- how to use the length of sentences and punctuation to create the rhythm in your prose that is nearer to talk in print;
- how to use words to convey your meaning accurately.

When some students reach this stage, all too often they're ready just to shrug their shoulders and give up on their writing, dismissing it despairingly with the words, 'I just haven't got a very good style, that's all!', as if this was somehow God-given, encoded into our DNA. It probably comes from our early schooling when children were given prizes for their compositions, and from that moment on we came to believe the world is somehow divided between those who have writing talent and those who have not – and there's not a thing we can do about it.

But this is just not so. There is much we can do to improve our style. The simplest thing is just to read more: the more literature we read, the better our style. Like a process of photosynthesis it filters down through our consciousness, enriching our thought processes and sharpening our use of words without us being aware that anything significant is happening. Get into the habit of reading well-written novels, so that you're always in the middle of reading one. Just fifteen to twenty minutes a night before you go to sleep will in time have a marked impact on your writing.

▶ Writing lightly – the guiding principles

Nevertheless, for some people this might seem a far too mysterious process, reaching fruition only for those who have spent a lifetime dedicated to unravelling the arcane secrets of writing. Although this is far from being the case, there are still other practical steps we can take. But first, to do this we need to establish certain guiding principles, definite markers, that we can use when we choose our words and phrases. After applying them in two or three pieces of work, you should be seeing quite noticeable improvements in your writing.

Each of these guiding principles is focused on one pre-eminent goal: to avoid all heavy, unreadable prose. Make your writing as light as your subject allows. The result is likely to be a more enjoyable experience for the reader and a memorable, effective piece of writing. Keep in mind the three main guiding principles, which can be summed up in just three words:

- logic
- interest
- brevity

The first of these you've already met if you've planned well and written an introduction that lays out the logical map that you will be following throughout the essay. As we've said, as you pick up each topic in this map in the first sentence of each paragraph, indicating with transitions what you will be doing in the paragraph, the reader can follow you, step by step, without fear of being lost.

As to the second, interest, we shall discuss this in Chapter 29 when we look at the type of evidence you might use. For now, our concern is with brevity – saying what you want to say in the fewest possible words. Here lies what most of us mean when we think of style. It means simplicity and economy in the use of language.

▶ Simplicity

The key to writing lightly is not to overcomplicate things; to remind yourself constantly that writing is nothing more than talk in print. Some of the best writing we've ever read seems to glide across the page as if it's just someone talking to you in the same room, even though the writer may be grappling with the most complex ideas and the deepest of emotions. When you read it, it seems the simplest thing in the world to do. But like most things that are done well, its simplicity disguises the hard work that's been invested: in this case in trying to overcome the difference between written and spoken communication.

▶ Written v. spoken

We're all aware of the problems this difference creates for a student writing an essay. As we're not sitting next to our readers, we're not able to tell them what we really meant to say each time they stop to struggle with one of our more difficult expressions. This is made even more difficult if our work is being marked by an external examiner, who won't have the same familiarity with and sympathy for our ideas as our tutor does.

But perhaps the most elusive aspect of normal speech, that's difficult to capture in our written work, is any emphasis we might express through tone or gesture. This has to be conveyed through our choice of words and phrases, and through sentence rhythm and punctuation. And, of course, unlike the oral explanations we might give in answer to a question, in our written work readers can go at their own pace; they can even go back and re-read one of our arguments. All of which makes writing a much more concentrated form of communication than speech.

Given these problems you couldn't be blamed for putting your hands up in the air in despair; it seems a frighteningly difficult task. But the truth is, it's a lot simpler than we allow ourselves to think. If, when we come to write, we have convinced ourselves that it *is* a difficult task, this is exactly what we will find. We'll tend to complicate the task unnecessarily, making it virtually impossible to do a good job. This is what Matthew Arnold says about style and the business of writing:

> People think that I can teach them style. What stuff it all is! Have something to say, and say it as clearly as you can. That is the only secret of style.[1]

▶ Sentences

Most students find writing difficult because they're convinced that it's much more complicated than Matthew Arnold describes it. And it always appears that way, when anyone explains what you should do and what you should try to avoid. But this is all part of an effort to get back to what will eventually come easily, if not naturally, which is to produce writing that is talk in print. This may seem difficult to start with, but it will get easier as you apply these basic guiding principles.

For most of us the problems seem to start when we graduate from one level of learning to another. We convince ourselves that, as this involves understanding more complex ideas and arguments, we must therefore use long and complicated sentence structures, and difficult and unusual words to convey them. In reading students' work I regularly come across mammoth sentences of more than 200 words, replete with a confusing array of multiple clauses and phrases that come tumbling out on top of each other. Reading this, examiners are likely to be confused and lost amidst this jungle of words.

But, equally serious, they will probably walk away from this kind of essay convinced of three things: first, that students who produce this sort of work are not clear about what they want to say; second, that they haven't planned their ideas with any care; and third, that they didn't think through the ideas in the planning stage before they wrote them. In fact it would be reasonable for examiners to conclude that they are only now working through these ideas for the first time as they write.

It should be obvious, then, that the key to writing sentences, as it is to writing paragraphs, is not to lose your reader. A complex sentence full of multiple clauses is a difficult and perilous terrain for examiners to negotiate. Not only are you likely to lose them as they pick their way gingerly through this difficult terrain, but by the time they have reached the end of the sentence they will have forgotten your original point. To prevent this, try to do two things: keep sentences relatively short and, wherever it needs it, use a logical indicator ('but', 'if', 'however', 'therefore', 'moreover', 'similarly', etc.) to indicate what you're doing.

Length

Take the first of these points – length. Wherever possible make your sentences short and their structure clear. For example, read the following sentence:

It's possible to argue that almost all advertisements, with the exception of a few, are informative, indeed, as we have already seen, some appear to be wholly concerned with this, although government bodies releasing warnings about smoking or the use of domestic fire alarms are clearly intent on changing our behaviour they are still concerned to give the public what they believe is vital information.

It's not difficult to see that it would benefit, first, by being broken up into three shorter sentences, and then, by punctuating the last of these to make its structure clearer:

It's possible to argue that almost all advertisements are informative. Indeed, as we have already seen, some appear to be wholly concerned with this. Although government bodies, releasing warnings about smoking or the use of domestic fire alarms, are clearly intent on changing our behaviour, they are still concerned to give the public what they believe is vital information.

Of course, sometimes this just isn't possible: occasionally, to develop a complex argument you can't avoid using a complex sentence structure. But if this is the case, beware of the dangers and do all you can to make sure the sentence can be negotiated easily, without any danger of confusion, by using logical indicators and the signposts of punctuation to indicate the structure. Indeed, as you grow in confidence you will probably want to achieve more than this with your punctuation – it will certainly pay dividends. Experiment using the rhythm of your words and punctuation to convey the meaning. The 'white space' you create through your use of dashes, colons, semicolons, full-stops (periods) and commas helps to create a rhythm that is nearer to the spoken word. And the nearer you approach this the easier it is to understand what you've written.

In much the same way you can experiment using different lengths for your sentences to achieve different effects. Although shorter sentences are easier to follow, it's not necessary to make every sentence the same length. If your ideas are well thought out and organised logically – which they will be if you've planned your essay – your sentences will have a rhythm of their own. But remember, longer sentences tend to be soothing, whereas shorter sentences tend to be abrupt. So, if you want to get your point across in a way that makes the reader really think about it carefully, use a shorter sentence, particularly after developing an argument with a series of longer sentences. But don't overdo it – it easily devalues.

Logical indicators

As to the second point – the importance of logical indicators – the problem is not just that we fail to use them, believing that the reader can follow our train of thought without difficulty, but that they get lost in our sentences. When you read your work through, check that the logic is clear. If it isn't, try moving your logical indicator to a more important position in the sentence, say to the beginning. In the revision stage, if you find it still doesn't read logically and smoothly, read it out aloud, record it and play it back to yourself, or get someone else to read it to you. You'll soon recognise the abrupt transitions, the lost or missing words, and all the other problems that keep your writing from being talk in print.

In a nutshell

- Aim to create writing that is talk in print.
- Don't lose the reader in long sentences.
- Wherever possible use short sentences with clear structures.
- Experiment with your punctuation, words and sentence length to create the rhythm of talk in print.
- Make sure your logical indicators don't go missing.
- Read it aloud to make sure it reads logically and smoothly.

Practice exercise 18
Sentences

Read the following passage. At times you will find it difficult to understand its meaning exactly. Sentences tend to be long and confused, the punctuation is not as helpful as it could be, and logical indicators tend to go missing.

Without actually rewriting the passage, by just attending to the sentence length, punctuation and logical indicators, make the passage more readable, more like talk in print.

When you've completed this, compare your version with the answer given below.

Passage

Peeling the Onion – Art in Western Liberal Democracies

The problem for liberal democracies is that they have an inveterate habit of dissipating the social context that seems so important if art is to flourish. They break down the interpersonal, isolating each individual both from one another and from society. In such societies art must out of necessity turn away from public themes towards private pursuits and preoccupations the exploration of emotions, the glorification of sex, even the invocation of death.

In these individualised cultures talk of uncovering our essential selves has become the orthodoxy of the age our struggle for self-fulfilment has led us to believe in a form of essentialism that there lies a hard core of reality within all of us if we can only strip away the successive layers of misleading appearance and reveal it. Psychoanalysts seem to regard the self as an entity that is always striving for self-realisation and fulfilment – an essential nature bursting to get out.

Our easy acceptance of these assumptions conceals two serious problems. Talk about revealing our essential selves might in fact be quite meaningless like stripping away each successive layer of an onion, we might find at the end we're left with nothing at all. If this turns out to be the case, we will then be forced to accept the challenge that we are only what we make ourselves in the world as we find it.

The second problem, however, is even more worrying it strikes at the very viability of art in these individualised cultures. We talk of self-realisation as if it is the common-sense rationalisation of every artist struggling for self-expression. In effect, it leaves the artist cowering from the real world, sheltered within the safe, though barren confines of solipsism. If we believe that all we can ever really know is our inner personal states, then the outside world can only ever be a product of our own consciousness. This is incompatible with a language to express it, whether in music, painting or literature.

In effect it can only be expressed through a private language, the terms of which are defined by reference to our private sensations and whose meaning can only be known to us. As Wittgenstein points out in *Philosophical Investigations*, such a language is not logically possible, because a language is designed to communicate with others, and this requires commonly accepted rules. In a private language, where whatever seems right can only be decided by referring to the exclusive personal states of the user, there can be no such rules.

Despite its internal coherence any art built upon exclusively personal experience is in danger of having no anchor in a common shared reality its flotilla of symbols adrift with no charts. The modern liberal artist is left with the problem of trying to communicate what being alive is like without the assurance of a common social frame of reference without an identity etched in the complex interactions of social relations of family, friends and acquaintances, he is left with just his abstract humanity known only to himself.

Answer

Peeling the Onion – Art in Western Liberal Democracies

The problem for liberal democracies is that they have an inveterate habit of dissipating the social context that seems so important if art is to flourish. They break down the interpersonal, isolating each individual both from one another and from society. Consequently, in such societies art must, out of necessity, turn away from public themes towards private pursuits and preoccupations: the exploration of emotions, the glorification of sex, even the invocation of death.

As a result, in these individualised cultures talk of uncovering our essential selves has become the orthodoxy of the age. Our struggle for self-fulfilment has led us to believe in a form of essentialism, that there lies a hard core of reality within all of us, if we can only strip away the successive layers of misleading appearance and reveal it. Psychoanalysts seem to regard the self as an entity that is always striving for self-realisation and fulfilment – an essential nature bursting to get out.

But our easy acceptance of these assumptions conceals two serious problems. First, talk about revealing our essential selves might in fact be quite meaningless. Like stripping away each successive layer of an onion, we might find at the end we're left with nothing at all. If this turns out to be the case, we will then be forced to accept the challenge that we are only what we make ourselves in the world as we find it.

The second problem, however, is even more worrying: it strikes at the very viability of art in these individualised cultures. We talk of self-realisation as if it is the common-sense rationalisation of every artist struggling for self-expression. Yet, in effect, it leaves the artist cowering from the real world, sheltered within the safe, though barren confines of solipsism. If we believe that all we can ever really know is our inner personal states, then the outside world can only ever be a product of our own consciousness. But this is incompatible with a language to express it, whether in music, painting or literature.

In effect it can only be expressed through a private language, the terms of which are defined by reference to our private sensations and whose meaning, therefore, can only be known to us. But, as Wittgenstein points out in *Philosophical Investigations*, such a language is not logically possible, because a language is designed to communicate with others, and this requires commonly accepted rules. In a private language, where whatever seems right can only be decided by referring to the exclusive personal states of the user, there can be no such rules.

Despite its internal coherence any art built upon exclusively personal experience is in danger of having no anchor in a common shared reality, its flotilla of symbols adrift with no charts. The modern liberal artist is left with the problem of trying to communicate what being alive is like without the assurance of a common social frame of reference. Without an identity etched in the complex interactions of social relations of family, friends and acquaintances, he is left with just his abstract humanity known only to himself.

▶ Words

The same problems that make sentences difficult reappear in our use of words. We believe that as we advance to higher levels of learning we will need to use more complex, even abstruse, language. And it's true that as we graduate from one level to another we will be expected to use and explore more complex ideas and concepts, and these will demand a more subtle use of language and a more careful and deliberate choice of words and phrases. Clearly, words like 'nice', 'good' and 'bad' are inadequate vehicles for conveying subtle distinctions and for all but the crudest of meanings. But this doesn't mean that we're driven to using a plethora of multi-syllabled words or the most convoluted sentences that conceal more than they reveal.

This can give rise to all sorts of problems, not least the use of jargon and other words that are empty of real meaning. The following sentences illustrate this. The first is taken from a student's essay, and the second, ironically, is drawn from material for a course on talking and writing.

> Negative feedback brings about an opposite action as a consequence of having sampled the output through the feedback loop.

> Concepts and the language that infuses and implements them give power and strategy to cognitive activity.

You can probably glean some sense from these sentences, but there will be few of us who don't have some problem unwrapping their meaning. They both suffer from the use of jargon, which has been substituted for genuine, explicable thought. In fact in most cases when we're confronted by jargon it's not surprising we fail to see the meaning clearly, because the truth is it's not there to start with.

And, even when there is meaning, the jargon only serves to obscure it. In these sentences, phrases such as 'negative feedback' and 'feedback loop', and words that are used vaguely, such as 'infuses', 'power' and 'strategy', are all substitutes for genuine thought. The authors have evaded the responsibility to think clearly about the subject, choosing instead to rely upon jargon to convey what meaning there is.

This underlines what we've emphasised in previous sections, that clear and effective writing depends upon clear and effective thinking. Language is the vehicle for your ideas: if your ideas themselves are muddled and confused, then so too will be your language and style. This brings us back to the interpretation and planning of the essay. Now that you've done these successfully, you're better placed to make clearer demands upon your style, and this is more likely to result in clarity and precision in your use of language.

Choosing the right words

Nevertheless, that's still only half of the problem. Now that you've got the inside clear, your ideas, you need to be clear about the outside, your words. As you search for the right word, don't settle for something that doesn't capture your specific idea accurately. Of course, you don't want to interrupt your flow of ideas and words, and you can leave much of this tidying up to the revision stage, but you will need to get close enough to your idea to recall exactly what you were trying to say, when you come to revise.

So, when you find yourself using the familiar generality that approximates roughly to what you want to say, stop and search for a word that is more accurate and specific. Otherwise your readers will conclude that you simply haven't got the intellectual determination to pin your ideas down precisely or, worse still, that you have few interesting ideas of your own. Either way, they're likely to assume that the vague sweeping generalities you've used mean one thing, when you really mean another.

If you were to claim, for example, that 'Modern business methods are destroying communities and exploiting the poor', this could mean a number of different things to different people. To pin down exactly what you want to say you would have to be more specific. What methods in particular? In what way are they destroying communities? And what specific groups are being exploited? Without this your readers might broadly agree with you, but place little significance in what you're saying.

Clichés

And, what's more, the benefits of striving for greater clarity and precision in your use of language don't end there. The more you force yourself to search for a word that is the perfect vehicle for your idea, the more you will have to draw on in the future. As a result, you'll be less likely to fall back on the familiar, reassuring, although empty, cliché. Like jargon, clichés are often a sign that you haven't pinned your idea down accurately, or that you haven't searched thoroughly for the exact word that will carry your idea perfectly.

Yet, as most of us know, it's not always easy to avoid clichés. Indeed, it may not always be wise to. Cutting out all the clichés in your writing can often make your prose sound stiff and cumbersome. A familiar cliché conveying just the right emphasis and meaning will help you produce prose that is nearer to talk in print, with a natural rhythm that's not strained and difficult to read.

Unfortunately, all too often the impact is quite the reverse. An empty cliché, that does no real work beyond sounding cosy and familiar, can sap our writing of its life and vigour. If you want your ideas to have impact and your readers to appreciate that you really do have interesting and original ideas, then avoid any word or phrase that doesn't do justice to your ideas, and this includes clichés.

So ask yourself, when a cliché comes to you in the middle of a passage, does this convey what I want it to, or is this familiar phrase encouraging me to adopt a thought structure that I didn't want? And, of equal importance, will it lead my readers gently down a familiar path which I didn't really want them to go down? Like everything else in your writing, if you use a cliché, mean to do it: have a clear reason, a purpose, for doing so.

Assignment 10
Style

In the last assignment you wrote the introduction, the conclusion and the first two paragraphs that followed the introduction to the essay you've chosen to work on. In this assignment write the next three paragraphs, that follow on from the two you wrote for the last assignment.

Make sure that the structures of your sentences are clear and your words convey your meaning accurately.

After it's written, read it over to yourself aloud or get someone else to read it to you. As you listen to it search for two things: first, any passage where the rhythm is clumsy and it's not possible to read it fluently; and secondly, where logical indicators go missing, making it difficult to decipher your meaning.

▶ In the next chapter

Once you've completed this assignment you will be more aware of just how effective these techniques can be in making your writing lighter, more like talk in print. Writing lightly often means catching the rhythms of speech and, at times, this can be done just by shortening a sentence, or moving a logical indicator, or using your punctuation to make more white space.

In the next chapter we will consider the other element of style, economy. We will examine the various ways we can improve our style, giving our writing greater clarity through a more economical use of language.

Note

1 Matthew Arnold, quoted in G. W. E. Russell, *Collections and Recollections* (London, 1903), ch. 13.

28 Style – Economy

In this chapter you will learn:

- how to make sure your arguments are not obscured by superfluous words and phrases;
- a simple practical guide to improve your style;
- how to use the active voice wherever possible;
- how to avoid watering down your prose with too many adverbs, adjectives and prepositions.

▶ Improving the readability and impact of your writing

In the last section we examined the importance of simplicity in our writing, the first of the two elements of style. This brings us to the need for economy. Once you've thought your ideas through and planned them carefully, your major concern thereafter should be to express them clearly, concisely, with an economical use of words. In this lies the essence of what most of us understand by 'style' – what the Reverend Samuel Wesley once described as, 'the dress of thought; a modest dress, neat, but not gaudy'.[1]

Even so, many students still find it difficult to abandon the belief that somehow a good style is full of superfluous flourishes and filigrees of 'tasteful' affectation. Nothing could be further from the truth. As the Reverend Wesley rightly points out, a good writing style is elegant, but not ostentatious. Each component of a sentence should have a reason for being there: it should have a clearly defined function. There should be no wasted effort: no unnecessary words or phrases that obscure the meaning of the sentence. Otherwise the clarity of your thought will be lost, leaving the reader wondering what it all means.

Understandably, in the discussions we have with people in our normal lives we all use superfluous words and phrases that cloud and obscure the issues. This is often necessary to give us the thinking time we need to summon up our thoughts while we speak. Modern politicians, confronted by a throng of probing TV microphones and a posse of journalists, have long learnt how to buy themselves extra thinking time with wordy phrases, like 'this moment in time'. Now even sports people, pop stars, and managers of football teams have discovered how useful this can be. But at least they have some excuse in that they need to buy time to gather their thoughts. For the rest of us who can enjoy the luxury of careful, time-consuming thought as we write our essays, there is no excuse for phrases like 'most importantly of all' and 'in modern America of today'.

Knowing what to leave out

Along with simplicity, then, economy should be our paramount concern as we write. A. N. Whitehead described style as the ultimate morality of the mind. By this he implied that the mind should adjudicate rigorously on our use of words and our choice of phrases to ensure that each phrase has a well-defined function, that sentence structures are direct, and that words are chosen for their absolute economy of expression.

Indeed, knowing what to leave out is as important as knowing what to include. In effect, Whitehead's ultimate morality of the mind is the art of knowing what not to do. Therefore, if clauses and phrases can be summed up in a word, replace them. You'll be surprised by the effect. It's worth having a sign on your computer screen or a notice pinned over your desk reminding you constantly that the readability of your work increases in proportion to the unnecessary words you eliminate.

But this is not the only bonus that comes from economising. Equally important, the really significant words will no longer be smothered, and your points and arguments will no longer be obscured by unnecessary words and phrases. They'll stand out more, and they'll have impact to make the reader think and wonder. Take the following sentences, remove the unnecessary phrases and see the impact. The resulting sentences are sharper and more direct.

Advertisers will tell you, if you're thinking of making a purchase, what's good about their product, but omit the weaknesses.

Advertisers will tell you what's good about their product, but omit the weaknesses.

A report from a consumer association might heavily criticise a product for one reason or another, but if it contains just a single sentence of praise, this is likely to find its way into promotional literature.

A report from a consumer association might heavily criticise a product, but if it contains just a single sentence of praise, this is likely to find its way into promotional literature.

All this means that as you write you should constantly censor yourself and monitor your choice of words, asking yourself, 'Is this word or phrase necessary and does it convey my meaning exactly?' Although this is difficult at first, it will get easier. And you've always got the revision stage to come when you can clean up your work.

▶ Style in practical terms – the dos and don'ts

All of this makes sense in general terms – it gives us a clear idea of what we need to do throughout our work to avoid heavy, unreadable prose. But it still helps to have some simple practical rules by our side to help us produce work that is light, concise and interesting; work that grabs the reader's attention and keeps it to the end of the essay.

To help you do this, try using the following as a simple practical guide. It may not be possible to apply each rule all at once – you might need to concentrate on two or three of them, until they become established. Then you can move on to the others, until you're applying all of them in every piece of work. But you must try to keep your inner editor at bay as you write, so you can release your creativity. If you find the fluency of your writing begins to break up as you check on these things, remind yourself that you've still got the safety net of the revision stage.

▶ 1 Choose the short simple word over the long obscure one

If the short simple word carries the same meaning as the long obscure one, use it, otherwise you're in danger of producing prose that sounds unnecessarily pompous. But whatever word you choose, your primary concern should be to ensure the meaning is clear – avoid words that are vague, whether short, simple, long or obscure.

▶ 2 Use the active voice

Wherever possible use the active, rather than the passive voice. All too often the passive voice produces passive readers, who sleepwalk their way through your prose. The active voice is almost always clearer and more direct, so there's no need, as many students writing academic essays tend to believe, to convert every sentence into the passive form.

In the active form it's the doer of the action who is the subject of the sentence, rather than the receiver of the action, or the action itself, as in the passive form. For example,

Passive: The party was made more enjoyable by Rita's outrageous stories.

Active: Rita's outrageous stories made the party more enjoyable.

Passive: The blue getaway car was described by the bank clerk.

Active: The bank clerk described the blue getaway car.

Passive: An atmosphere of deep gloom is created by the novelist in the last paragraph of the chapter.

Active: The novelist creates an atmosphere of deep gloom in the last paragraph of the chapter.

Notice how the passive form is almost always less direct, positive and concise. For example, you might say,

My first car will never be forgotten by me.

But when you convert this into the active voice with the doer of the action the subject of the sentence, by being more direct it is more concise, and also more positive:

I will never forget my first car.

But that's not to say that the passive voice should never be used. There are times when what is done is more important than who did it. For example, the statement,

Professor Jenkins and Doctor Taylor of University College, London, last month achieved the most significant breakthrough yet in the treatment of colon cancer

would be better in the passive voice:

The most significant breakthrough yet in the treatment of colon cancer was achieved last month by Professor Jenkins and Doctor Taylor of University College, London

because the most important fact in the statement, what has been achieved, has been placed at the front of the sentence, and the doers at the back.

Practice exercise 19
Passive or Active?

Listed below you will find three pairs of statements. Rewrite each pair into a single sentence in either the active or the passive form. Choose which you think is the most appropriate in each case and then briefly give your reasons for your choices.

Once you've finished, compare your choices and the reasons you've given with those in the answer below.

Statements

1 Nigel Brown scored the goal.

   The decisive goal was scored in the last minute of the game.

2 Chief Justice Taylor was driving home.

   He was stopped by the police and found to be driving under the influence of alcohol.

3 John Douglas was stopped on his way home and robbed at knife point.

   He was robbed by a gang of eleven-year-olds.

Answers

1 Passive sentence: The decisive goal was scored in the last minute of the game by Nigel Brown.

Reason: The most interesting fact in these two statements is that the goal was scored in the last minute of the game.

2 Active sentence: While he was driving home Chief Justice Taylor was stopped by the police and found to be driving under the influence of alcohol.

Reason: The most interesting fact is not that someone was caught driving under the influence of alcohol, but that it was a prominent member of the judiciary.

3 Active sentence: A gang of eleven-year-olds stopped John Douglas on his way home and robbed him at knife point.

Reason: That he was robbed by a gang of eleven-year-olds is more interesting than the fact that he was robbed at knife point.

▶ 3 Rely on nouns and verbs to carry your meaning

Verbs

Wherever you can, try to build sentences around verbs that are specific and active. Weak verbs have to be shored up by adverbs and adverbial phrases, that can water down the image. But beware of your choice of verb: don't overstate the case by choosing one that is too strong.

In the following sentences, by replacing the weak verb and its adverb with a stronger verb, the sentence is made sharper and its meaning clearer.

Yet we still might be right in thinking suspiciously that behind all this information lies a covert message.

Yet we still might be right in suspecting that behind all this information lies a covert message.

Our desire for status and our respect for authority has given advertisers an effective way of deceptively taking advantage of our feelings to promote all manner of products.

Our desire for status and our respect for authority has given advertisers an effective way of exploiting our feelings to promote all manner of products.

Nouns

In the same way, make sure the nouns you use are specific and definite, not general. They must produce a clear image. Like the use of adverbs, if you have to use adjectives to shore up your noun, modifying or qualifying it, you've probably chosen the wrong one in the first place. The danger is your meaning will lose impact, or will be difficult to see, beneath the camouflage of adjectives and adjectival phrases.

In the following sentences, by replacing the noun and its adjective with a single noun that is more specific, a clearer image is produced, one which carries much more meaning.

By appealing to their strong tastes advertisers successfully by-pass the consumer's capacity to make rational choices.

By appealing to their passions advertisers successfully by-pass the consumer's capacity to make rational choices.

It's not just tastes that you're discussing, but passions – a particular type of taste which is much stronger than all the rest, at times even irresistible.

They may give us information on the latest technology, but they are also covertly suggesting that we can't afford not to keep up with the latest developments.

They may give us information on the latest technology, but they are also covertly suggesting that we can't afford not to keep up with progress.

It's not just the latest developments, but the whole idea of progress and whether this is necessarily a good thing.

► 4 Replace prepositional phrases with prepositions

Like adverbs and adjectives, too many prepositional phrases water down your prose and obscure your meaning. Many of these we use in our normal speech simply because they give us more thinking time. But if you use them in your writing they will clutter up your prose and give the reader a bumpy, uncomfortable ride through your arguments and explanations. This will make it difficult for your reader to understand your meaning.

Therefore, wherever possible replace the prepositional phrase with a simple preposition. For example,

replace 'with regard to' with 'about',
'for the simple reason' with 'because', and
'on the part of' with 'by'.

This is not to say that such phrases are always inappropriate, but you should pose yourself the question, 'Can I replace these with a simpler preposition without any loss of meaning?' If you can, do it!

You will also find, particularly in the revision stage, that it helps to collect prepositional phrases in your notebook. When we're asked to produce them, most of us are hard pressed to think of one. It helps, then, to list them in your notebook as you come across them in your reading, so you know what you're looking for when you come to revise.

► 5 Create fluency through transitions

In Stage 3 (Planning) we discussed the importance of transitions in creating fluency between paragraphs, thereby giving your essay the coherence and continuity it must have to achieve a high grade. They are also important as a means of giving your readers the literal signposts they need to negotiate your essay successfully without getting lost.

As you come across transitions in your reading, note how other writers link their paragraphs, perhaps even keeping a record in your notebook so you can use them yourself. Below is a list of the most common linking words and phrases that are useful as transitions:

But, However, On the other hand, Yet . . .	indicating contrast
For example, That is . . .	indicating illustration
Similarly, Moreover, Furthermore,	
In addition, By extension, What is more . . .	indicating extension
Therefore, Consequently,	
As a result, Thus . . .	indicating conclusion
Then, After that, It follows . . .	indicating the next step

Others you'll find useful include 'likewise', 'correspondingly', 'hence', 'accordingly', 'nevertheless', 'incidentally', 'otherwise', 'nonetheless', 'obviously'.

Compound transitions

The more you look for transitions to record in your notebook the more compound transitions you will come across. As the name implies, they are made up from one or more words or transitions. There is, therefore, almost an inexhaustible variety of them, indeed you can make up your own as easily as you can collect them. Their value lies in giving you a much wider range of transitions to choose from, allowing you to navigate exactly the right passage through your arguments with just the right changes in emphasis and direction to reflect all the subtleties of your arguments. The list below is broken up into the more obvious changes you're likely to use in your arguments.

Conjunction	And, moreover, – And although – And in one respect – And once – And so – And while some – And as it is
Extension	So, even though – It follows then – In this way – From that angle – By the same token – On that account – Given this
Endorsement	Not surprisingly – Of course – And moreover – Most important of all – Even more – In particular
Contrast	But instead – But at the same time – And yet – But even – But then again – But perhaps – Yet still – But while
Narrative	Following this – And after that – But then – So began – But so far – More recently

▶ **In the next chapter**

The final two rules in our practical guide concern our use of evidence. In the next chapter you will learn how to use evidence to change the pace of your writing and engage your readers in your arguments. You will see how your use of evidence not only supports and illustrates your arguments, but makes your work more interesting and persuasive.

Note

1 Revd Samuel Wesley, *An Epistle to a Friend concerning Poetry* (London, 1700).

29 Working with Evidence

In this chapter you will learn:

- how to use the different types of evidence to support your arguments effectively;
- how to make your work more readable by varying the type of evidence you use;
- how to make the seven practical rules part of your writing strategy.

The last two of our seven practical rules for improving our style are concerned with the way we use evidence. Without doubt this is one of the most neglected aspects of our writing. We tend to assume that all we have to do is select our evidence and then insert it into our essay when our arguments need support.

Yet the evidence we use serves to do much more than just support and illustrate our arguments. Used thoughtfully, it can help us change the pace of our writing, making our essay more readable. And there is no other component of our essays that can so effectively engage our readers' empathetic responses. You will find, then, that by looking carefully at the way you use evidence not only can you make your work more interesting, but you can give it real impact.

▶ 6 Don't overstate or understate: match your words to the strength of the evidence

Choose your words consciously and deliberately to convey accurately the strength of your ideas and the evidence that supports them. Often, when we fail to think through our ideas with sufficient care, we're inclined to see issues in the form of simple absolutes: all/nothing, right/wrong, yes/no. But rarely is there sufficient evidence to support such claims.

There are, of course, categories of sentences in which you can use words like 'all', but they're more restricted than we generally acknowledge. Either they're sentences describing a particular known group of things: 'all of my friends', or 'all of the coins in my pocket', or they're trivially true, that is they're true *a priori*, by virtue of the meaning of their constituent parts.

For example, it would be quite correct to say that 'All bachelors are unmarried men, ' or that 'All cats are animals,' or that 'All bicycles have two wheels,' because this is what we mean by these terms. These sentences are true by virtue of what we agree to put into them in the first place. The fact that we agree the word 'bachelor' shall mean 'male' and 'unmarried', makes the sentence true. In the same way, when we unwrap the meaning of other words like 'cat' or 'bicycle', we find that their meaning too links two or more characteristics in 'all' cases.

Beyond these 'analytic' truths, we're faced with the problem of using simple absolutes, like 'all', in empirical propositions, that is propositions that go beyond the meaning of the terms they use, to make statements about the real world. As we've already seen, it's safe to use words like 'all' in sentences that make a claim about a particular known group of things, like your friends or the coins in your pocket. So you could safely say that 'All the people in this room are male', or 'All the members of the party voted for Mr X as their candidate', because the evidence for these claims is easy to verify.

But most of the claims we make are not like this: they involve an element of judgement on our part; they cannot be verified either by demonstrable fact or by analysis of the meaning of their constituent parts. They're claims like 'Nobody believes it's right to kill dolphins,' 'Everybody agrees that terrorists should receive capital punishment,' or 'At no time over the last seventy years has anybody seriously doubted the value of the automobile.' Each of these claims is too strong for the evidence we have, or even could have. You need find only one person who believes dolphins should be killed, or that terrorists should be sentenced to life imprisonment, or that the automobile has damaged the quality of our lives, to have disproved them.

Another sign worth sticking to your computer screen or pinning above your desk might read:

> **The more difficult I make it for the examiner to dismiss my arguments, the higher my marks.**

Clearly, then, you must make every effort to match the strength of your statements to the strength of your evidence, using words like 'much', 'many', 'some', 'frequently'. In this way you avoid the risk of overstatement, which will weaken your arguments and lead the examiner to dismiss them for lack of sufficient evidence.

You can do this in three ways in descending order of evidential strength.

6.1 Hard evidence

This is the strongest form of evidence, which includes statistics, examples, quotations, even anecdotes. Obviously, wherever possible use this form of evidence to support your arguments. Although readers can challenge your judgements and the interpretation you place on this evidence, they cannot criticise you for dispensing mere opinion. The hard evidence you use shows that there are serious grounds for someone to consider the arguments and points you've developed.

6.2 Explication

However, often it's simply not possible to support an argument with the sort of hard evidence it needs. Nevertheless, you may still believe it's a valuable argument to develop, one that most people will accept for good reasons. It may not even be possible to gather any evidence of any kind to support it: it's just that most of us accept that it's reasonable to believe that this is the case. Of course, common opinion is not always common-sense, but in these cases it is more a question of what makes *reasonable* sense.

For example, you might claim that most people believe that tobacco companies should not target their products at children. Now there may be no hard evidence for this claim: there may have been no surveys ever done, or government statistics issued about what people believe. Yet it's obvious you're probably right. All you can do, therefore, is to reveal the reasonableness of this claim through careful explication of your argument. In this way you show that your assumptions are reasonable, that they're based on common-sense, and there are no flaws in your arguments.

In our claim about tobacco companies, for example, we might argue that most people are aware of the long-term health problems that smoking creates; that children are not in a position to evaluate all the information and make a free and informed choice; and that once hooked at an early age most smokers find it difficult to quit and, therefore, end up suffering from these health problems, some of which may be terminal. Given all this, it now seems a reasonable claim to make. It's founded on a common-sense understanding that you share with others, including the reader, and you've demonstrated that the case is argued consistently.

6.3 Report

However, if you lack hard evidence, or you're in a timed exam and you can't remember any, and you don't feel confident enough to argue for the reasonableness of your case, then you're left with only one alternative: shift the weight of responsibility from your shoulders onto someone else's. You do this by attributing the view to some named authority or, if you can't remember who advocated the view, to some impersonal authority, like 'many believe. . . .', 'some people claim. . . .', 'it is argued. . . .' and so on.

Clearly this is the weakest form of support for your argument and, although it can be useful under timed conditions, you must be aware of the degree to which it weakens your argument. Hard evidence and explication will earn higher marks, because, as you take on the responsibility of defending the argument as your own, you are obliged to use the abilities in the higher cognitive domains to argue and justify it with evidence of the appropriate quality and strength.

In contrast, by shifting the responsibility to others you merely exercise abilities in the lower cognitive domains: you're merely recalling and describing a case developed by somebody else. Nevertheless, without this, without any attempt to support your argument, it will be dismissed as merely a statement of opinions, of no particular value, beyond the fact that you can remember it. And, as we said before, anyone can express opinions.

Practice exercise 20
Explication

Listed below you will see three statements. Give three or four reasons why you think these might be reasonable statements to make. Most of us believe these statements are reasonable, but, if you don't, set aside your doubts and give the sort of justification that you think someone would give who does in fact believe them.

Compare your reasons with those listed in the answer that follows.

Statements

1 Most people believe we're right to try to protect the environment.

2 Most of us are opposed to the systematic use of very young children in the labour force.

3 Most of us accept that we should not be cruel to animals.

Reasons

1 The environment.

Because of:

1.1 the increasing levels of pollution;
1.2 the rise in the incidence of health problems related to environmental pollution, e.g. asthma;
1.3 the depletion of resources, like rainforests;
1.4 the damage to the ozone layer and the related increase in skin cancer;
1.5 the effect of changes in the ecological system, e.g. the changes in weather patterns supposedly as a result of the 'greenhouse effect';
1.6 endangered species whose habitats are disappearing.

2 Child labour.

Because:

2.1 children should be in education;
2.2 children are easily exploited;
2.3 they should have a childhood, rather than be forced into the adult world too early;
2.4 they are likely to work in dangerous and unhealthy conditions;
2.5 in some circumstances they will take work away from adult workers who need it to support their families.

3 Animals.

Because:

3.1 we believe we have a moral responsibility to try to maximise the well-being of all, not just promote our own self-interests;
3.2 this involves the moral obligation to minimise all unnecessary suffering;

3.3 all sentient beings – including animals – have a capacity to suffer as a result of physical pain, and emotional and psychological distress.

▶ 7 Know how much evidence to use

In view of what we've just said, the standard advice to novelists applies equally to those of us who write essays – wherever possible *show*, rather than *tell*. Don't just state something is the case, demonstrate it with evidence. It's worth reminding yourself that you're not just describing an event, just explaining *what* happened; you're explaining *why* it happened – you're giving reasons that will, hopefully, convince the reader that you're right.

Equally important, this has a significant bearing on the second of our guiding principles – interest. Quotations, statistics, anecdotes, all make your work more readable. Not only do they break it up with changes of pace and content, but they allow the subjects to speak for themselves. Your readers can then respond empathetically, and with their emotions and feelings engaged in your work this can lend untold support to your arguments.

But make sure the evidence you use has a point: that it is related to and reinforces your arguments. Any quotations, statistics or anecdotes you use must do real work. You may like a quotation for the impact you know it will have on the reader, or an anecdote for its pathos or poignancy, but if it doesn't reinforce a point or advance your argument, drop it. You'll always find a use for it later.

And don't overdo it with evidence. There's always the danger that you just might bury your readers under information, making it impossible for them to take on board everything you want them to, thereby wasting a lot of the good evidence you've dug up. If you pile one unrelated piece of information on another, your readers will have no means of dealing with it successfully. They will lose themselves and, in turn, you will lose marks. Whereas if you strip out all the unnecessary information, what remains will stand out and will have more impact.

As we've seen a number of times already, the key to this is structure. If your readers are clear what part the information plays in the overall scheme of things, they can process it successfully and put it in its appropriate place. But if the structure's weak, they'll have to re-read it to make sure they've understood it, or, if they're not so scrupulous, they'll just miss much of what you're saying. The key to this, then, is to create a clear structure within which you use only those facts, quotations and statistics that do real work, and write them out as succinctly as possible.

In a nutshell

- Show rather than tell.
- Make your work more readable by varying the type of evidence you use.
- Make sure your evidence does real work.
- Try not to bury your reader under an avalanche of information.
- Create a clear structure for your evidence so your reader knows how to process it.

▶ Using the seven practical rules

All of this is a great deal to remember, particularly while you're writing. So don't, if it interrupts your creative flow. Just start by reminding yourself of two or three of the rules as you write. Eventually, with these well under your control, you can move on to the rest. And you've always got the revision stage after this to clean up your work. Indeed, you'll find as you revise one essay after another, all seven rules will gradually filter through into your writing. This is not to say you shouldn't bother to remind yourself that the active voice is better than the passive, or that nouns should be specific and definite, not general. If you can do this without interrupting your flow, then do it.

Assignment   11
Style

In this assignment finish writing the remaining paragraphs of the essay you've chosen to work on. Before you start, remind yourself of the seven practical rules we've outlined in this section. However, write as freely as possible: don't let your editor in to disrupt the flow of your ideas.

Once you've finished, put them aside for a day or so, then read them through to check how well you've done with the seven practical rules. For this exercise you're not actually revising them, but you should go through each rule to see if you could have done better.

▶ In the next chapter

Now that you've finished writing your essay, before you put it aside until you're ready for revision, you need to deal with all the material that you've borrowed from the texts you've used. In the next chapter you will be shown how to avoid the problems of plagiarism and how to decide when you need to cite your sources.

30 Plagiarism

In this chapter you will learn:

- about the dangers of plagiarism and how to avoid them;
- how to decide when you need to cite sources and when you don't need to – the six-point code;
- how to organise yourself to lessen the chances of plagiarism.

By definition the research we undertake to write an essay involves us in borrowing material in one form or another. So, before we pack away our notes, relieved that we've done most of the hard work, we need to remind ourselves that we have certain ethical responsibilities to meet. We have an obligation to acknowledge all those who have helped us by giving us material in the form of ideas, quotations, figures and anecdotes. Failure to do this will mean we have committed just about the worst form of academic dishonesty.

▶ What is plagiarism exactly?

There can't be many students at universities who are unaware of the meaning of this. But still there are things we do that we don't always recognise as plagiarism.[1] Therefore, we ought to have a clear idea of the various activities this includes. In its simplest form it is the attempt to present someone else's ideas or arguments as your own. This might be using an idea you've read in one of your sources without acknowledging it, copying paragraphs directly into your own work without quotation marks or a reference, or just quoting from a paper without quotation marks, even though you may have cited the paper appropriately elsewhere. In effect it involves any activity which amounts to you taking credit for work that is someone else's.

Fortunately, most examples of plagiarism are not deliberate. Some students are just unaware of the rules of acknowledgement. Others fail to organise their work well enough, so that when they come to research their essays, they take their notes in a rushed and careless manner. As a result they blend their own ideas with those they take from the texts they use. They fail to put these ideas into their own words, so that the paraphrases and summaries that find their way into their essay are not sufficiently different from the original.

The problem is, as we saw in Chapter 10, that the solution can be almost as harmful in its impact on a student's work as plagiarism itself. In other words, we come to believe that the only way to avoid plagiarism is to give a reference for every idea not only quoted or paraphrased, but borrowed in any possible way. This gives us the impression that there is nothing new in education and our role is just to recycle received opinion. In this way, by demonstrating that our ideas are not original, we hope to make them invulnerable: as they have been thought by others, their authority gives our arguments the protection we cannot. Education, then, appears to be more concerned with *what* we think, than with *how* we think.

Even so, there are other sources of advice, more tolerant of our own ideas, and in this we begin to see the depth and complexity of the problem. The *Greats Handbook* at Oxford advises students: 'The examiners are looking for your own ideas and convictions, and you mustn't be shy of presenting them as your own: whether you are conscious of having inherited them from somebody else doesn't matter one way or the other.'[2]

▶ So, where should you draw the line?

It's simply not enough to tell students, as one university does, that they must use references whenever 'the knowledge you are expressing is not your own original thought'.[3] This would mean that you are left giving references for just about all the ideas you will ever use. You've probably used words like 'gravity' or 'ideology' many times before, but they are not your original thoughts. Does this mean you must provide a reference from Newton's *Principia* or Marx's *The German Ideology*, respectively, each time you use them? You may know that the distance from London to Edinburgh is 378 miles or that Jupiter has 16 moons, but you have never measured or counted them yourself, so should you give the reference to the person who has, each time you use this information? Of course not. So where should you draw the line?

With specific information or data, in the form of facts, statistics, tables and diagrams, it's easier to decide. You will have found them in a specific publication, which you will need to cite, so your reader will know who gathered the information and where to find it. The same applies to any information, or set of ideas, that have been organised in a distinctive way. The information may have been known to you, but you have never seen it presented in this form or argued in this way. And in this lies the crucial principle:

> Whenever the author has given something distinctive to the information or its organisation, cite the source.

In citing the source you are acknowledging the author's distinctive contribution. By the same token, this applies to a phrase or passage that you use verbatim. It has its own distinctive form that you must acknowledge. This is true even of a single word, if this is distinctive to the author's argument.

▶ Common knowledge

But with most ideas and thoughts the situation isn't so clear cut. There may be nothing distinctive about them or their organisation. So you may believe quite reasonably that, although you got the ideas from a source you've read, you can use them without acknowledgement.

One justification for this is that all knowledge in the public domain, all 'common knowledge', need not be referenced. But this seems to do little more than give the problem a different name. So, what is 'common knowledge'? This brings us back to our original distinction. Common knowledge is all those facts, ideas and opinions that are not distinctive of a particular author or a matter of interpretation. They may be familiar ideas or just easily found in a number of common reference works, like dictionaries, basic textbooks, encyclopaedias, or yearbooks.

For example, you need not give a reference for the fact that the French Revolution began in July 1789, but you would have to for a particular historian's account of the causes of it. You might not need a reference if you were to explain that the Wannsee Conference in January 1942 cleared the last obstacles for the application of the Nazis' Final Solution to the whole of Europe, but you would need evidence and references if you were to make the unfamiliar claim that Hitler knew nothing about it.

It wouldn't even be necessary to give a reference for a distinctive contribution made by someone in a particular discipline, if this is well-known within that discipline. In politics or sociology, for example, it wouldn't be necessary to give a reference for Marx's concept of 'alienation', or in philosophy for Kant's 'categorical imperative', but if you were to refer to an author's particular interpretation of either, this would need a reference.

Take the word 'paradigm', meaning a dominant theory in an area of study, which sets the conceptual framework within which a science is taught and scientists conduct research. It was first used in this sense by T. S. Kuhn in his seminal work, *The Structure of Scientific Revolutions* (1962). Today the term has spread throughout the social sciences and philosophy. But in none of these areas would you be expected to cite the reference to Kuhn, if you were to use the term; so common has it become within each of these disciplines.

Other types of common knowledge come in the form of common or familiar opinion. It may seem to you undeniable that the vast majority of your fellow citizens are in favour of staging the next Olympic Games or the World Cup in your country, but no survey may ever have been done or referendum held. Similarly, it might generally be held that the elderly should receive special treatment, like free bus passes and medical help. In appealing to such common knowledge you would have to judge how familiar it was. The rule is, 'if in doubt, cite'.

▶ The six-point code

To make it easier for you to decide exactly when you need to cite, use the following simple six-point code. This is another of those notes worth sticking to the side of your computer screen or pinning to the notice-board above your desk. Wherever you keep it, make sure it's just a glance away.

When to cite

1 **Distinctive ideas**   Whenever the ideas or opinions are distinctive to one particular source.

2 **Distinctive structure or organising strategy**   Even though you may have put it into your own words, if the author has adopted a particular method of approaching a problem, or there is a distinctive intellectual structure to what's written, for example to an argument or to the analysis of a concept, then you must cite the source.

3 **Information or data from a particular source**   If you've gathered information from a source in the form of facts, statistics, tables and diagrams, you will need to cite the source, so your readers will know who gathered the information and where to find it.

4 **Verbatim phrase or passage**   Even a single word, if it is distinctive to your author's argument. You must use quotation marks and cite the source.

5 **If it's not common knowledge**   Whenever you mention some aspect of another person's work, unless the information or opinion is widely known, you must cite the source, so your readers can follow it up.

6 **Whenever in doubt, cite it!**   It will do no harm, as long as you're not citing just to impress the examiner in the mistaken belief that getting good grades depends upon trading facts, in this case references, for marks.

▶ Minimising the chance of an oversight

Nevertheless, even with this simple code and every good intention, there is always the possibility that you just might overlook the need to cite a source. Most examples of plagiarism are probably accidental oversights of this kind. The solution, for the most part, can be found in what we've said in previous chapters.

It's more than likely that most of these oversights come about through poor organisation. If we start working on our essay just days before it is due to be handed in, we're likely to cut corners as we take notes and gather our material. At this point it's all too easy to blend the author's ideas in with our own, thereby overlooking the need to cite the source. Organising our time, as we did in Chapters 17 and 18, is the most effective way of minimising this danger.

But there are other things we can do, too. In Chapter 12 we examined the importance of actively processing the ideas we read and note, not only taking out structures, but criticising and evaluating the ideas we read. This, too, can minimise the chances of an oversight. Not only does it reduce the amount you're likely to borrow, but more important, you will integrate the ideas into your own thinking, imposing your own distinctive organisation and structure on them.

However, as we saw in Stage 1, this, in turn, depends upon interpreting the question in the first place. Having analysed the implications of the question and revealed not only what you know, but the questions you want answered in the texts, you can avoid being dictated to by your authors. Armed with your own ideas, you're less likely to adopt their ideas wholesale.

Even so, as you note down material from your sources, you can still take simple, practical steps to avoid oversights. The most important of these is just to mark out clearly in your notes the ideas you borrow, to distinguish them from your own. For example, it will help if you can put the material you borrow from your sources in a different colour, if not on different sheets of paper, or even in different computer files.

For similar reasons, and to save you time when you come to search for the details of a reference, record at the top of the page the title of the text, the author's name, the page numbers and the date of publication. This will not only save you the nightmarish stress that comes from trying to track down a single reference to a quotation, or an idea, that you took down hastily, but it will also serve to remind you that you are working with a source. This is often all we need to take more care to separate our ideas from those of our source, and to record accurately what we borrow.

▶ In the next chapter

Now that you know how to avoid plagiarism and how to decide which of your sources you need to cite, you can turn to the techniques involved in citing your sources and compiling a bibliography and a reference list, both of which should enhance your essay for you and your reader.

Notes

1 One of the most useful and comprehensive accounts of referencing and plagiarism is Gordon Harvey, *Writing with Sources: A Guide for Harvard Students* (Cambridge, Mass., 1995). I am indebted to this for the more perceptive distinctions that follow.

   You can find it at: http//www.fas.harvard.edu/~expos/sources
2 *Greats Handbook* (Oxford: University of Oxford, 2000), p. 42.
3 Jan Regan, *Essay and Report Writing: What is Expected of You* (Lismore: Southern Cross University, 2000), p. 9.

31 Referencing and Bibliographies

In this chapter you will learn:

- the various ways of citing sources;
- how to create reference lists and useful bibliographies;
- how to acknowledge uncited sources.

Now that we've dealt with the most difficult judgements that we need to make in managing our sources, we're left with the simpler problems of how we cite each reference and list the details of each text we use.

▶ The different systems for citing[1]

There are a number of systems governing the way we cite references. All seem to insist on their own conventions with the strength of religious fervour. Some insist a comma be used in places where others use a semicolon. Many expect the date of publication to appear at different points and would be scandalised if it appeared elsewhere. So, check with your department to see if they have certain expectations, a system they would like you to use. You might refer to your course guide, or its equivalent. Failing that, ask your tutor.

Most tutors won't mind what system you use as long as it meets three cardinal objectives: it must be clear, accurate and consistent. Remind yourself why you're doing this: first, to give credit to the author for the original ideas; and secondly, to give your readers clear and sufficient detail for them to locate the exact reference for themselves.

▶ Footnote or endnote system

This is probably the most well-known system, certainly the most elegant. Each reference is cited in the text by a number, which refers to either a footnote at the bottom of the page, or a list of references at the end of your essay. Its main advantage, beyond its simplicity, is that it doesn't disrupt the text as much as other systems that enter the details of the reference in the actual text itself. These tend to clutter up the text, breaking the flow of ideas as you read. What's more, the footnote or endnote system has the advantage that most word-processing programs create and position footnotes or endnotes automatically for you.

Footnotes
When you write a footnote, it's usual to abbreviate authors and titles. In doing this you can choose from two alternative styles, but the same advice follows as before: choose one and stick to it – be consistent. You can either cite the full title on the first occasion you cite the work and then cite the abbreviated title each time after that, or you can adopt what's known as the Harvard, or the 'name–date', system. Using this, you cite in the note the author's name, the date of publication, and the relevant page. In both cases the full details of all the titles referred to would appear in the reference list and bibliography.

Abbreviation system
In this system the first reference to a book would appear as:

P. Rowe, *The Craft of the Sub-editor* (Cambridge, 1997), p. 37.

Later references to the same book could be abbreviated to:

Rowe, *The Craft*, pp. 102–3.

A reference to a journal article would appear as:

Brian T. Trainor, 'The State, Marriage and Divorce', *Journal of Applied Philosophy*, vol. 9, no. 2 (1992), p. 145.

A later reference to the same article could be abbreviated to:

Trainor, 'The State', *JAP*, pp. 138–9.

The Harvard system

Under this system the same references would appear as:

Rowe, 1997, p. 37.
Rowe, 1997, pp. 102–3.
Trainor, 1992, p. 145.
Trainor, 1992, pp. 138–9.

Endnotes

This is by far the simplest of the three systems. The numbers inserted into the text refer to a numbered reference list at the back of the essay. As with the footnotes system, repeated references to a text can be abbreviated, but in this case you use three well-known Latin abbreviations. When you first meet these they can seem arcane and forbidding, but use them once or twice and you will see how much time and effort they can save.

Say your first reference was as follows:

1. P. Rowe, *The Craft of the Sub-editor* (Cambridge, 1997), p. 37.

A number of references later you may want to refer to this text again. In this case you would use the Latin abbreviation 'op. cit.', meaning 'in the work cited', instead of repeating the detailed description of the text, which you've already given. Let's say it was the fifth reference on your list:

5. Rowe, op. cit., pp. 102–3.

If, in the next reference, you wanted to refer to the same text again, this time you would use another Latin reference, 'ibid.', meaning 'in the same place':

6. Ibid., p. 84.

If, then, in the next reference, you wanted to refer again to the same page of the same text, after 'ibid.' you would use the Latin abbreviation 'loc. cit.', meaning 'in the passage just quoted':

7. Ibid., loc. cit.

▶ In-text citing

Like the second form of footnotes, in-text citing uses the Harvard system, but puts the name of the author, the year of publication, and the page number in the actual text itself in parentheses, after the material you've borrowed. Then a list of these references appears at the end of the essay, where the full details of the texts to which these abbreviations refer, can be found.

On some occasions you may decide that the author's name will appear in the actual text with only the year of publication and the page number in brackets. The following examples illustrate the various ways this can be done.

> Perhaps artists need to feel politically motivated against oppressive regimes in order to etch their identity clearly against a social and political reality they deplore. In the words of Theodore Roethke, 'In a dark time, the eye begins to see' (1966, p. 239).

> Perhaps artists need to feel politically motivated against oppressive regimes in order to etch their identity clearly against a social and political reality they deplore. After all, 'In a dark time, the eye begins to see' (Roethke, 1966, p. 239).

> As Roethke (1966) points out, perhaps artists need to feel politically motivated against oppressive regimes in order to etch their identity clearly against a social and political reality they deplore. After all, 'In a dark time, the eye begins to see' (p. 239).

Paraphrasing

When you paraphrase an author's words, only the author and the year need to be included. For example:

> Certain diets that reduce the levels of serotonin in the brain appear to produce higher levels of aggression. Historically, periods of famine, and carbohydrate and protein malnutrition, have been associated with significant increases in crime and violence (Valzelli, 1981).

> Valzelli (1981) argues that those diets responsible for reducing the levels of serotonin in the brain appear to produce higher levels of

aggression. Historically, periods of famine, and carbohydrate and protein malnutrition, have been associated with significant increases in crime and violence.

If your material comes from more than one source by the same author

In this case arrange your sources chronologically, separated by a comma.

> Homelessness was shown to have increased as a result of the change in legislation and with the tighter monetary policy that doubled interest rates over a period of two years (Williams, 1991, 1994).

If the author has published more than one work in a single year, then cite them using a lower-case letter after the year of publication.

> Williams (1994a, 1994b) has shown that higher interest rates, while doing little to arrest the decline in value of the currency, have seriously damaged companies engaged in exports and increased the levels of home repossessions.

When a reference has more than one author

When it has two or three authors, give all the surnames, separated by commas with the last one separated by the word 'and'.

> Recent evidence has shown that cinema attendance in the 1950s declined less as a result of the impact of television, than through increasing affluence and mobility (Brown, Rowe and Woodward, 1996).

> Computer analysis has shown that the hundred most used words in the English language are all of Anglo-Saxon origin, even the first words spoken when man set foot on the moon in 1969 (Lacey and Danziger, 1999).

If there are more than three, cite them all the first time – for example: (Brown, Kirby, Rowe and Woodward, 1991) – but when you cite them again, use just the first name followed by 'et al.' (and all the others) – for example: (Brown et al., 1991).

When an author cites another author
In this case, if you want to use the comments of the cited author, then you acknowledge both authors, but only the author of the text in which you found the comments is listed in the reference list.

> In describing recent studies that tended to show that men become dangerous when their personal aggressiveness is unnaturally contained, Masters (1997, p. 37) cites a comment by Anthony Storr, who says, 'Aggression is liable to turn into dangerous violence when it is repressed or disowned.'

> Anthony Storr (cited in Masters, 1997, p. 37) argues that, 'The man who is able to assert himself in a socially acceptable fashion is seldom vicious; it is the weak who are most likely to stab one in the back.'

When a number of authors present the same idea
In this case arrange the authors in alphabetical order, separated by semi-colons.

> If a child does not receive love from its parents in the early years it will neither integrate their standards within its behaviour, nor develop any sense of moral conscience (Berkowitz, 1962; Farrington, 1978; Rutter, 1981; Storr, 1972).

▶ Acknowledging uncited sources

Before we finish with referencing, consider just one more source that might need acknowledging. At times some of our best ideas come from discussions we have with friends, colleagues and tutors. Many of these may just be informal occasions when an idea might fire your imagination, or you might try out an idea on a tutor, who shows you how to develop it further and in ways you hadn't even thought of. Alternatively, an idea might come from one isolated comment in a lecture, or an example that opens up possibilities you hadn't seen before. Or you may just get inspiration from a novel you may have read, or an article you might idly skim while you wait for someone.

All of these sources can play an important part in generating your ideas and giving them shape. So, if they have played a significant role, think about whether you need to acknowledge this. If the help is of a general nature, say the original insight that motivated your thinking in the first place, or an idea that revealed for you the way to tackle the problem raised by the essay, then you can place a reference number after the title or when you state the main idea. You can then pick this up at the bottom of the page or at the top of the list of endnotes with a few words acknowledging your debt. Alternatively, you may just be acknowledging the source of a particular point, one of many in your essay. In this case the note will appear in the middle of the sequence of footnotes or endnotes.

The following are examples of the sort of comments you might make, although there is almost no limit to the sort of help you might acknowledge.

I am particularly indebted to Dr David Dockrill for many of the ideas on transubstantiation in this section.

My understanding of intentionality is largely influenced by discussions I have had with Dr Joe Mintoff.

I have benefited from Dr John Wright's criticisms of the first draft of this passage.

I owe this example of the Prisoners' Dilemma to Prof. C. A. Hooker, who used it in his lectures on Commercial Values at the University of Newcastle in the first semester 2000.

▶ Bibliographies and reference lists

At the end of your essay it's usual to give both a bibliography and a reference list, although in some pieces of work you may just be asked for a reference list alone. This contains only those authors and works you've referred to in the essay, while a bibliography is a list of all the material you've consulted as background for the topic.

The latter can be very useful both to you and to your readers. Later you might want to check back on certain points or expand and develop some of your ideas. The aim of the bibliography is to tell your readers in the clearest possible way what you've used, so don't pad it out with items to impress them. Nevertheless, it will no doubt help you in your future assignments if you make it as comprehensive as possible. If it's appropriate, divide it into primary and secondary material.

Primary material includes government reports and statistics, research material, historic documents, and original texts, while secondary material includes books, articles and academic papers, which usually discuss or throw light on the primary material.

If you've been systematic from the start, the bibliography is quite easy to compile. But if you haven't recorded your sources carefully, then it can be quite a nightmare. You will find that the habit of recording the details of your sources at the top of the page before you take notes, or better still, using a section in your card-index system to compile a bibliography, will make the job much more straightforward.

Use just one card for each source, with all the details you need. You will even find that recording your own impressions of the usefulness of the text in one or two sentences will help you when you come to research other assignments, for which this source might be useful. These impressions will be lost to you within a short time, so by recording them as soon as you finish with the text you will know exactly how useful it is and what you can use it for in the future.

Listing the sources

Whether you're compiling a reference list or a bibliography, as we said before, the key is to be consistent. There are different conventions governing the way you list the texts, but as long as you follow a regular sequence for citation, there should be no problem. Below you will see one of the most common methods of citation. As you list them, arrange your references alphabetically, and where there is more than one book by the same author, arrange these chronologically under the author's name.

- *For books or other free-standing publications*: first names or initials of the author, the author's surname, full title of the work (in italics or underlined), place of publication, name of the publisher, and date (in brackets).

  Where you're using a later edition than the first, indicate the date of the first publication.

- *For periodical articles*: first names or initials of the author, the author's surname, the name of the article (in quotation marks), the title of the periodical (in italics or underlined), volume number of the periodical (if published in volumes), the year of publication (in brackets unless no volume number is given), the page numbers of the article.

i.e.

> N. Author, *Title of Book* (place of publication: publisher, and date).
>
> N. Author, 'Title of Chapter', in *Title of Book*, ed. X. Editor and Y. Editor (place of publication: publisher, and date), pp. ••–••.
>
> N. Author, 'Title of Article', *Title of Periodical*, vol. 2, no. 1 (date), pp. ••–••.

Of course, if you are compiling a reference list and you're using end-notes, you will also have to include the page reference to locate the passage or quotation you have used.

Practice exercise 21
Compiling a reference list

Arrange the following list of sources into a reference list, using the method of citation we have just outlined.

Once you've completed it, compare your list with the answer given below.

List of sources

1 Author: R. E. Robinson and J. Gallagher
   Title: *Africa and the Victorians: The Official Mind of British Imperialism*
   Publisher: Macmillan
   Date and place of publication: 1962, London

2 Author: Peter Singer, ed.
   Title: *Ethics*
   Publisher: OUP
   Date and place of publication: 1994, Oxford

3 Author: Charles Darwin
   Title: *The Origin of Species*
   Publisher: John Murray
   Date and place of publication: 1859, London

4   Author: Leo Alexander
    Title of the article: Medical Science under Dictatorship
    Title of the periodical: *New England Journal of Medicine*
    Volume number: 241
    Year of publication: 1949
    The page numbers of the article: 39–47

5   Author: Peter Singer
    Title: *The Expanding Circle*
    Publisher: OUP
    Date and place of publication: 1981, Oxford

6   Author: Allen Wood
    Title: Marx against Morality, in *A Companion to Ethics*, ed. Peter
       Singer, pp. 511–24
    Publisher: Blackwell
    Date and place of publication: 1994, Oxford

7   Author: Peter Curwen
    Title of the article: High-Definition Television: A Case Study of
       Industrial Policy versus the Market
    Title of the periodical: *European Business Review*
    Volume number: vol. 94, no. 1
    Year of publication: 1994
    The page numbers of the article: 17–23

8   Author: John C. Ford
    Title of the article: The Morality of Obliteration Bombing
    Title of the periodical: *Theological Studies*
    Year of publication in the periodical: 1944
    Title of volume of essays in which reprinted: *War and Morality*
    Editor: Richard A. Wasserstrom
    Date and place of publication: 1970, Belmont
    The page numbers of the article: 1–18

9   Author: Peter Singer
    Title: *Practical Ethics*
    Publisher: CUP
    Date and place of publication: 1979, Cambridge

10   Author: Geoffrey Parker
   Title of the article: Mutiny and Discontent in the Spanish Army
      of Flanders, 1572–1607
   Title of the periodical: *Past & Present*
   Volume number: vol. 58
   Year of publication: 1973
   The page numbers of the article: 38–52

Answer

1   Leo Alexander, 'Medical Science under Dictatorship', *New England Journal of Medicine*, vol. 241 (1949), pp. 39–47.

2   Peter Curwen, 'High-Definition Television: A Case Study of Industrial Policy versus the Market', *European Business Review*, vol. 94, no. 1 (1994), pp. 17–23.

3   Charles Darwin, *The Origin of Species* (London: John Murray, 1859).

4   John C. Ford, 'The Morality of Obliteration Bombing', *Theological Studies* (1944); reprinted in Richard A. Wasserstrom (ed.), *War and Morality* (Belmont, 1970), pp. 1–18.

5   Geoffrey Parker, 'Mutiny and Discontent in the Spanish Army of Flanders, 1572–1607', *Past and Present*, vol. 58 (1973), pp. 38–52.

6   R. E. Robinson and J. Gallagher, *Africa and the Victorians: The Official Mind of British Imperialism* (London: Macmillan, 1962).

7   Peter Singer, *Practical Ethics* (Cambridge: Cambridge University Press, 1979).

8   Peter Singer, *The Expanding Circle* (Oxford: Oxford University Press, 1981).

9   Peter Singer (ed.), *Ethics* (Oxford: Oxford University Press, 1994).

10   Allen Wood, 'Marx against Morality', in *A Companion to Ethics*, ed. Peter Singer (Oxford: Blackwell, 1994), pp. 511–24.

Assignment 12
Reference list and bibliography

Now that you've completed this exercise, compile your reference list and a bibliography for the essay you've chosen to work on in these assignments.

▶ The next stage

With your essay completed, along with the reference list and bibliography, it's time to put it aside for a day or two, so that you can come back with a fresh mind to revise it.

In the next stage you will learn how to revise your essay without killing off your most creative ideas and without breaking up the fluency of your prose. Indeed, you will see how effective revision can be in giving your work the sort of polish that elevates your essay from being just a good piece of work into one that is interesting and thought provoking.

Note

1 For the most detailed account of many of the systems used, refer to Gordon Harvey, *Writing with Sources: A Guide for Harvard Students* (Cambridge, Mass., 1995).

Available at: http//www.fas.harvard.edu/~expos/sources

Stage 5
Revision

INTRODUCTION

Now that you've written your essay you will realise that one of the most difficult problems is to remind yourself of all those things we've talked about to improve your style, while at the same time writing as freely as possible. The key to doing this successfully is to separate the writer from the editor.

▶ The writer v. the editor

In this stage you will learn to use these two distinctly different sets of skills without fearing that one is getting in the way of the other. This reinforces, again, the importance of breaking up essay writing into its distinct stages. Separating the writing and revision stages frees our hand, allowing us to write without the burden of having to produce the final polished version all in one go. Knowing that we can polish up our prose later, we can be more creative. It allows our ideas to flow and our minds to explore all the contrasts and connections between our ideas, that give our writing impact.

But to do this effectively we have to learn to shift the focus from the writer to the editor without endangering our best ideas. The rich insights we saw in our ideas, which engaged our interest and commitment when we first began to plan and write them, are likely to engage our readers too. Therefore, we have to learn to edit our work without killing the very thing that's likely to grab our readers and make them think.

To help you in this, and to make revision simpler and more manageable, you will learn to revise with a purpose: with a clear strategy of those things you want to work on in each revision, rather than attempting to revise everything at the same time. To make this easier, you will be shown the five-stage revision strategy, the first two revisions of which deal with the structural features of the essay, while the last three deal with the content.

▶ Structure

In the first revision you will be shown how to identify those passages where our talk in print breaks down and it's difficult to continue to read fluently with the right emphasis and rhythm. Once this is done you will move on to the second revision, in which you learn how to revise the structural features of your essays, like the introduction, the conclusion, the logical structure of the essay, and the relevance of your arguments and evidence.

With these two revisions completed you will be keenly aware of the impact the types of changes you've made can have on your essay. By tying in paragraphs to the introduction with clear topic sentences and transitions, an essay which might have been just a loose list of points, becomes a taut, cohesive piece of work, in which readers are never in danger of getting lost and every argument counts for marks. Similarly, if you have wrapped the structure up in a conclusion that completes the circle by coming back to issues first raised in the introduction, you will leave readers not only convinced that you have kept your promises, but with the satisfaction that everything has found its appropriate place.

You will also be shown how to revise your evidence, so that you use it to the best effect. If it's relevant and varied you will have made your work more interesting by breaking it up with changes in pace and content. And if you use evidence that allows people to speak for themselves, your readers are likely to be more involved in your work. They can respond empathetically, with their emotions and feelings engaged, which can lend untold support to your arguments. Nevertheless, you have to be sure your evidence does real work and you don't bury your readers beneath too much.

▶ Content

In the final three revisions our main concern is to remove all unnecessary words and phrases that are likely to obscure the meaning of our sentences. If we fail to remove all of this, the clarity of our thinking will be lost, and our readers will be left wondering what it all means. With it removed, those words we use to carry the greatest significance in our work will no longer be smothered. They will stand out more and have sufficient impact to make our readers think.

As we saw in the last stage, knowing what to leave out is as important as knowing what to include. The readability of our work will increase in proportion to the number of unnecessary words we eliminate. Therefore, in this revision our aim is to ensure that our meaning is being carried by strong nouns and verbs, rather than shoring it up with too many adverbs, adjectives and prepositions.

Removing these, replacing long words and sentences with shorter ones, and identifying all those sentences that would be better in the active voice, we can make our writing not only clearer and more concise, but more direct.

32 Preserving your Best Ideas

In this chapter you will learn:

- about the importance of revision in allowing you to be more creative;
- how to shift the focus from the writer to the editor without endangering your best ideas;
- how the five-stage revision strategy makes revision easier and more effective.

▶ Using your mind more effectively

A surprising number of students still seem quite unaware of just how much the writing stage depends for its success on the revision stage. As we thump the page with our last emphatic full stop there are those of us who breathe a deep sigh of relief that the essay's finally done, without a thought for revision, beyond a cursory check to see the spelling is all right.

But, if nothing else, revision has the effect of freeing your hand, allowing you to write without the burden of knowing you have to produce the final polished version all in one go. Knowing that you can polish up your prose later, you can be more creative, allowing your ideas to flow and your mind to make the logical connections and comparisons that give your writing impact.

In this lies an interesting parallel with the invention of the word processor. Before the modern home computer and the word-processing packages we now use, you were condemned to write with pen and ink, or on a manual or electric typewriter. Either way you went into the task of writing knowing that unless you were prepared to go through the whole process of typing your essay out again, what you were producing was your final draft. It not only had to be right the first time, it also had to be presentable. This meant that as soon as you'd made a mistake, your flow of ideas had to stop while you got out the *tip-ex* to correct the error. Your creative flow was constantly interrupted both for the correction of errors and to give you time to find exactly the word you wanted, along with its correct spelling.

Now, with the word processor, it's possible to divide up the task one step further than we've already done with our stages of writing. By having a planning stage, distinct from the writing stage, we've already separated the two most difficult things in writing: on the one hand, summoning up our ideas and putting them in a logical order, and on the other, choosing the right words, phrases and sentence structures to convey them accurately. But now we can go even further: we can separate the ideas entirely from the choice of words and their correct spelling. You don't even have to worry too much about the sentence structure and punctuation, because these too can be cleaned up later.

▶ Freeing your ideas and creativity

If you think about this carefully, you'll see that the whole process of dividing writing into the five distinct stages of this book (interpretation, research, planning, writing, and revision), along with all the advantages that a word processor gives you, is designed to free you from responsibilities at each stage. As a result you can be more creative and use more of your own ideas, many of which, you'll no doubt be surprised to find, like most students when they first do this, are full of insight and intelligence.

We've all had the experience of writing the old way with pen and paper or with a manual typewriter. All too frequently the words would get hopelessly tangled up with the ideas as they began to flow like a torrent. Your mind would make connections, analyse issues, synthesise arguments and evidence, and draw all sorts of interesting contrasts, all of which you would struggle desperately to retain and use. But as fast as you fought to find the right words and their correct spelling in order to capture these ideas, they would be gone and others, equally evanescent, would replace them.

The mind simply moves much faster than our inadequate techniques will allow us to record. Breaking the essay up into stages, and using a word processor, both gives us the same advantages as using pattern notes in the interpretation stage, rather than linear notes: it's a more effective way of keeping up with the mind and using more of its creativity.

The same can be said for revision. The importance of this stage lies in the fact that it allows you the freedom to focus more of your attention on the ideas in the writing stage and on your creative use of language. If you make mistakes with your grammar, your spelling, or your sentence structures, don't worry, you can pick them up and sort them out in the revision stage.

▶ Cooling off

The shift from the writer in you to the editor, then, involves a shift of focus from the creative activity of converting your ideas into language to a more self-conscious focus on the way you've used words, phrases and structures. The editor inside you should be asking, how does it sound, is it fluent, does it move logically from one stage in the argument to another, are there sections that need more evidence, or more development?

With this in mind, you've got to allow yourself to undergo a conversion from the writer to the editor, from the artist to the craftsman. To do this, the first thing is to put your essay aside. Allow yourself a cooling off period of at least a day, so your editor can surface. It's not that you're trying to create objectivity between yourself and what you've written. This would endanger those rich insights you saw in your ideas when you first began to plan and write them. It's these that first engaged your interest and commitment, and they're likely to engage your readers' too. So, if you were to revise in an objective, dispassionate frame of mind, you might kill the very thing that's likely to grab your readers and make them think.

Nevertheless, aware of these dangers, try to approach your work as you believe the examiner or any reader will approach it. Allow yourself to feel the impact of your original insights as you expect the reader to be affected too.

▶ Revise with a purpose

However, once you begin to revise you will soon find your most difficult problem is that there are so many things to check – so many questions to ask of your work. The only effective way of making this simpler

. and manageable is to revise a number of times, each time checking on a different range of things.

This may seem a lot of work, but it will certainly pay dividends: each extra revision always improves your work. The effortless feel of talk in print that flows across the page in light elegant prose only comes from multiple revisions undertaken with a clear purpose in mind each time. But that's not to say that this is an endless process. As your writing improves you'll know when it's time to stop and put it aside – you'll know when it's finished.

▶ In the next chapter

What follows is a strategy of five revisions, each one looking for different things. You may find you want to do more than five, because you can see there are still improvements coming through each time, but you should regard five as the minimum. In the next chapter we will tackle the first two revisions, which deal with the structural features of the essay.

33 Revising the Structure

In this chapter you will learn:

- about the importance of listening to your essay being read aloud, to identify those passages you will need to work on;
- how to revise the structural features of your essay, like the introduction, the conclusion, and the logical structure of the essay;
- how to make sure your arguments and evidence are relevant and effective.

▶ First revision – revising for reassurance

This is the lightest of all revisions. After we've finished writing an essay most of us are keen to read it through to see how it sounds. We like to be reassured that it reads well, so we can give ourselves a mental pat on the back. This may sound like aimless self-indulgence, that we should train ourselves to do without, but, in fact, this sort of revision and the reassurance it brings does have a valuable point to it.

It allows us to set down a marker: not only are we reassured that it reads well and it's interesting, but we're also clearer about those areas we need to work on to improve it. More often than not these may just involve a clumsy word or passage that needs tidying up, but they can be more serious.

They may indicate that you haven't thought through your arguments clearly enough, or your ideas have developed further since you wrote the passage, and you now see the issues differently. This revision is not just about making sure what you've written is clear from the outside, but also about ensuring that your writing expresses clearly the ideas on the inside. If you were not entirely clear about them when you wrote the passage, then your writing is likely to be unclear, too. Either way, at this stage you just need to mark the passage so that you can come back to it later.

After the cooling off period, then, read it through for reassurance. But as you read through, tolerate your mistakes. Don't stop and start working on them. Just jot down notes on mistakes and weak areas that you must look at later.

Practice exercise   22
First revision

Take the essay you completed in the last assignment. First, read it through to yourself, then get a friend to read it to you. As he or she reads it, note those passages where your talk in print breaks down, where it's difficult to continue to read fluently with the right emphasis and rhythm. Remember, your ear can often pick up awkward passages much more effectively than your eye.

Although you'll pick up other problems as you go through each subsequent revision, this lays down clear markers that these are problem passages and you will have to look at them.

▶ Second revision – the larger questions

In the second revision your main concern is with the larger structural features of your essay – the introduction, the conclusion, the logical structure of the essay, the relevance of your arguments and the evidence you use.

With this in mind, as you work through your essay concern yourself just with the following things.

Introduction
Check that you've interpreted the implications of the question clearly and haven't missed anything. Your examiners will want to assure themselves that you have thought this through thoroughly and that you haven't begged questions, taking some things for granted that you shouldn't have. Then, having done this, check that you've outlined the structure, the map of the essay, clearly, so the reader knows not just what you're going to do, but why.

A clear logical structure

Now, as you move on to read the body of the essay, you're checking that you've delivered on all these promises. You must be sure that you've led the reader clearly through the essay. Of course, this is helped if you've organised the material in a clear, logical sequence that the reader can follow. But it also depends on the direction signs you erect in your essay to make sure the reader is never lost.

Keeping this at the front of your mind, in addition to checking that there is a logical sequence in your arguments, a clear pattern to your essay, also check your transitions and topic sentences. If your structure is clear, you won't need transitions for every paragraph, but if in doubt use them. They help the reader follow the route you're taking without getting derailed and side-tracked. The same can be said of topic sentences – they allow the reader to see clearly what the following paragraph is going to be about. But check that everything else in the paragraph supports it.

Your arguments

Having checked that you have made clear the relevance of what you're doing through the overall structure of your essay, now look at the content of each paragraph. Read the arguments contained in each paragraph checking two things. First, make sure that all the arguments bear directly on the map of the essay outlined in the introduction. If they don't, it will dilute the overall approach of the essay and it will tend to confuse the reader. Secondly, check that you have developed each argument sufficiently and that they are clear. If there are difficult passages that could be clearer, rewrite them. This will include most of those you identified as a problem in the first revision.

Your evidence

As you read these arguments you should also be concerned that you've supported them with enough evidence. But make sure you haven't used too much – remember, pruning all unnecessary detail means that what remains stands out. It's the art of knowing what not to say. For similar reasons, make sure you haven't given the reader irrelevant information. This will blur the focus of your arguments and weaken the structure of your essay.

Now, make sure your evidence is specific. If you're developing arguments that employ generalisations, perhaps involving fairly abstract concepts, your examples should be as specific as possible, so that they pin your arguments down. Not only have your examples got to support your arguments, but they must illustrate them vividly. This will make them more believable and interesting – they will grab and hold your reader's attention.

Finally, check that, wherever possible, your arguments have *shown* your readers what you mean, rather than simply *told* them. For this, make sure you've used enough quotations and anecdotes. They will make your writing more readable, but they must make the point you want them to make. Therefore, make certain they all do *real* work. And remember, like other forms of evidence, too many are as bad as too few.

Your conclusion

Having checked all of this, when it comes to your conclusion it should be plain sailing. The key thing you must be certain of is that the introduction and conclusion relate to each other, giving your essay a tight cohesion. If you haven't achieved this, then rewrite it so that you come back to the issues you raised, and the anecdote you may have used, in the introduction. But avoid raising any new issues that weren't raised in the body of the essay. The key to conclusions is to let your readers know that you have delivered on all the promises you made in the introduction.

► Checklist

1 Have I interpreted the implications of the question thoroughly? Have I missed anything?
2 Does the introduction analyse the implications clearly and give the reader a clear indication of the structure of my answer?
3 Have I arranged the material logically?
4 Does the essay move fluently from one section to the next, from paragraph to paragraph?
5 Does each topic sentence introduce the subject of each paragraph clearly?
6 Have I developed each argument sufficiently?
7 Have I made my arguments clear, or are there difficult passages that would benefit from being rewritten?
8 Do I support each argument with sufficient evidence and examples?
9 Do all my examples and evidence do real work?
10 Have I *shown*, rather than *told*, the reader wherever possible?

11 Have I answered this particular question relevantly?

12 Have I dealt with all the implications of the question that I identified in the interpretation stage?

13 Have I covered these in enough depth?

14 Have I spent too much time on less significant issues, while only dealing superficially with any of the major issues?

15 Have I presented a convincing case which I could justify confidently in a discussion?

16 In the conclusion, have I avoided introducing new ideas that haven't been dealt with in the body of the essay?

17 Have I tied my conclusion in with my introduction?

Assignment 13
Revision – the structure

Now revise your essay carefully again. This time go through each of the stages outlined here.

Start with the introduction, checking all those things we've talked about. Once you've done this, tick off the items on the checklist. Then move on to the logical structure, checking the logical sequencing of the arguments, the topic sentences and the transitions. Tick them off on the checklist and then move on to consider the arguments, evidence and conclusion, ticking these off on the checklist too.

▶ In the next chapter

With this done you should feel more confident that all your ideas, what's on the inside, are now clearly and logically developed in your essay. You can now turn to the outside, the language and style through which you've expressed these ideas.

34 Revising the Content

In this chapter you will learn:

- about the importance of checking factual accuracy, spelling and grammar;
- how to make the revision of your style simple and straightforward, yet comprehensive;
- how to make your writing more vivid;
- how to use the checklists to make sure you haven't overlooked anything;
- about the importance of the appearance of your essay to the final mark.

In the next two revisions your attention shifts to the smaller questions, like factual accuracy, grammar, and the use of words. Although this means you'll be focusing on fewer things, this is a more meticulous and slower read.

▶ Third revision – checking the details

In the third revision your concern is for the accuracy of your facts and quotations. Particular care needs to be taken in checking these. If you lose your readers' trust over these details it may infect all of your work. They may conclude that they must be cautious about everything you say.

In addition, you will also be checking your spelling and grammar. You must be sure that if you break the rules of grammar, it's deliberate – that you're doing it for reasons of style, to produce a certain effect – and it's not the result of a lack of knowledge. But whether you keep to the rules or decide to break them, the key is clarity: it must be the best way of making your meaning clear.

Checklist

1 Is the content accurate?
2 Are the grammar, punctuation and spelling correct?
3 Have I distinguished clearly between my own ideas and those of others?
4 Have I acknowledged all sources and references?
5 Have I omitted any text from my bibliography?

▶ Fourth revision – style

For most of us this is the most difficult and confusing of all revisions. There's just so much we need to focus on. To make it easier, just work from a simple list of things you're looking for. Eventually, you may want to include other things that you come to realise are significant problems in your writing. But at this stage just confine yourself to the following simple list of the most important things that you need to pay attention to – they will have an immediate impact on your writing, making it light, interesting and easy to read.

It's worth reminding yourself that the more you take out at this stage, the more readable your work becomes. What remains becomes more vivid, grabbing and keeping the interest of your reader. In view of this you will almost certainly need a number of revisions of this type. I find the more of these revisions I can do the better it becomes, until I reach a stage when I realise all too clearly that I need do no more.

Unnecessary material

As you go through your work, keep asking yourself if there are any unnecessary words, phrases, sentences, or even paragraphs, that ought to be removed. Again, remind yourself that the readability of your work will improve in proportion to the unnecessary material you eliminate.

In the advertising essay you might have a sentence like the following:

A small sign nailed to a village tree announcing where and when the local village fête will take place might be giving just information, but beneath it lies a covert message, an appeal to people, who might be reading it, to come along and support local causes in their fund-raising activities.

By taking out the unnecessary words the meaning is made clearer, sharper and more direct.

> A small sign nailed to a village tree announcing where and when the local village fête will take place might be giving just information, but beneath it lies a covert appeal to come along and support local causes in their fund-raising activities.

Long sentences

With long sentences you run the risk of confusing, even losing, your readers, who will then be unable to give you marks for your good work. They may even lose patience with you as they struggle to find their way through the unfamiliar terrain of your thinking. To guard against this, cut up every long, complex sentence that can be reduced to two or more shorter sentences.

For example, although it's not impossible to understand the following sentence, its meaning is difficult to track at times. But once you've broken it down into three sentences, it presents no problem at all.

> Appeals are made to some imagined social consensus, to 'basic' or 'shared' values, it's assumed we all want to drive the latest and fastest car on the road and our lives will be unfulfilled unless we have a 'multi-valve engine' and 'ABS braking' and to sustain these appeals myths have to be created by the media.

> Appeals are made to some imagined social consensus: to 'basic' or 'shared' values. It's assumed we all want to drive the latest and fastest car on the road and our lives will be unfulfilled, unless we own a 'multi-valve engine' and 'ABS braking'. And to sustain these appeals, myths have to be created by the media.

Long words

Much the same advice goes for long words, although they have a different effect on your writing. They may not confuse your readers quite as much as long sentences; nevertheless they can leave them wondering whether you really meant to say what you did, and they will often make your writing sound unnecessarily pompous. It makes sense, then, wherever possible to replace long obscure words with short and simple ones.

The following example presents no problem in understanding what is meant, but it does sound slightly pompous:

Our constant demand for material possessions and a higher standard of living has bestowed on politicians an effective way of influencing the way we vote.

It would be simpler and more direct to say:

Our constant demand for material possessions and a higher standard of living has given politicians an effective way of influencing the way we vote.

This example not only sounds pompous, but leaves you wondering whether you are clear about what the writer really meant to say:

An advertiser will work to establish a close contiguity between driving a certain car, or drinking a certain drink, and a full, active social life.

Once you've substituted a more familiar word, the meaning is immediately clearer.

An advertiser will work to establish a close association between driving a certain car, or drinking a certain drink, and a full, active social life.

Strong nouns and verbs

Enough has already been said about the importance of writing with strong nouns and verbs, rather than shoring them up with adjectives and adverbs. So, check that you have used strong nouns and verbs with the minimum of modifiers. And constantly remind yourself that the fewer verbs you have to modify with adverbs, and nouns with adjectives, the better your writing will be.

You might argue,

A manufacturer of computer printers will be keen to tell you that theirs is the most advanced printer on the market, but be really nervous about revealing that their print cartridges cost on average five times as much as any other printer.

But your meaning will be clearer if you argue,

> A manufacturer of computer printers will be keen to tell you that theirs is the most advanced printer on the market, but be reluctant to reveal that their print cartridges cost on average five times as much as any other printer.

'Nervousness' manifests itself in many different forms. So, in the first sentence, where you really wanted to identify one particular form that was relevant to the printer manufacturer, it was too vague to do this. In fact shoring it up with the word 'really' didn't help much either, because, although you might be interested in the intensity of nervousness, what you really wanted to convey was the type of nervousness involved.

In the following sentence there are examples of both weak nouns and weak verbs. By substituting stronger, more specific words, see how the sentence gains in clarity and directness.

> Theatre promoters are likely to comb through unfavourable reviews looking carefully for any isolated expression of a favourable comment that can be used to promote their plays.

> Theatre promoters are likely to comb through unfavourable reviews in search of any isolated expression of approval that can be used to promote their plays.

The active voice
The same can be said of the active as opposed to the passive voice – we have already spent some time stressing the importance of the active voice in making your points clearer, by making them more concise and direct. Therefore, as you revise ask yourself, have you used the passive voice on only those occasions when what is done is more important than the doer. Wherever possible make the doer the subject of the sentence.

In the following example the most important information is what was actually done, rather than by whom. So, re-forming the sentence in the passive form makes the point more effectively.

> In the 1970s managers in some US supermarkets, in order to reduce shoplifting, recorded subliminal messages onto the music played throughout the store.

In the 1970s subliminal messages were recorded onto the music played throughout some US supermarkets by managers, who wanted to reduce shoplifting.

Checklist

1 Have I removed all unnecessary words, phrases, sentences and paragraphs?
2 Have I cut up all the long complex sentences that can be cut up?
3 Have I replaced all long, obscure words with short and simple ones?
4 Have I removed all unnecessary modifiers in favour of good strong nouns and verbs?
5 Have I written in the active voice?

Practice exercise   23
Revising the content

Read the following passage and then revise its content by going through the stages we've outlined above. Wherever you find unnecessary material, long sentences, long words, weak nouns and verbs, and passages that should be in the active or passive voice, revise them. Then go through the checklist to see if you've covered everything.

When you've finished, check your revised version against the answer given below.

Revising the content

Cultural change in modern Europe

In the second half of the nineteenth century as labour and information moved more rapidly and easily across borders new pressures for change were generated bringing with them unprecedented social and cultural fragmentation rarely seen before. Towns grew at inconceivable rates into vast cities drawing workers in from the countryside to interact with the new foreign migrant labour flooding in from all over Europe, developing a new urbane, cosmopolitan culture, fuelled by rising literacy and a popular press with mass readership. Not only were traditional social classes changing with movement up and down the social structure, but cultures and traditional customs were being threatened by an exodus away from the rural areas into cities, and by international, cosmopolitan influences that flowed across borders.

The forces for uniformity in tastes, culture and fashion that touched just about every European society that engaged in trade and commerce was fuelled by the revolution in communications alone. Consumers demanded the best of what they bought irrespective of where it was produced, so architecture, clothes, fashions, even the ways of solving problems, were discovered to be increasingly the same and, except where they were consciously prolonged, national styles slowly faded. Even in the 1930s it was already apparent that a time was approaching when it would be impossible to tell one country's towns and cities from another and, add to this the impact of dance music, the cinema and the wireless, even the cheap recreational literature that more and more drew its inspiration from the US, and it became clear to a growing number of people that their social and cultural identity, once a source of patriotic pride and a sense of belonging, was disappearing beneath a uniform, cosmopolitan culture, that was constantly changing.

Answer

Cultural change in modern Europe

In the second half of the nineteenth century as labour and information swept across borders, new pressures for change were generated, bringing with them unprecedented social and cultural fragmentation. Towns grew at inconceivable rates into vast cities drawing workers in from the countryside to interact with the foreign labour flooding in from all over Europe. Here a new cosmopolitan culture developed, fuelled by rising literacy and a popular mass press. Not only were traditional social classes changing with movement up and down the social structure, but cultures and customs were being threatened by movement away from the countryside into cities, and by cosmopolitan influences that flowed across borders.

The revolution in communications alone was fuelling forces for uniformity in tastes, culture and fashion that touched just about every European society that engaged in commerce. Consumers demanded the best product irrespective of where it was produced. Architecture, clothes, fashions, even the ways of solving problems, were increasingly the same. Except where they were consciously prolonged, national styles slowly faded. Even in the 1930s it was already apparent that a time was approaching when it would be impossible to tell one country's towns and cities from another. Add to this the impact of dance music, the cinema and the wireless, even the cheap recreational literature that more and more drew its inspiration from the US, and it became clear to a growing number that their social and cultural identity, once a source of patriotic pride and a sense of belonging, was disappearing beneath a uniform, cosmopolitan culture, that was constantly changing.

▶ Fifth revision – revise by ear

Finally, your last revision! This appears to come back to your first, because you're reading your work through to see how it sounds. You're interested in its flow and rhythm. Hopefully, it should read like talk in print, with light effortless prose that glides across the page with a pace and rhythm that holds the reader's attention.

Unfortunately, most of us get so close to what we write and the thought patterns our sentences represent, that we find it's difficult to read it as another person would. If you have this problem, ask a friend to listen while you read it out aloud or, better still, ask your friend to read it out aloud to you.

This is the best test of all: if it doesn't come across fluently to someone who has never seen or heard it before, then it will need to be changed. This reading will certainly identify clumsy sentences or where you might have dealt with your ideas in an illogical order. The other advantage of this is that, because you're not reading it yourself, you'll be free to note where in your work it was difficult to understand the meaning of what was written. Failing this, if you haven't got a compassionate friend, or you're afraid to risk your friendship in this way, then record it on a cassette and play it back to yourself as if you were listening to it for the first time.

But beyond the question of whether your work can be read and understood easily by someone reading it for the first time, think about one other thing. You may want to change the pace of your work at certain times in order to make your points more effectively. You may want to speed up or slow down in some sections by varying the length of sentences. Long sentences are very comforting and reassuring. They may be best suited to the development of the core elements of your arguments, which need to be analysed and elaborated carefully. But when you want to be abrupt, to grab your reader's attention with a vivid piece of detail, or an insight that you feel is a key point to get across, use a short sentence – don't let it get drowned in the words that surround it.

Checklist

1 Does it read well for someone reading it for the first time?
2 Is the pace and rhythm right for the arguments I want to make?

► Using the checklists

As we've seen in previous stages, it always helps if you have a simple, clear strategy to work with: even though you may know what you're looking for, it helps to have a checklist so you can deliberately ask yourself questions which you just might overlook. It will also help you to assess how well you've completed each stage of the process, so you can see where you need to spend more time in the next assignment. With these advantages in mind, get into the habit of using checklists and try to answer the questions as you think your examiners might answer them when they assess your work.

► Appearance

Does your essay have a neat professional appearance?

Amid every other consideration, this last question appears to be the least significant. And, of course, it is, or it should be. But first impressions count, however unfair this may seem. Despite every effort made to ensure that each essay is subjected to the same objective criterion for assessment, marking still contains an element of subjectivity. Most people find it difficult to shake off their first impressions as they read an essay.

What's more, there may be an inductive truth here. There are people who're convinced that experience shows that a sloppily presented essay is more than likely to be sloppily argued. It's likely to lack sufficient attention to detail in terms of accuracy and the evidence used to support arguments convincingly. Whether these views have any credence or not, you can avoid the danger of dropping a grade by making sure your essay is clearly and neatly presented, with as few mistakes in it as possible. Your work must look like the work of a fastidious person.

Assignment   14
Revision – the content

Take the essay you've been working on in the assignments and go through the final three stages revising the content.

In your first revision look for all the unnecessary words, phrases and sentences. Check for readability. If sentences are long, cut them up into shorter, more manageable lengths. Remember the key is to keep your readers engaged and not to lose them.

On the second revision check for strong nouns and verbs, and where you find too many adjectives and adverbs see if you can think of stronger nouns and verbs, that would make these unnecessary. The same goes for the active and passive voices in your writing. Check wherever you've used the passive voice that it is more appropriate than the active voice.

Then, once you've completed that, move on to the last revision. Get someone to read your essay to you, so that you can see how well it sounds.

▶ **The final step**

With this done you will have completed the five-stage revision on your essay. As a result you should be seeing a marked improvement in your work. The introduction should outline a clear structure for your readers to follow. Your paragraphs should have transitions and topic sentences that clearly signpost the direction of your argument and its relevance to the question. And your conclusion should tie up the issues raised in the introduction, producing an essay that has a tight, convincing structure.

Equally important, your writing should be much lighter. You should be able to see that it is getting closer to talk in print. You will already notice that with fewer modifiers and prepositions it's possible to read your ideas without the bumpy ride you might be used to. What's more, knowing how to use your punctuation, and sentences of different lengths, you will begin to enjoy more confidence in your ability to develop your arguments and make your points in a way that holds your reader's attention.

In short, you will begin to realise that you can produce an essay that not only does justice to your ideas, but leaves your readers knowing they have read something that is interesting and thought provoking.

Conclusion

We started this book by drawing attention to the value of writing essays both in what you can learn from them and in terms of the abilities and skills you develop along the way. Now that we've worked through each of the stages, it should be possible to see more clearly the benefits that can be derived if each of these stages is done well.

In the first stage, *interpreting the title*, you were shown ways of developing the skills you need to analyse the most difficult concepts. As a result, you should now feel confident that you can reveal not just the key issues involved in any question, but also the sort of insight which marks your work out as interesting and original. What's more, you should now be able to build on this with the brainstorming skills you learnt in this stage. These will help you mobilise your ideas, arming you with your own thoughts, so you're no longer tyrannised into accepting uncritically the opinions of the authors you read.

In the *research* and *planning* stages you were shown how to develop the sort of intellectual skills that will give you the confidence to tackle any assignment no matter how difficult. Having researched the topic, not only will you have learnt a great deal about it and many of the peripheral issues, but you will have developed the capacity to use your research skills with more flexibility to meet a wider range of intellectual tasks. Similarly, by planning your essay you created a structure of ideas you can draw upon not only in your written work, but in discussions and examinations. Around this you can now build your own understanding of the subject.

As to your ability to capture your ideas in writing that is clear, fluent and interesting, now that you've worked your way through the *writing* and *revision* stages you will know that by separating the writer from the editor you can use the skills involved in each much more effectively. Having done this once, you should be able to repeat it in all your work, producing essays that are clearly structured, logically argued and written in clear, light prose that holds the reader's attention. You will know now, having worked through each of the five stages of revision, that you can allow yourself to write freely, knowing that you can significantly improve your essay later, when you let the editor in.

In the wider context of the courses you're studying, all of this means you are now equipped to get the most from each essay you write. Once your essays have been returned, you can use your tutors' comments for further learning. They might, for example, suggest new ideas, fresh examples or different opinions. All of these need to be considered while your ideas are still fresh in your mind. There may be simple corrections of factual or logical mistakes. There may be comments on your writing style, suggesting how you could express your ideas more clearly. Or there may be detailed remarks on the structural aspects of your essay.

But, as you realise by now, like most other aspects of learning, you will get the greatest benefit from these comments if you organise yourself to respond to them effectively. This might mean nothing more than noting in your notebook those problems that arise regularly in your work, like spelling mistakes, transitions, and punctuation. If you then make a point of consulting your notebook as a matter of routine before the revision stages of all your essays, you can more easily identify and correct the problems. Similarly, if your tutors leave you with fresh ideas to pursue, this might involve further reading, or at least developing your own response in your journal.

The key to this, as we've seen, is to give your thinking the opportunities it needs to grow and develop. Each discrete stage of the writing process provides fresh opportunities, as do the journal and the notebook, so that when you come to look back over them you can see just how far you have come, how much more you understand, and how much better equipped you are to research and write about those things that interest you.

And, just one final word: remember, you can never do a perfect job. To do this you would have to wait until all the facts are in – and, of course, they never will be. All you can do is to add to our understanding of what we *do* know. *Your* insights and *your* interpretation of the facts add to this understanding: they are just as valuable as anyone else's. Therefore, be bold – don't be cowed by the fear of authority.

Bibliography

Dorothea Brande, *Becoming a Writer* (London: Macmillan, 1984). Even professional writers admit they are indebted to this book for its help in freeing their most creative insights.

Tony Buzan, *Use Your Head* (London: BBC, 1979). One of the first to popularise pattern notes, or 'mind maps'.

Stuart Chase, *Guides to Straight Thinking* (New York: Harper, 1956).

Stella Cottrell, *The Study Skills Handbook* (Basingstoke: Macmillan – now Palgrave, 1999).

Edward de Bono, *Parallel Thinking* (London: Penguin, 1994).

Edward de Bono, *Serious Creativity* (London: HarperCollins, 1995).

Manya and Eric De Leeuw, *Read Better, Read Faster* (Harmondsworth: Pelican, 1973).

Jean M. Fredette (ed.), *Handbook of Magazine Article Writing* (Cincinnati: Writer's Digest Books, 1990). Learn from the professionals – this is full of sound practical advice from professional writers.

Bruno Furst, *The Practical Way to a Better Memory* (Marple: Heap, 1977). One of the most renowned books on concentration and memory training.

Harry Maddox, *How to Study* (London: Pan, 1967).

John Peck, and Martin Coyle, *The Student's Guide to Writing* (Basingstoke: Macmillan – Palgrave, 1999).

William Strunk, and E. B. White, *The Elements of Style* (New York: Macmillan, 1979). Once known as 'the little book', this sold over two million copies in its first edition – learn how to write clearly and concisely.

Robert H. Thouless, *Straight and Crooked Thinking* (London: Pan, 1958).

John Wilson, *Thinking with Concepts* (Cambridge: Cambridge University Press, 1963).

Index